MODI vs INDIRA GANDHI

MODI vs INDIRA GANDHI
On Becoming Prime Minister

Y. C. HALAN

GYAN

Published, 2020
Published by

Gyan Publishing House
5, Ansari Road
Daryaganj, New Delhi-110002
Phone: 011-47034999, 9811692060
www.gyanbooks.com
E-mail: books@gyanbooks.com

Printed at: G. Print Process, Delhi.

Cataloging in Publication Data—DK
Courtesy: D.K. Agencies (P) Ltd. <docinfo@dkagencies.com>

Halan, Y. C. (Yogesh Chandra), 1936- **author.**
Modi vs Indira Gandhi : on becoming prime minister / by Y.C. Halan.
pages cm
ISBN 9788121219624 (PB)

1. Modi, Narendra, 1950- 2. Gandhi, Indira, 1917-1984. 3. Prime ministers—India—Biography. 4. India—Politics and government—1947- I. Title.

LCC DS481.A1H35 2019 | DDC 920.054 23

Contents

Acknowledgements 7
Foreword 9
Preface 11

1. Early Life of Narendra Modi 15
2. Indira Gandhi: Early Life 27
3. Modi: Political Life in Making 39
4. Political Training of Indira 61
5. Modi Becoming PM 81
6. Indira Becoming PM 139

Epilogue 151
References 155
Index 171

Acknowledgements

This book was possible because of my daughter, Monika supported by her husband, Gautam, who persistently persuaded me to write the book based on the happenings that I witnessed during my long career of journalism beginning in 1970 and lasting up to 2014. I am thankful for their provocations which made this book possible. Meera, my granddaughter, has always been a source of strength to me. Affectionate love to her.

My wife, Mridula, read and reread the manuscript of the book several times and made me to rewrite more than half of it. If it has taken a publishable shape, it is because of her. Thanks to her in more ways than I can ever say.

Special thanks to Mr. Amit Garg, Director, Gyan Books Private Ltd for publishing the book and his editorial and production team that gave such a nice shape to the book.

Finally, thanks to all those numerous friends, colleagues and sources, who from time to time, fed me with stories during my long journalist career.

Foreword

I feel honoured to be asked to contribute a Foreword to a very interesting study coming from the perceptive pen of Dr Yogesh Halan. Among the most eminent journalists of the country, Dr Halan is an old friend. He had long innings in the senior-most editorial positions of leading national dailies. Later, he played a significant role in the growth of the electronic media as well. Characteristically full of struggles and fights for truth and national interest, his life had a glorious record of never compromising on basic principles of personal and journalistic ethics, whatever the cost in terms of material benefits.

This is probably the first comparative study of the making of two really "strong" Prime Ministers during the last 72 years of the largest parliamentary democracy on earth. Indira Gandhi and Narendra Modi came from very different and even diametrically opposite family, social and economic backgrounds. The routes they followed, the roads they traversed and the ladders they used to get to the top had little similarity.

I had the proud privilege of being in the service of Parliament right from the days of the first Prime Minister, Jawaharlal Nehru in the first Lok Sabha (1952 - 1957). I could brag about having known personally almost all the Prime Ministers - some of them not so closely. Of the two - Indiraji and Modiji, I was in office throughout the periods of the Prime Ministership of the former and came to know her somewhat well but the latter i.e. Modiji I have known only from outside and from a distance. While all comparisons are a little dicey and odious and individual perceptions and assessments of powerful personalities involved may vary, I can say with full confidence and with a sense of responsibility that Dr Halan's analysis is non-partisan and objective. It is deep, incisive and based on facts gathered through personal interactions and life-long experience of communicating - on and off the record - with the political class of decision makers. As a journalist, he has been privy to much that happened behind the scenes and outside the public domain during the last seven decades.

As the author takes us through the childhood, adolescence and youthful days of Indira Priyadarshini and Narendrabhai, large parts of the script read like an engrossing novel. Very appropriately, political training and increasingly active participation in party activities by the two leaders preparing to assume the highest office are covered at some length. As the author clarifies in his Preface "The book is on the environment in which the two grew up and the political and peer system that helped them to become PM. It does not go into their functioning as PM."

I commend this book most unhesitatingly as an informative, educative and joyful reading for all those concerned with the history of contemporary political management in India. I have no doubt that it will be read very widely with great interest.

New Delhi.
4 March, 2019.

Subhash C. Kashyap
Former Secretary-general
Lok Sabha

Preface

Prime minister (PM), the head of the government in a country, is the most powerful leader whose main responsibility is to project the vision of his Government.Cardinal de Richelieu, who became the French PM in 1624, is known to be world's first Prime Minister. Later, Britain also introduced prime ministership in 1721 when the King stopped chairing the meetings of his ministers and Robert Walpole became the first PM. Though Britain did not introduce the institution of prime ministership, it is known as the country that introduced prime ministership in a parliamentary democracy.

Prime Ministers became increasingly powerful when they began to control the policy-making as economies developed and governance became more complex. How the PMs controlled the political system and managed the country during crises, domestic and international, separated strong and weak prime ministers. Strong prime ministers acquired considerable constitutional powers like the power to change the structure of ministries as an executive action without seeking new legislation and focused on the most high-profile and strategic aspects of the government like foreign relations, major defence decisions, macroeconomic policy and the government's legislative timetable and priorities. They also steered the country out of crises successfully.

Weak prime ministers had no control on their ministers and, therefore, on governance. They were also not able to solve the critical economic and security-related problems and could not manage crises successfully. Such PMs were mostly in coalition governments because they had to balance representation among the various coalition party partners, doling out cabinet and junior ministerial appointments in numbers sufficient to ensure the support of all parties within the government. A new model of weak PM emerged during the Manmohan Singh regime when the PM had no control on ministers or the Party. In fact, the functions of the PM were performed by the Party President, who became more powerful and the real centre of power.

What makes a PM strong?

Difficult, but a good question.

Difficult because politics is a tough game needing distinctive areas of expertise. Governing a country, particularly a highly complex and pluralist like India, needs an immense range of skills to become a strong prime minister. Foremost is communication because the PM has to convince various sections, inside and outside the country, about the stand point of his government. Secondly, he must develop a package of policies linked to its Party's values appealing to the widest possible segmentsof the electorate.Thirdly, he must possess boundless energy and the ability to respond to unexpected crises. Fourthly, during a crisis, he must be taciturn to criticisms and attacks from the media. Fifthly, he should show highest degree of integrity in his public and private lives. He should also unite the people and everdivide them for political reasons. Therefore, a good PM should always perceive elections as a cricket match and not like a battle. Lastly, a PM must work hard to ensure that democratic institutions remain alive and blooming by not curbing free speech.

Strong PMs in India

India, during the past 72 years, had 16 Prime Ministers. The first was Nehru and the 16th is Narendra Modi. Lal Bahadur Shastri, Morarji Desai, Charan Singh, V. P. Singh, Chandra Shekhar, H. D. Deva Gowda and Inder Gujral were short term PMs. Only seven Prime Ministers—Jawaharlal, Nehru, Indira Gandhi, Rajiv Gandhi, P. V. Narsimha Rao, Atal Bihari Vajpayee, Manmohan Singh and Narendra Modi enjoyed full one or more terms in office. Out of the seven, only two, Indira Gandhi and Narendra Modi, could be called strong Prime Ministers.

Though a large number of books have been written on both, Indira and Modi, none, as far as I know, has tried to analyze the path both took to become Prime Ministers. I decided to try my pen to analyze how they became prime ministers. I discussed the idea with my friends—political analysts, journalists and psychologists—and realised that the personality of a person was decided by the earlier life of the person. Parents, peers and friends play a large role in shaping the behaviour, actions and beliefs of the person. The negative and positive impacts of upbringing in the family decide what type of person s/he would become. The influences of peers motivate the person's determination, efforts and discipline, all in a combined way decide the final outcome of person's personality.

The second area that makes a person strong was the training one gets in political organisation, personnel management and handling public issues. Lal Bahadur Shastri (who remained PM only for 19 months) and Indira Gandhi were strong prime ministers because they got training under stalwart as Mahatma Gandhi, and Jawaharlal Nehru. Rajiv Gandhi, despite receiving strongest mandate from the people could not be a strong PM as he never got any political training as he never thought of entering politics, not to talk of becoming PM.

An old friend of mine suggested that I must write the book as I have been following political developments since 1952 when I became a student of political science and worked as a volunteer in the first general elections of that year. Later, as an academician and journalist, I had close proximity to national political leaders and knew what was going on behind the curtains. The book, in fact, is based on my observations and discussions with fellow journalists, political leaders and bureaucrats during my journalist career.

The book is divided in three sections. The first section of chapter one and two describes and analyses the early life of Narendra Modi and Indira Gandhi. The second section of chapter three and four investigates their political exposure and training. The third section of chapters five and six describes the forces that made them prime ministers.

The book is on the environment in which the two grew up and the political and peer system that helped them to become the PM. It does not go into their functioning as PM.

Chapter one

Early Life of Narendra Modi

Nine months after India ceased to be the territory of the United Kingdom, on 17 September 1950, the house of Damodardas Mulchand Modi and Hiraben, reverberated with the cries of a male child. There was not much rejoicing because it was the birth of a third child, though, the happiness at the male child's birth always was.

Vadnagar, in Mehsana district of the then Bombay State, was a non-discrepant, dusty and sleepy temple-town with patched narrow lanes, old two-storey houses and a lake in the heart of the town. The family lived on meagre means; the father, Damodardas Mulchand, owned a small grocery-cum-tea kiosk near the Vadnagar railway station. The eight-member family lived in a small three-roomed mud-bricks house (approximately 360 square-feet), deep inside narrow and winding lanes of the town. It was poorly lit and had very little natural light; the kerosene lamp in the night worsened the already existing smoke and soot.The family bathed and washed clothes in a nearby lake and struggled to make both ends meet. Mother Hiraben worked as house-help at the houses of others. It was in these ignoble surroundings that the 14th Prime Minister of India was born and spent his childhood.[1]

Damodardas' forefathers had come from a family named Ranchoddas and had settled in Vadnagar in the late nineteenth century. The family belonged to the low-caste *Ghanchi* community, traditionally involved in operating pressers and selling cooking oil. The community, due to modern technology, began to lose market and became a marginalised section of the society and was included in the 'Other Backward Community Schedule.' Damodardas, to compensate his diminutive income, decided to run a grocery-cum-tea-shop at the railway station.Hiraben and the children operated the oil presser and Hiraben also worked as maid in neighbouring well-to-do houses.[2]

Gujarat, the state of traders, has been responsible for introducing two foreign communities that changed the face of India.

The first were Parsees who practiced Zoroastrian religion. In the seventh century, when the Arabs conquered Persia, the conversion began and more and more Zoroastrians converted to Islam. But many brave-hearts, to escape persecution, left their homes in Khorasan and moved out to look for an abode where they could practice their religion freely and in peace and also earn income. They travelled south and reached the port of Hormuz from where they sailed for India. They landed on the island of Diu and spent a few years there. But they did not feel secure and comfortable there and moved towards Gujarat around 936 A.D.[3]

Jadi Rana who was ruling Gujarat at that time, was fair, liberal, sagacious and intelligent. He welcomed them and patiently listened to their story and request for an asylum. Jadi Rana asked them to explain their religious beliefs and rituals and was struck by many resemblances between Zoroastrian and ancient Vedic rituals. He allowed them to stay in his kingdom on four conditions: They would adopt the local language (Gujarati); their women will wear Gujrati dresses; they would not bear arms and, would perform their marriage ceremonies in the evening. The Parsees accepted the conditions and founded the settlement of Sanjan.[4]

One interesting legend, probably fictional, is that Jadi Rana, was apprehensive of allowing so many foreigners to settle down in his kingdom. So, he asked the *valet de chamber* to bring a bowl filled with milk up to the brim to signify that his kingdom was already full and would overflow if more people are added to it.One of the Zoroastrian priests understood the message and added a small amount of sugar to the milk. The sugar dissolved in the milk, sweetening it without causing it to overflow. The priest sent a message to the king that his community, if allowed to stay, will make the lives of the citizens sweeter without disturbing the peace in his State. Jadi Rana gave shelter and permitted them to practice their religion and traditions freely.[5]

The second were the Europeans. Almost 562 years later, in the afternoon of 22 April 1498, a Gujarati Kanji Malam, led Captain-Major Vasco di Gama to Gujarat. Malam was a trader of cotton and indigo from Kutch and made regular voyages to the African coast to barter his goods for gold and ivory.Vasco da Gama had lost his way in Africa and was wandering for four months up the continent's south-eastern coast, from Mozambique to Mombasa, facing the hostility of local rulers and Arab and African merchants. He met Malan, who was also a good navigator, at Malindi on east African coast and Malan navigated him to Calicut.[6]

Gujaratis' had an aptitude for navigation and Gujarati merchants had established trading routes stretching from the Persian Gulf to present-day Malaysia and Indonesia. For two-thousand years before the Portuguese arrived, Gujarat had been at the junction of the world's two main trading axes: The Silk Road and the Spice Route, and it was a principal distribution centre for goods from African, Arab and Asian ports that entered the subcontinent. From the coast, one inland trade route went east to Bihar; another north to Mathura; and a third south to Marathwada. Merchants from Greece, Arabia, Persia, Africa and China came to do business in Gujarat centuries before European explorers set foot in India.[7] No doubt, it was the most prosperous region in India in the ancient times.

****

Situated at a distance of 112 km from Ahmedabad, Vadnagar is steeped in history. Several archaeological excavations, since 1950's, have shown that Vadnagar's known history goes back to 2,500 B. C when settlements of agricultural community existed. Pottery, textiles, fragments, ornaments and tools were found during these excavations from various sites suggesting that it was one of the many Harappan sites. It was so important and thriving Buddhist centre that the Chinese traveller Huan Tsang, stayed there and wrote about it in his travelogues that 'it is rich in Buddhist centre with as many as 10,000 Buddhist monks in the town.' It was a vibrant centre of learning and spirituality having all the elements of a famous city—legends, battles, temples, forts, gates and large water bodies. A prosperous trading city, it was a cultural centre and patronised artists, sculptors, musicians, dancers and actors.

The town remained in obscurity till Xi Jinping on his first meeting with Modi in Gujarat in September 2014, told him that "your birthplace has a special connection with my birthplace in China. Chinese traveller HuanTsang stayed at Vadnagar during his India visit and when he returned to China, he stayed in Xian (the hometown of Jinping)."[8]

****

The early childhood of Modi was like of any other boy in an ordinary poor family— literally dark, hard and full of struggle. But the never-tiring child, as Modi was, did not bemoan and took upon himself the task of working and earning money for the family. Every day, the six-year boy would get up before the sun-rise and open the tea stall by the Vadnagar Railway Station. His father would come later and prepare tea and ask Modi to go to the station when the first train would arrive.Modi, with *kullarhs* (handle-less terracotta cup) in the basket and tea-kettle in hand would reach station. Shouting '*garam chai*' (hot tea) he was selling steaming-hot and much-needed tea to half-awake passengers. As the train would be steaming off the station, the school-bell would ring and he would just cross over the railway track to go to the class.[9]

Modi described his childhood on the official Instagram page of 'Humans of Bombay.' (A team of storytellers concentrating on the journey of individuals, showing that each and every person is unique, inspirational, and relatable. It is a community of more than one million people that believe in the power of humanity) Modi writes:'My family of 8 lived in a 40x12 feet house–it was small, but enough for us. Our days began at 5 AM when my mother would provide traditional forms of curing and healing to newborns and small children. All night, my brother and I would keep the '*chula*' going for her to use. She didn't have the fortune of getting an education, but God was kind and she had a special way of curing ailments. Mothers would line up outside our home because she was known for her healing touch.'

'Then, I would open my father's tea stall at the railway station, clean up and go to school. As soon as school ended, I would rush back to help him, but what I really looked forward to was meeting people from all over India. I would serve them tea and listen to their stories–that's how I learnt to speak Hindi. I would hear some traders speak about 'Bambai' and wonder, 'Will I ever get to see the city of dreams?'[10]

Modi was free in the evening and there was no activity of the station as no train arrived. He would still go to the station and spent hours with *sadhus* staying there. Serving them tea, he would listen their fascinating stories that enthralled him. The stories had lasting impact on his adolescent mind and he increasingly became religious and spiritual. His interaction with them made him aware of Swami Vivekananda and he realise that his new life would only come from working among people.In this way, *Sadhus* left a strong imprint on Narendra Modi and he became inquisitive about Swamiji and spent long hours in the school library reading about his life and works. The readings took his thoughts and dreams beyond a conventional life. He decided not to confine his life in the surroundings of classroom and office and became determined to move out and find out the real world and the people and make a difference to the society. When other boys were thinking of life after finishing education, Modi was developing an inclination towards spiritualism and abstemiousness. As an experiment, he gave up eating salt, chilies, oil and jaggery.[11] In the words of Modi: 'While growing up, I had a lot of curiosity but very little clarity. I would see army men in their uniforms and think that this was the only way to serve the country. But as my conversations with the saints and *sadhus* at the railway station grew deeper, I realised that this too was a world worth discovering.'[12]

The second impressionable effect on his mind was the 1962 war with China. When the Chinese attacked India he was just 12-year old and saw soldiers in trains, passing through Mehsana station, going to fight the enemy. He found the soldiers enthusiastic to fight the Chinese, happy and singing marching songs. He would ensure that every soldier was served tea and was so impressed by their patriotism and heroic fighting stories that he joined National Cadet Corps (NCC) in the school Whenever he can, he went to army camps to spend hours with soldiers.

The impression of soldiers was so strong that he decided to join army and fight for the nation. But the destiny did not fulfil this desire of his and he could not manage adequate money to deposit the fees at the Sainik School in Jamnagar. His family was also strongly opposed to his joining the army.[13]

The third event that impressed his mind at the age of seven and made him to join *sangh* was the discourses by Laxmanrao Inamdar, *pracharak* (preacher) of RSS (Rashtriya Swayamsewak Sangh—National Volunteer Society). Popularly known as '*Vakil Sahib*' (advocate sir), Inamdar visited Vadnagar and Modi went to listen his sermons and was deeply impressed by his knowledge and logical reasoning. The influence was so strong that instead of celebrating Diwali with his family he went with Inamdar to different places he visited. At his instigation, on the Diwali day, eight-year old Modi took the oath of *bal swayamsevak* (child volunteer) at Vadnagar *shakha*. He was so fond of *shakha* that after coming from school, he would dump his books and rush for *shakha*. This gave him an opportunity to do something different, more than what others do in a daily routine way in life.[14]

Modi passed his higher secondary examination in 1967. More than academics, Modi had special interests in co-curricular activities. His special interests were debating, swimming and theatre. He was one of the regular students at the debating club of the school.[15] He was a good debater, with a gift of pomposity, that made him noticeable in the school. He also had deep interest in theatre and liked to play larger-than-life roles. He had an inquisitive mind and spent long hours in the library. Unlike other students he would query the teacher and would ask many clarifications to understand concepts and problems. Sometime he would even question the way the subject was taught in the class. He also believed in hierarchy and challenged the class monitor when he wanted to check his homework. He told him curtly that only the teacher had the authority to check a student's work and other students do not have that power. With teachers also, he was bold and suggested many innovative and unconventional ideas ranging from teaching to washing clothes, for which he was scolded by teachers as well as his mother. As a young child, he was quite liberal in his religious belief and celebrated both Hindu and Muslim festivals. This enabled him to make strong network of friends and neighbours in both the communities.[16] Modi, when eight years old, met Lakshmanrao Inamdar, popularly known as *Vakil Saheb* (lawyer sir), and was greatly impressed by his personality and views. He joined the RSS on his suggestion, as a *bal swayamsevak* (child volunteer) and began attending its local *shakha* (daily gathering of RSS members for games, debate and discussions). Inamdar also became his political mentor. While attending *shakha,* Modi came in contact with two Bharatiya Jan Sangh (earlier version of Bharatiya Janata Party) leaders, Vasant Gajendra Gadkar and Nathalal Jaghda. Both were the founding members of the BJP's Gujarat unit in 1980.

After selling tea at the railway station every day, he attended *Shakha,* that enabled Modi to develop his debating skill. It also made him brave and so daring that he would swim in *Sharmishtha* lake through crocodiles. One day he was hit by the tail of a crocodile and as a revenge he caught one small crocodile and took it home. His mother was greatly annoyed and asked him to drop it back in the lake. A story is told about him about the flag on the top of a temple situated on a small boulder in the middle of the crocodile-filled lake. Modi with his two friends swum through the crocodiles to the temple, changed the flag and swum back to the shore. It was a daring feat that everyone refused. He received a thunderous ovation by the villagers, who wanted the flag to be changed.[17]

The *shakha* in Vadnagar was established in 1944 by Babubhai Nayek, a school-teacher. He was one of several Sangh activists from Maharashtra who fanned out across India and enrolled themselves in public educational institutions to recruit young men into the RSS. After Gandhi's assassination, Nayek kept a low profile, concentrating on his job but occasionally hosting *Vakil Saheb*, the state leader, to address new recruits. On Diwali day in 1958, one of the young boys who lined up to take the oath of *balswayam sevak* from *Vakil Saheb* was Narendra Modi. "Narendra always wanted to do something different. Something more than what we did on a daily routine at home and school. And the RSS *shakha* just provided him that," Sombhai Modi, Modi's oldest brother told Vinod K Jose of *Caravan* magazine in an interview.[18]

Modi's impressionable mind was shaped by strong influences from three persons—*sadhus*, soldiers and RSS *pracharak* Inamdar. Renunciation by the former, serving the nation and the people by the second and dedicated service by Inamdar. All the three determined the future course of his life. An opportunity came running to Modi in 1959, when Tapti river swelled and the floods caused havoc in Surat. The nine-year old Modi, installed a food stall with the help of a group of friends and donated the income for relief work.[19]

When Modi was still a young child of six, his father consulted an astrologer about his future prospects. When told that he would either become a hermit or do something great for the country. This made Damodardas panicky and he decided to fix his marriage. So, he decided to finalise his marriage with Jashodaben, four-year daughter of Mafatlal Patel from Brahmanwada, who lived close by in Mehsana district. Seven years later, both were married but she entered the home of Modi in 1968, after *gauna,* when Modi was 18-year old. Modi was not in favour of the marriage but did not have the courage to defy his parents. This resulted tension in the family and Modi left home, without consummating the marriage.[20] After a few days, she was sent back to her parents' house to continue her studies.This was the beginning and end of Modi's married life. Parting with Jashodaben was without fights between them.[21] And there was no communication thereafter.

Though Modi never accepted Jashodaben his wife, she has always, even today, considered Modi as her husband and met him a few times, thinking that he would accept her. She even went to meet him with Hiraben at the RSS *shakha* in Vadnagar. He had hurt his hand and she put medicine on it. Another time she attended a play '*Ek Phool, Do Maali'* (One flower, two gardeners), in which Modi had acted. After the play she met and told him that his acting was good. *(Ibid)* She met him for the last time in 1987 and he apologized her for not staying with her and asked her to consider divorce and remarriage and carry on with her life. She however replied saying, 'Why would I re-marry? You move forward on your path and I will on mine.'[22]

An emotional pressure because of the cumulative impact of the three influences—*sadhus*, soldiers and *shakha* was fully built in him by the time he finished his schooling. And the forced marriage by parents made him to leave his home to become a monk. The 17-year boy carried a small bag that had only basics—a set of clothes to change, a pair of shorts and shawl and a photograph of his mother. The money in his pocket was only sufficient to sustain him for fifteen days. And he wandered cross-country for two years to become a monk.[23]

Modi left the family, telling them that he would become a '*sanyasi*'(mendicant) and wander in Himalayas. The shocked family had no option but to accept his wish to leave the home. The day he left, his mother prepared a sweet dish that is cooked on special occasions and applied the customary '*tilak*' (a red mark on the forehead).[24]

For the next two years, Modi travelled across Northern and North-eastern India and the family was completely unaware about his whereabouts and travels. First, he went to Belur Math, the headquarters of the Ramakrishna Math, located on the west bank of Hooghly River, founded by Swami Vivekananda in Calcutta (now Kolkata). But he was turned away because he was not a graduate. After staying there and wandering in Calcutta, travelled through Siliguri, and Gauhati (now Guwahati) and passed through a dense forest where he met a *sanyasi* (hermit) and stayed with him for a month. He worked on his garden and had spiritual discussions on celestial matters. From there he moved to another hermitage, Advaita Ashram, set up by Swami Vivekananda in Almora near Nainital in the Kumaon region of Uttarakhand, passing through Bihar and Uttar Pradesh. Here also he was refused admission on the same pretext, that he was not a graduate.

The disappointed Modi left Almora and decided to explore the country to understand the people. He travelled through Himachal Pradesh, Delhi and Rajasthan and after a year reached the Ramakrishna Mission in Rajkot in the Saurashtra region of Gujarat. Here also he was refused admission and was bluntly told by Swami Atmasthanandaji Maharaj, who headed the Ashram, that he should give up efforts to become a monk because he was completely unsuited for it. He also told him that he was meant for other things and he should make pursue it.[25]

It seems that the three monks gave a direction to Modi who got an awakening and abandoned his pursuit to get into the world of spiritualism. For two years, Modi live a life that was spartan, harsh, forlorn but made him extrovert. 'But it was two years well spent because it decided him on his course at a deep psychological level. These travels left a lasting impression on the youngster. He travelled across the expansive landscape of India exploring the various cultures in various parts of the country. It was also a time of spiritual awakening for him that connected him further to a man he always admired- Swami Vivekananda. He had rewired his brain and gained an understanding of himself that removed any doubts about his future.'[26] It was some sort of *nirvana* (awakening or rebirth), though towards materialist world. It was also a time of spiritual awakening for him that connected him further to a man he always admired- Swami Vivekananda.[27]

Modi returned home after wandering for two long years which left a lasting impression on his youngmind. He explored various cultures in various parts of the country. He told his biographer, Andy Marino: 'There was no comfort in my life. I had a small bag and my whole life was in that bag. I was not keeping anything else with me.[28] And Modi was not exaggerating because when he returned after two years, his mother, as soon as he left for the town, began to search his bag. 'It contained almost nothing: a change of clothes, a pair of shorts and a shawl (for the cold mountain nights). There was also – she had no clue from where he got it – a photograph of her that Narendra carried with him all the time he was away.'[29]

Though he returned to Vadnagar, via Delhi and Rajasthan, he unexpectedly left for Ahmedabad just after two week stelling the family that he was ending his *sanyas* to join his uncle Babubhai's business, who ran a canteen at the Gujarat State Road Transport Corporation; this time his destination was fixed and the mission was clear. He was going to Ahmedabad, determined to work with the RSS.

He did not stay with his uncle for long and soon left him to run a tea shop on his own on a cycle. Here he came in contact with a few *pracharaks* (campaigners) who stopped at his tea cart while returning from the morning *shakha*. Soon he disbanded his cart and joined RSS headquarters as an assistant and stayed at Hedgewar Bhavan where 12 to 15 people lived together. He was 21 at that time.[30]

Shortly before the 1971 War, Modi took part in a non-violent protest against the Indian Government in New Delhi and was arrested. This made Inamdar to adopt him as his understudy. Although he was never asked to do so, he washed *Vakil Saheb's* clothes and cleaned his room to derive inner happiness. So strong was his influence on Modi that many years later, in 2001, he co-authored a biography of Inamdar.

With the support and backing of *Vakil Sahib*, he became a regular member of the RSS after the Indo-Pak War of 1971 and became full-time *pracharak* in 1972. He worked under Inamdar in Hedgewar Bhawan and shared his room with other *pracharak* and followed a rigorous daily routine, getting up at five in the morning and working till late night. He was given the responsibilities of preparing tea, breakfast and evening snacks for the seniors in RSS. He also swept and cleaned the ten-roomed building. In the midst of such a hectic routine, he was given responsibilities for the massive summit organised in Siddhpur in 1973. He met top leaders of the Sangh. The networking helped him in his future upward movement in the RSS. He rose rapidly because he was adept at picking his mentors and using them for moving up.[31]

While Modi was involved in the RSS activities. *Vakil Saheb* recognised his potential and persuaded him to restart his studies for higher degrees. At his urging, he commenced his studies through correspondence course and passed the BA (Pass) examination from the University of Delhi in 1978 with political science as one of the subjects. Five years later, in 1982, he received a Master's degree in political science from Gujarat University. Though in the graduation he could get only the third division, he passed his master's in the first division.

This was the beginning of Modi as a staunch RSS follower and because of his hard work he got increasing responsibilities in Gujarat. He helped *sangh* leaders in their travel arrangements, helped them in getting bus and train tickets. Within a year, at 23, he was selected for one-month's Officer Training Camp (OTC) at RSS national headquarters in Nagpur. This level-one training was essential before one was given any official position in the Sangh. After completion, he was appointed RSS *pracharak* in-charge for the Akhil Bharatiya Vidyarthi Parishad (All India Students Council, ABVP) wing in Gujarat. He held this position till the Emergency.[32]

End note

Modi spent his early life in poverty, scarcity and hard work, developing him a dedicated, hardworking and sincere person. Even today, when he is 68, he works 365 days 16-to-18 hours a day. Even when he is fasting for nine days on *navratras* (nine days before Lord Ram's birthday), his work-pattern remains the same. During his first visit to the United States in September 2014, the fasting Modi was busy in meetings from morning till evening; when others were eating breakfast or dinner, he was just sipping water, showing no weakness in his voice and behaviour. The Americans could not believe that a hungry man was full of that strength and energy that they all had.

Determination and fearlessness were two traits that he imbibed from early childhood. As a child, he helped his father and brother in their tea stalls. The crocodiles did not deter him swimming the canal. This fearlessness still survives in him, be it demonetization or GST reforms. He also learnt to lead a disciplined life. Even as a small child he would get up early, open tea stall, sell it at the railway platform and attend classes. As a *Bal Swayamsevak* in RSS, he learnt to follow a stricter disciplined regimen.

His early life made him determined to make it big. Developing a no-nonsense approach, he became highly passionate about what he does. He became a go-getter and seldom failed to achieve the targets that he fixed. He identified threats to his objectives quite early and took corrective measures to achieve them. No doubt, he is a deadly combination of preparedness, assertiveness, oratory, and articulation. He can handle various adversities, face multifarious challenges and possible issues. He is assertive, self-assured and confident without being aggressive. He learnt to transform obstacles into opportunity, have commitment in whatever he does and never looks back. In brief, he has taught himself to be a master strategist.

****

Chapter Two

Indira Gandhi: Early Life

Farrukhsiyar, great-grandson of Emperor Aurangzeb, became the Emperor after killing his uncle Jahandar Shah and his son Azizuddin Shah in 1713. After three years, he went to Kashmir to enlist the support of Mughal ruler to strengthen his power. He met Pandit Raj Kaul and was greatly impressed by his knowledge of Sanskrit and Persian and invited him to Delhi in his royal court. Within a few months, twenty-one-year-old Raj reached Delhi. The Emperor gave him a big *havali* (mansion) on the banks of the *nahar* (a canal), built for carrying Yamuna water to the Red Fort for royal members. He was asked to teach Persian to royal members and was granted a *jagir* (estate) to have a status among nobles. In a short time, Raj became closer to the Emperor, who himself was a scholar of Persian, and, this made Raj quite influential in the Mughal Court. He was better known as Kaul-Nehru in the Royalty as he lived on the banks of *nahar*. His clout in the royal court ensured jobs in the Mughal Courts for next generations. His grandson dropped Kaul and was simply known as 'Nehru.' And thus, began the Nehru dynasty, later to rule India for a long time.[1]

Raj's great-grandson, Laxmi Narain Nehru, saw the declining power of the Mughal Emperor and realised that the future rulers would be the British. Therefore, he shifted loyalties and became the *vakil* (lawyer) of the East India Company to look after its interests at Delhi. But he did not want to annoy the Mughals. So, he allowed his son, Ganga Dhar, who was a good horseman and fencing expert, to work as Kotwal of Delhi under Emperor Bahadur Shah Zafar.

The Mutiny against the British broke out in 1857 and despite their initial setbacks, the British ultimately defeated the rebels, regained power and deposed the Emperor Bahadur Shah Zafar. Ganga Dhar, being a Mughal employee, feared killing by the British and flew to Agra with his wives and children. Since his both daughters, Patrani and Maharani were very fair and beautiful, the British troops intercepted him and thought that he was kidnapping two British girls. His son, Nand Lal, had fair knowledge of English and explained the situation to the British sergeant and saved the family from annihilation. Ganga Dhar died young and three months after his death, Motilal, his third son, was born.

Motilal was brought up by his elder brother, Nandlal, an advocate at High Court in Agra. After passing the Pleader's examination of the Allahabad High Court, began practicing at Kanpur under Pt. Prithvi Nath Chak. But soon he moved to Allahabad (the capital of United Provinces till 1920), where the High Court had shifted from Agra, to help Nandlal in his lucrative practice. But unfortunately, Nandlal died a year later and Motilal took over his practice. Being close to the ruling power, he was approved for appearing at the Privy Council in London and soon began to plead the civil cases of big landlords and had a roaring practice as his clients were big Zamindars, Taluqdars, Rajas and Maharajas. This made him famous and rich and he bought a huge mansion in the Civil Lines, just a few minutes' drive from Government House.[2]

Motilal was an archetypal British aristocratic: wore Savile Row expensive suits, ate English food prepared by a Christian cook, lived in a 42-roomed, English manorial estate type mansion on 20 acres of extensive land, had a retinue of servants, an English chauffer and was served by a group of liveried servants. The dining table was set with antique Sevres porcelain, crystal glasses and silver cutlery. The house had a huge piano in the drawing room and an oversized library of leather-bound books. His three children were taught at home by an Irish tutor and reared by a British governess.[3]

Jawaharlal was the eldest and being the only son had a sheltered and uneventful childhood. He grew up in an environment of privilege at wealthy homes including the large palatial Anand Bhawan. Until he was sixteen, his education was by British tutors and governesses and under the influence of a tutor, Ferdinand T. Brooks, he became interested in science and theosophy. He also had Indian tutors who taught him Hindi language and Sanskrit language. Later, he attended the Harrow in England and got an honours degree in natural science from the Trinity College in Cambridge University. Jawaharlal qualified as a barrister after two years (1910-12) at the Inns of Court School of Law in London.[4]

In such an immensely rich, high born and foreign-educated family, Indira Priyadarshini was born on the stormy night of 19 November 1917 (the month of Russian Revolution), to Jawaharlal, the most pampered son of Motilal. Though she was the first child of the only son of in the most prosperous and elite family of the town, there was not much rejoicing in the house because despite the Nehrus being westernised, the family wanted a male heir. Later, she wistfully commented, a few decades later in her memoirs: 'While my family was not orthodox to consider the birth of a girl child a misfortune, it did regard the male child a privilege and a necessity.'[5] Jawaharlal was an exception to the family as he wrote to her on her 13th birthday that the very month in which she was born, thousands of miles away a major revolution, that changed the history, came about in Russia. Kamla, later began to habitually dress her like a boy. Many a times she was taken as a boy and she herself signed her early letters to her father as 'Indu-boy.'[6]

Like his father, she had the best of British-style education at home, India, Switzerland and England. As a child she had a team of waiting liveried servants at her beck and call, moved in a British pram, and drove around in an English chauffer driven car, the only one in the city. Though her mother and grandpa adored her, she was a neglected child, lonely, self-effacing and inconspicuous as she was neglected by aunts and cousins. She grew up a lonely child and being the only child in the most affluent and influential family in the city, she did not go out to play with other children in the park or neighbourhood. In fact, there was no neighbourhood culture in that part of the city and parks did not exist. So unlike other children she solitarily played games like giving political speeches to the assembled servants or mocking lathi charge or police raids.

Before her formal education began in Anand Bhawan, she had the first political learning when she was four months short of three years. In August 1920, Gandhiji launched the nonviolent non-cooperation movement against the British Government that included boycotts not only of British manufactures but of institutions operated or aided by the British in India: legislatures, courts, offices, schools. Gandhiji asked people all over the country to have a bonfire of English dresses and cloth. A bonfire was also organised at Anand Bhawan. As she saw the fire's flames rising and Savile Row suits, made-in-England satins and chiffons burning, she brought her French frock and tossed it in the fire. When told that her doll was also foreign-made, she clasped it for many days. At last she realised that it must be set on fire if it was foreign made. She carried it to the roof, and with a heavy heart, set it on fire. For a long time, she felt unhappy that she burnt it, as she accepted in her memoirs.[7]

Though her grandfather adored her, she did not grow as a normal child in Anand Bhawan because she was usually disregarded and looked down upon, particularly by her aunt Vijayalakshmi. She also felt lonely as her father was involved in political activities and tours and when at home surrounded by people. Kamla was either accompanying Nehru or not keeping well. The atmosphere in the house was also tense because his father many a times did not agree with Motilal on many political issues.

Bibi Amma, widowed at the age of 18, was another depressing effect on her. Bibi Amma was her grandmother's elder sister who lived in Anand Bhawan and had complete control on her sister. She was a sadist and troublemaker and got pleasure in making others sorrowful. She took special interest in making Kamla and Nehru unhappy. Indira, always avoided, considering her an evil.[8]

Most of her education was at home. She joined St Cecilia's when she was seven, a school run by three British spinsters, but was withdrawn because Jawaharlal protested that she should not be taught at a British school. She then was taught by Indian tutors at Anand Bhawan only. About a year later her studies were disrupted again as she had to go to Geneva with her mother who had developed tuberculosis.

In Geneva, she was admitted to *L'École* Internationale, a multilingual school for the children of those who were involved in the League of Nations. The school was far away from Indira's pension house and she had to trudge the long distance by foot, tram and bus. The life was hard for her as there were no servants and relatives to look after her. But she quickly adjusted to life in Geneva, took complete charge of her mother, who was bed-ridden and looked after the house with the help of a maid. Geneva was good in one sense: She became close to Jawaharlal, who, for the first time, was able to give her his full attention and there were no hostilities from grandmother and Bibi Amma. In the beginning, Jawaharlal accompanied her to school and took her for excursions. But later she began to travel alone with her backpack. It made her independent and she, being on her own, learnt how to be enterprising. She also learnt to manage the house as she had to assist the maid and go with her for shopping. When back from school, she read stories to Kamla and gave her medicines on time. This brought her closer to her mother.[9]

Indira liked her stay in Geneva because she could discard coarse *khadi* Indian dresses and shift to European outfits. She began to wear Swiss dresses, knee shocks and strapped patent leather shoes. She also came in contact with world known poets like Ernst Toller, German-Jewish poets, novelists like Roman Rolland, French biographer and critic and a large number of radical Indians who were exiled from India and were living in Switzerland.

Another addition to her personality was coming closer to nature and developing a love for beauty, high snow-clad mountains and dark green forests. She attended three schools, all surrounded by apple, pear and chestnut trees, learnt French and German and was exposed to foreign cultures. She also became tougher as she had to walk long distance to walk to school, go for running and skiing under the guidance of her father and had to take icy showers, no matter what the weather was. She also went with Nehru for long hicks in mountains. All this made her more fit than any other ten-year Indian girls. She also met V. K. Krishna Menon, who played an important role in her life later.[10]

Though Kamla was not fully recovered, Nehru decided to come back to India as he was missing important political developments. So, on a chilling early December morning, he left from France for India with Kamla and Indira and reached India after 23 days. As Indira was sailing from Marseilles just two weeks after her tenth birthday, she was leaving her childhood behind. She now was a precocious, physically stronger child with an independent mind. She had come to Europe as a meek depressed child but left as a confident, resilient to face any situation and the flexibility to adjust as need arose. She had realised the importance of building good and healthy relationships with others and collaborating with them rather staying by herself.[11]

Back in India, Indira entered in the second phase of her life. She was again in the same old rut—gloomy environment, witnessing sordid neglect of her mother despite her falling health and growing disagreement between Motilal and Jawaharlal, sometime even in the presence of guests. She was all the time humiliated by her aunt, Vijaya Lakshmi Pandit, who used to call her 'ugly and stupid,' making her a silent, moody teenager.

She now was missing her school and wanted to resume her education and was admitted to St Mary's School, a convent run by British and German sisters who detested the Indian culture. She felt as if she was in Europe again as majority of the students were either British or Anglo-Indian. Only a handful were Indian girls. She was not happy in the school because she was the only girl wearing khadi dresses for which she was mocked by the fellow students because of which she felt dreadfully isolated.[12] She also found a complete disharmony between home and school; the former completely in Gandhian culture and the latter completely westernised. She also could not develop roots in the school because she travelled with the family to Mussorie every year during summer months. She also toured different parts of the country with her family for political purposes.[13]

Three years after her return to India, her grandfather, Motilal, died, whom she venerated and loved absolutely and whole heartedly. With the major protector away, humiliations by aunt Vijayalakshmi (Nan) increased and one day she even called her 'ugly and stupid.' Indira overheard the scorn and felt wounded and was completely withdrawn and became grumpy. Kamla and Nehru, when came to know about it, decided to send her away from Allahabad. Both were particularly concerned because with increasing political activity both could be arrested any time. Both were worried to think of what would happen to her if both were arrested. And the possibility was high as the political activity was intensifying and increasing every passing day. So, both decided to send her to Pupils' Own School in Poona now (Pune), that was close to Sabarmati Ashram, where Gandhiji was living. And, thirteen-and-a-half-year-old Indira landed at Poona to study at Pupils' Own School.[14]

The school was run by a Parsi couple, Jehangir and Coonverbai Vakil who were trying to inculcate socialist ideas in students. Though good in French, she was an indifferent student. But she came to be known as the most caring student and all needy students thrived under her care. She was particularly attached to a *Harijan* (lower caste whom upper caste would not even touch) girl whom she bathed and picked lice from her hair. Feroze, realising the political potential of the Nehru family, was impatient to marry Indira. So, he proposed to her when she was studying at Poona. Kamla and Indira, both, did not approve it and he was snubbed by both saying that she was too young to think of marriage.[15]

When Indira matriculated from Pupils' Own School, Nehru did not want her to go to any Indian University, including Allahabad and was much impressed by Rabindranath Tagore and the school established by his father at Santiniketan. He visited him when he took Kamla to Calcutta (now Kolkata) for special medical treatment. Though he did not think high of academic standards at Santiniketan, he decided to send her there till she was sent to Europe for higher studies. It was at Santiniketan that Indira developed deep interests in fine arts and culture, particularly in classical Indian dance of ancient Manipuri school. She also liked Indian and European music, theatre, painting, and crafts of all types. This made her impassioned with colours. Later, when she became the Prime Minister, she was very particular in selecting the colour of her own clothes, particularly sarees.

In Santiniketan, she became a matured adolescent girl with natural adolescent-passionate emotions. She began to feel sensual craving for a male and, like any normal girl, had a teenage crush on her middle-age French teacher, Frank Oberdorf, who also showed his love for her. He too seems to have realised the political significance of the Nehru family and like Feroze, wanted to benefit. Both continued to exchange letters still she finally decided to marry Feroze.

She also developed inner strength as, away from intense political activities, crowds and ill-treatment by Nan and cousins, she was living in peace, harmony, happiness and beauty. She felt safe and learnt to live quietly introspecting within herself.[16] She learned to live like a commoner; sleep on mats, taking cold bucket baths and sweeping floors.

The third phase of Indira's life began when she spent one month at Bhowali with Feroze, whose parentage was suspicious. Though known to be the son of Jehangir Faredoon Ghandy, he was believed to be the son of Jahangir's sister Dr Shirin Commissariat, a famous surgeon in Allahabad and a girl friend of the leading advocate Raj Bahadur Kakkar. Feroze first came in contact with the Nehru family in March 1930, when Kamla and twelve-year old Indira, along with a group of women demonstrators, were picketing outside Ewing Christian College. Feroze, sitting on the College wall, was enjoying the fun. It was a hot sunny day and Kamla fainted as she could not bear the midday heat. Feroze, ran to her, comforted her and took her and Indira to their home.

Feroze was handsome, energetic, hopeful and helpful and became a devotee and hanger-on of Kamla. In fact, he was infatuated by Indira and realised that the best way to win her was becoming faithful to her mother. He also realised the importance of the Nehru family in the emerging national politics and looked for an opportunity to marry her. So next day he left his studies and became a Congress volunteer to actively participate in the freedom movement. He also changed the spelling of his name from 'Ghandy' to 'Gandhi.'[17]

Her education at Santiniketan was interrupted twice. First, when within a month of her joining Santiniketan, Kamla was down with pleurisy and Indira left for Allahabad. Though everyone from the family was there, Indira was pained to see that everyone was involved in himself/herself and did not come forward to help Kamla when she was suffering and needed help. She even wrote to Nehru that 'though the house was full of people, no one came to help her till you arrived, when everyone showed utmost care and concern. Now that you have again gone…there is some danger of mummie being left to herself…As soon as Mummie is strong enough she should be removed to any place outside Allahabad.'[18] Things, however, did not change and Kamla remained lonely and uncared. Consequently, Kamla again fell seriously sick within three months. So, she was taken to Bhowali sanitorium.

Feroze and Indira accompanied her. Indira went back to Santiniketan after a month.

During the one month stay at Bhowali, Indira came closer to Feroze. She saw him attending and caring for her mother like a nurse. Probably it was Feroze's care for her mother, who was neglected by everyone including Jawaharlal, that drew her closer to him. Realising her soft corner for him, he again proposed her at Bhowali when she was Eighteen, but she again cold-shouldered him.

Second time she left Santiniketan for ever, when Kamla was not responding to the treatment at Bhowali and was to be moved to Europe for surgery. After a month-and-a-half she left for Germany with her mother and Kamla's cousin, Dr Madan Atal. Feroze accompanied them up to Bombay to see them off. He resolved to join them later and reached Germany after seven months.

Kamla was operated in Berlin after about a month of leaving India and was sent to Badenweiler in southwest Germany for further treatment. Nehru wanted Indira to move out from the melancholic atmosphere of Badenweiler which was surrounded by TB patients. She was moved to Switzerland and she travelled alone through its several cities. This was the time when Nehru thought of sending her to Oxford and asked a few of his friends to explore the possibilities. She was back with her mother after a month.

Feroze, in India, was exploring the possibilities of joining Indira in Germany. He was persuading his aunt Dr Commissariat to send him to London School of Economics (LSE). Meanwhile the doctors suggested that Nehru should join Kamla, who, they thought, was nearing death. He was released from the jail on compassionate grounds reaching Badenweiler to be with her in her last days. Kamla improved after his arrival and Indira went to London to explore the possibilities of joining Oxford. She returned end-December and suddenly left for Wengen to secretly meet Oberdorf. Almost at the same time, flabbergasted Kamla and Nehru, saw Feroze suddenly turning up at Badenweiler. He followed Indira to Wengen, and returned the same night and stayed at Badenweiler, dropping the plan of going to London as promised to his aunt.

The arrival of Feroze alarmed Kamla and she discussed with Nehru about her future. She told him that Indira should not be married to Feroze because he was inconsistent and would not be able to support her. Matter ended there because he wanted to return India as he was elected Congress President. But destiny wanted the other way. Kamla died the day he was to leave, 28 February 1936. Only twenty days earlier, both had celebrated their 20th wedding anniversary. Feroze was at her bed-side along with Nehru and Indira. After cremating her, Jawaharlal and Indira left for Montreux (Switzerland) and Feroze for London. Nehru returned to India with Kamla's ashes and Indira came to L'Ecole Nouvelle at Bex (Switzerland). Soon, she left Bex for London to prepare for Oxford. On way, she met Feroze who was in Paris.

After four months, she appeared for a test for Oxford, but failed in Latin. She joined Badminton School but did not like the atmosphere which was stifling like a prison camp. Shortly after joining Badminton School, she went to Bex to collect her stuff. On her way to Bex, she stopped at Paris to spend two days with Feroze. Both returned to London where they lived close by. Love grew between them and they visited concerts, theatre and opera with an old friend of Indira, Shanta Gandhi, no relation of Feroze, and spent time in Switzerland skiing.

Oberdorf had not given up the hope of marrying Indira and, a month later came to visit her in London as she had come back from Paris. He invited her to come to Germany at Christmas time, that was four months away. Old love came back to her and she was confused but soon decided in favour of Feroze. She wrote to him that she would not visit him as she did not want to love him 'even if he was the last man on earth.'[19]

She again appeared for Oxford admission test and failed second time and she had no option but to go to Badminton School that she strongly disliked. During Christmas she wanted to go to Switzerland with Feroze but the Headmistress, Miss Baker, did not give her permission, but had to allow her when Nehru intervened. Indira, Feroze and Shanta spent Christmas in Wengen, informing her father that she was with friends, not revealing who the friends were.[20]

She passed Oxford admission test in her third attempt, the last chance, and was selected for Somerville College of Oxford. Before joining Oxford, she visited India. She had come after two years and was forlorn because everything reminded her of her mother.[21] At Anand Bhawan, she found her father exhausted, tired and his robust health broken down. He had been touring India for eight-month for electioneering meetings and speeches. Now he desperately needed a break from all political activity. So, he, along with Indira, went for a month-long holiday to Burma (now Myanmar), Malaya (now Malaysia) and Singapore. During the vacation, she realised that the two were not as close as father and daughter as earlier. They never had a heart-to-heart talk and Nehru could not bridge the gulf. Later he accepted it and wrote to her that now onwards it wold be good if 'we meet infrequently.'[22] Probably, it was because she was in secret love with Feroze and he with Padmaja. The two did not share each other's secret, though both were aware about each other's affairs.

After six months, in September 1937, Indira sailed for England to join Oxford. Instead of going direct to London, she stopped at Paris where Feroze was living. Being autumn, both spend time roaming around the city. One evening, at the steps of the Roman Catholic Church of Sacré-Cœur Basilica, he proposed her third time. And, this time, she did not refuse and both were engaged, though secretly.

One month before she was 20, she joined Oxford's Somerville College. During her one-year stay, she was more interested in political activities than studies. Being Nehru's daughter, everyone wanted to make friendship with her and was regularly invited for meetings, public lectures, concert, and theatres. She also joined University Labour Club and Indian Majlis. She also visited London more frequently to spend time with Feroze and spent most of her time with him. She also met many of his left-wing friends. As a result, she could not pass her moderations (MOD) exam and wrote to her father that 'the thrill of Oxford has worn off and Oxford life, as it really is, is not a very attractive proposition.'[23]

Her inability to pass the moderations exam demoralised Indira because everyone else had passed the exam in the first attempt. She understood that now onwards she would have to study seriously and reduce here participation in social and political activities. She stayed more in her room to study. This made her unhappy and she began to lose weight. She also began to wear Indian dresses instead of western ones. She also became apprehensive about her secret engagement with Feroze as she began to worry the reaction in the family in India.[24] She reappeared in the Mod exam for the second time, but failed again in Latin.

By the spring of 1938, she was to take her the third and last chance of appearing Mod exam. She was not very confident about her Latin, and so, decided to drop out of the exam. Moreover, since she returned from Germany in January, she was feeling exhausted, weak and sick. She left for London the day she was to appear for her Mod exam, and with this her option of becoming an Oxford graduate ended. She remained un-graduated, though Somerville College had given an honorary degree in 1971.[25]

Almost the same time Nehru came to visit England and Europe. He was to stay and meet a host of important persons and Indira accompanied her father. She accompanied Nehru to Europe and travelled widely. The travels and long meeting followed by socialisation were strenuous and Indira almost collapsed when they reached Budapest and was admitted to hospital for two weeks. Because of her poor health, Nehru brought her back to India.

She was down with pleurisy when she returned to India and was sent to Almora, near Nainital, for treatment with aunt Krishna Hutheesing and her two kids. But she always insisted going back to London to be with Feroze. Nehru did not want her to go but she defied him and left for London after five months in April 1939. In London, she stayed close to Feroze, who had left his studies at LSE and was devoting more time to V. K. Krishna Menon's India League, a radical organisation that Menon had formed to fight for India's freedom. Indira came in contact with him and was greatly influenced by him and his work. Menon, fiercely intelligent but idiosyncratic person, played a significant role in her life for the next 35 years.[26] Menon, a shrewd man, realised the importance of Nehru's daughter, and involved her in India League. During her participation in India League, she developed friendship with a group of highly intelligent persons like P N Haksar, Nikhil Chakravartty, and Mohan Kumaramangalam. All played important role in her life when she became the Prime Minister.

Indira, after her return from India, was involved in two affairs; working for India League and spending time with Feroze. She stayed with Feroze in his one-roomed apartment, though Nehru was not aware of it. P N Haksar, a close confident and advisor of her till the emergence of Sanjay as the power centre during Emergency, was living close by. When Haksar visited them, she did not conceal what the sleeping arrangements were in 'Feroze tiny, book-filled flat.' She even thought of getting married with Feroze in London as 'both were living together as man and wife.' But Feroze was against it because he thought that Nehru would be hurt to see them husband-wife without his permission.[27] But the idea was still in her mind and had to be given up as she fell sick and began to have high fever. She was very scared that the old problem may be reviving again.[28] Finally, both left for India in early March. 'From Durban they steamed north into the Indian Ocean, past Madagascar and the Seychelles, up to the Arabian Sea, and finally reached Bombay on 16 April 1941. This time Indira was coming to India to stay. She was young, in love and on the verge of being someone else – Indira Gandhi.'[29]

She came back to India to stay for good, bidding adieu to UK.

Back in India, she wanted to get married to Feroze to which Nehru opposed because he was sure that the two were poles apart. Moreover, he considered Feroze loud, boisterous and a great user of expletives. Also, he had no university degree, a profession or even the prospect of a steady income and, therefore, he thought that he would not be able to support the lifestyle Indira had become accustomed to in the Nehru family. Then, he also thought that since Indira was continuously having poor health for the past several years, she may not be able to bear child bearing traumata. Nehru also thought that he would lose Indira if she marries Feroze and he did not want to live without her. Also, at the back of his mind was that Kamla was against this marriage and at the death-bed she had expressed to Nehru her fear that Indira would 'make the mistake of her life by marrying Feroze.'[30] Nehru diplomatically asked her to consult Mahatma Gandhi, whom she respected, hoping that he would persuade her to drop the idea. Nan even advised her to have an affair with him rather than having him a husband, because she was aware about his flirting with her daughters. Nehru also asked her to consult seniors in the family, all told her not to go for this marriage. But despite all, including Gandhi, advising her not to go in for the marriage, she stuck to her decision. In fact, after listening to all, she became more adamant to marry Feroze.

Jawaharlal had no option but to agree for the marriage. Ultimately, 141 days before Mahatma Gandhi launched the Quit India Movement, Indira was married to Feroze on the *Ram Navami* day, the 26th March 1942.

End Note

Though born in a political ambitious affluent family, her early life as a child was unsettled, isolated and dispiriting. Unlike other average children, her childhood was not a happy one. This was becasue her father was mostly away from home for his political activities and her mother, besides frequently suffering from bouts of illness, was not only neglected but ignored and insulted. She also could not develop a very warm relationship with her father, because she always blamed him for the negligent and affronting behaviour of the family towards her and mother. Naturally, she did not develop a warm and loving relationship with her father. She was fond of him, as a daughter should be, but the relationship could be called formal and detached. The environment in the family and the antagonistic and scornful relatives, particularly her aunt and cousins, who were most of the time there, made her imperious and cripplingly insecure. No doubt, she became defiant, self-reliant and arrogant in her later life. This may be one reason for marrying Feroze, which became disturbed at an early stage. In short, she was an unhappy child, weak in studies and reckless in decisions.[31]

Chapter Three

Modi: Political Life in Making

Modi owes his entry to politics to the enduring guidance of Vakil Saheb who became his idol when he was seven and remained so till his death. He was greatly influenced by his organisational capability built around renunciation, dedication and hard work.[1] The influence of Vakil *saheb* was so strong on his persona that when he returned after two years of self-exile, he first met his mother and then, instead of going to meet his father, he went to the *shakha* to contact Vakil *saheb*. Modi's political outlook was shaped by Vakil Saheb who taught him to discover other person's virtues and qualities and work on them. Inamdar became his mentor and protector and guided him to reach to his goal of making India of his dream.[2] In an interview to his official biographer Andy Marino he said: 'when I was working with the RSS, there was one gentleman who was my mentor—Laxmanrao Inamdar. Whenever I was facing any problem at that time, I used to talk to him. Now I have an autopilot system in my thinking process.'[3] Modi repaid his debt to Vakil Saheb by comparing him to *Ramsetu*, mythical bridge that Lord Ram built to Sri Lanka. Vakil Saheb died in 1984 and Modi paid his homage by writing his stimulating biography *Setubandh,* released by the then Prime Minister Atal Bihari Vajpayee in August 2001.

Modi learnt the art of oratory from Vakil Saheb who possessed flawless oratory skills as he addressed meetings in fluent Gujarati. As Modi writes in *Jyotipunj*, his 2008 compilation of the biographies of 16 RSS luminaries including Inamdar, Vakil Saheb had the ability to use everyday examples to convince his listeners. Modi was motivated by the way Inamdar convinced a reluctant RSS worker to take up a job: 'If you can play it, it's a flute, if not, it's still a stick.'[4]

****

Modi's interest in politics developed when, after wandering in the wilderness, he came back from two-year *'Bharat Darshan* (tour-India)*'* in 1969. During this time his inclination was more towards spiritualism, but now he finally decided to enter the materialist world and within a few days left for Ahmedabad and went to his uncle. With no money in his pocket, he travelled to Ahmedabad and stayed with his uncle, helping him in his business before he set up his own tea shop on his bicycle. It was mostly visited by RSS *pracharaks* who used to stop to have tea at his tea cart when returning from the morning *shakha*. Soon, they helped him to join RSS headquarters as an assistant. He, 21 at that time, stayed at Hedgewar Bhawan where 12 to 15 people lived together. His RSS connections took him to the BJP and to higher politics.[5]

After he joined the RSS, he began to take active part in their activities. The turning point was when he went to Delhi to participate in a *dharna* (sit-in strike) for allowing RSS workers to help army to fight on the Bangladesh front. Modi was arrested and sent to Tihar jail but was released soon. Modi's reaction was that 'instead of sending us to the warfront the government arrested us and sent us to Tihar jail.[6] It was that moment when Vakil Saheb noticed a potential in Modi and, at his initiative, Modi formally joined the RSS and was moved to Hedgewar Bhawan as an apprentice.[7] There was no turning back after that and Modi marched onwards on his political journey.

Modi's entry into politics was at the junior-most position. In his own words, the life was hard: 'Waking up at 5.00 a.m., fetching milk, waking up everybody up, participating in morning prayers, making tea and serving everyone. It was followed by cleaning utensils, going to the *shakha*, returning and making snacks for everyone. Then I served breakfast from 8.30 to 9.00 a.m., after which I had to clean up the entire building, consisting of eight to nine rooms. I swept and mopped the whole place, and washed both Vakil Saheb's and my clothes…For lunch, I used to go to some swayamsevak's house by rotation. After returning to Hedgewar Bhawan I again got to work and make tea for everyone. This was my routine for at least a year, and this was the time when I met many people.'[8]

Vakil Saheb had an immense influence over Modi, who gave him the same respect he gave to his mother. Both shared a special bond and Vakil Saheb became the main architect of Modi's political career. He always motivated Modi and told him never to refuse any responsibility, as they say in the army 'never volunteer, never refuse.' Modi won his confidence by working hard and sincerely under his supervision. 'Basically, whichever assignment is given to me, at that point of time, I am totally involved in it.

I never think about my past, I never think about my future,' he told Nilanjan Mukhopadhyay.[9]

Modi, under the benefaction of Vakil Saheb during the following 14 years, inherited his oratorial and organisational skills, his rapport with people, the ability to remember thousands of names and fine details. Among Modi's most precious possessions today are his mentor's diaries. Inamdar recorded his daily experiences during his life which was spread over decades. Modi also maintained a daily diary since the mid-1980s. When he moved to 7, RCR, one of his precious possesses was Vakil Saheb's diaries. These were his most valuable treasure.[10]

Modi a *pracharak*

Modi gained the complete confidence of Vakil Saheb after working tirelessly for eighteen-months. His work was rewarded when in 1972, Vakil saheb got him appointed a *pracharak*. As *pracharak,* Modi shared his room and meals with Manohar Lal Khattar, now the Chief Minister of Haryana. Khattar, an expert cook, prepared khichdi for Modi and Modi taught him how to operate a computer. This was the beginning of a long political process and struggle of 42 years that made Modi the Prime Minister of India, the most powerful and coveted position in India.

In 1973 Narendra Modi was given responsibility of working for a massive summit organised in Siddhpur where he met top leaders of the Sangh.

When Modi was cutting his teeth as an activist, the atmosphere in early 70's in Gujarat, in India as well, was very volatile. When he reached Ahmedabad, the city was reeling under one of the worst instances of communal riots. In the rest of the nation too, the Congress Party, which had already suffered reverses in the 1967 Lok Sabha Elections had spilt between the faction of Mrs Indira Gandhi and the erstwhile syndicate, whose leaders included Morarji Desai from Gujarat. Riding on the wave of a campaign to eradicate poverty, Indira Gandhi swept back to power in 1971 Lok Sabha elections winning 352 out of 518 seats in the Lok Sabha. In the Gujarat State Elections too she replicated the strong performance, winning 140 out of 182 seats and capturing a gigantic voteshare of over 50 per cent.

However, the euphoria of the Congress and Indira Gandhi faded as quickly as it was created. The dreams of quick reform and progress had given way to disillusionment amongst the common man in Gujarat. The struggles and sacrifices of political stalwarts such as Indulal Yagnik,

Jivraj Mehta and Balwant Rai Mehta had been undone by the politics of greed. By the end of the 1960s and early 1970s, corruption and misgovernance of the Congress government in Gujarat had reached new heights. The grand promise of '*Garibi Hatao* (Remove poverty)' turned out to be an empty one as it gradually changed into '*Garib Hatao*'. The condition of the poor worsened, and in Gujarat the misery was compounded with a severe famine, causing steep price rise thereafter. Endless queues for basic commodities had become a common sight in the State and there was no respite for the common man.[11]

****

Before he was appointed the *pracharak*, Modi was sent for one-month Officer Training Camp at RSS national headquarters in Nagpur. This national-level training was essential for getting any official position in the RSS. As *pracharak* Modi was to oversee the *Akhil Bharatiya Vidyarthi Parishad* (ABVP) in Gujarat. ABVP is Sangh's student wing in colleges and universities. He held this position throughout the Emergency. Modi was supposed to function like an underground guide, like a vein hidden under the skin. He had authority but had to remain unseen in public. But Modi was different person and did things to get attention and noticed.

A story was popular among *pracharaks*: ABVP was asked to organise agitations against the government in different close-by areas. Such a meeting was being held at the Bhullabhai Char Rasta in Ahmedabad. The speakers were asked to speak in a moderate tone against the government to avoid police and the intelligence agencies' action. When the meeting was in progress, Modi was going on a cycle and heard the speaker using restrained language. He jumped onto the stage, snatched the mike and gave an inflammatory speech, using abusive language and anger against the government and got warm ovation. But RSS took offence at his behaviour that night and was given a dressing-down by a senior for an underground *pracharak* coming out openly. He was brusquely told that he has broken the discipline of the RSS.[12]

It may be that higher-ups in RSS were annoyed because Modi was often breaking RSS' strict code. According to Shankar Singh Vaghela, a bitter rival of Modi: Modi was doing many things forbidden in RSS, for example, keeping a trimmed beard, wearing half-sleeve and not full-sleeves shirts, white and not khaki shorts and missing morning *shakha* by sleeping late. Also, he liked starched and ironed cloths that were not liked by many in RSS. He was also outspoken, took unilateral decisions and had bold approach to things.'[13] Things became so serious that *Sarsanghchalak* Madhav Sadashiv Golwalkar had to publicly question him for keeping beard.[14]

Two factors saved Modi for his incalcitrant behaviour: his organisational ability and the Emergency imposed by Indira Gandhi. Modi, during his apprenticeship and after becoming a *pracharak,* had thoroughly understood the RSS system of functioning from the lowest to the highest levels. No doubt, he became the most sought-after person if any thing was to be done. He assisted everyone in the office, supervised correspondence and organised party meetings from beginning to end.

There seemed to be no task he did not know to handle, no formality or process within the RSS he was unfamiliar with or found too mundane to take care. Some called him workaholic but he was steadily making himself indispensable.[15] His reputation of being efficient and a dutiful organiser overs had owed indiscipline in him. Though considered egoistic, rough and arrogant by many, more responsibilities were given to him due to his positive qualities and Vakil Saheb's protection.

The real Modi came up during the Emergency when Vakil Saheb, who was the Chairman of the Gujarat Lok Sangharsh Samiti (GLSS) appointed him its General Secretary. GLSS was a coordination committee for resisting Emergency. Then on Modi worked unseen and became very active in the agitation. He developed close contact with youth and student leaders and developed many safe abodes where underground workers could reside and work safely. Modi also developed a wide circle of sympathisers, friends for the safe lodging of underground leaders. He also raised funds to pay for their maintenance. He was instrumental in making several RSS leaders melted away in the Gujarati families.

Modi organised several secret adventures feats during the Emergency. One such story was that when a RSS leader, Keshavrao Deshmukh, with whom Modi was to coordinate, was arrested, Modi realised that another victim of the police may be Nathalal Zagda. Modi rushed to his house on his scooter and took him to a safe abode. Also, after the arrest of Keshavrao, it was realised that he was carrying papers containing details of the future programmes of GLSS and Modi was asked to retrieve them. Modi went to the police station along with a female volunteer who posed as his relative. Modi persuaded the police officer to let her meet him. While he engaged him in a discussion she retrieved papers despite police presence.[16] In another critical situation, when Nanaji Deshmukh was arrested, he was having with him a book containing the addresses of sympathizers. Narendra Modi had to remove everyone of them from the underground network and begin the difficult task of finding alternatives.[17]

Modi was also responsible to make travel arrangements for anti-Emergency activists to and from Gujarat, including Subramaniam Swami. Many a time he had to move in disguise so that he was not recognized. One day he would appear as a Sikh gentleman and next day a saffron-robed *sanyasi*. One time he was sitting in a railway carriage, hiding behind a thick-black beard, when his old school teacher sat down next to the grown-up urchin.' The disguise worked perfectly, but some years afterwards the teacher attested that as Narendra disembarked, he introduced himself and offered a hearty salutation.'[18]

Modi was also a part of the hidden campaign attempting to mobilize people and create widescale disaffection against Indira. A number of pamphlets were printed by him and distributed in the villages of Rajkot, where the saffron body assigned him to consolidate their base. During the period, Modi also wrote a book, *Sangharsh me Gujara*t (Gujarat under Emergency) which reminisces the horrific atrocities committed by the security forces during the emergency.

Emergency was a turning point in the life and career of Modi. It gave him an opportunity to work with leaders from different parties. Narendra Modi wrote on his blog on June 2013:'For youngsters like me, the Emergency gave a wonderful opportunity to work with a wide spectrum of leaders and organisations that were fighting for the same goal. It enabled us to work beyond institutions we had been brought up with. From stalwarts of our family, Atal ji, Advani ji, late Shri Dattopant Thengadi, Late Shri Nanaji Deshmukh to socialists like Shri George Fernandes to Congressmen like Shri Ravindra Varma, who worked closely with Morarjibhai....'[19]

Modi returned to Gujarat in the summer of 1979 at a time when the State was passing through a period of turmoil and change. After coming back to power Indira dismissed the BJP Government in February 1980 and in the following election in June Congress won 149 out of 180 seats. Madhav Singh Solanki became the CM. Solanki, thought of a political marvel of KHAM, Kahatriya (warriors), Harijans (underclass), Adivasis (tribals), and Muslims, strategy to combine these four poor and marginalised groups and provided them 18 per cent reservations. This alienated upper castes, (Baniyas, Patels and Brahmins) and caused State-wide riots causing killings and burning of property. But it brought the majority voters in the fold of the Congress.

When all this was happening, Modi criss-crossed Gujarat on his motorcycle, visiting every Taluka and almost every village to thoroughly understand the problems being faced by the people and observed the chaos generated by the Congress Government and the damage being done to the wider society. He thought over the entire problem and read widely and reached to the conclusion that development was the only solution to this problem that was becoming multifaceted year after year. He also understood that the only way to development was to strengthen the free market economy by formulating a rational resource management, human as well as physical, policy. For achieving this, a strong social and economic infrastructure was required to provide equal opportunities to the poor to prosper. It will automatically eliminate the social unrest caused by frustration. This brought him in direct conflict not only with Congress but with the conservative section of his own Party because he bluntly told all that the problems cannot be solved with the conventional solutions.

The assassination of Indira was a turning point in the life of Modi when a year later he became a key member of BJP. In the 1984 election Rajiv Gandhi, on the sympathy wave, got a historic victory by getting 414 Lok Sabha seats and BJP winning just two seats, Dr AK Patel from Gujarat and Chandupatla Janga Reddy from Andhra Pradesh. Post-assassination riots caused trouble in Gujarat also where the industry and business began to suffer severely. Modi travelled far and wide in Gujarat and BJP began to strengthen. It began to show results as BJP won local elections and also won the Lok Sabha by-election. But the riots were not subsiding in Gujarat and Rajiv Gandhi dismissed Solanki and appointed Amarsinh Chowdhry, an Adivasi, the CM. Though the riots subsided, social tension continued, particularly between Hindus and Muslims and by 1990 it was widespread. Both had barricaded their areas and Muslim areas were referred to as "border and Muslim neighbourhood were called 'Pakistan'".[20] This caused rifts in the Congress also.

When this was happening, BJP was lurching after the massive Congress victory in 1984 Lok Sabha election. Fortunately for BJP a relief came in February 1987 when Ahmedabad municipal elections were held. Modi was given the responsibility of organising the campaign. 'A meticulous calculation was made about how many Party workers were needed to canvas how many votes, and what percentage of success was likely from so much energy expended per ward. Such meticulous micro-planning helped the Party win two-thirds of the seats in the Ahmedabad municipality, a complete reversal of fortune.'[21]

This strategy was highly successful because every voter was connected to a party worker. It sent shockwaves to Congress and it realised the damages done to it because of its divisive policies. It also realised that BJP was benefitting because of polarisation of Hindu votes due to its policy of favouring minorities. 'Religious polarisation was rife. The ordinary citizen felt under siege. The mafia don (and later terrorist) Abdul Latif, even won an election for the Ahmedabad Municipal Corporation from his prison cell. The BJP would capitalize on the outrage.'[22] Political analyst Achyut Yagnik says: It has been the BJP's formula in Gujarat to portray the Muslim as an enemy and project the party as the protector of Hindus. All this began with Latif and moved on to Pervez Musharraf and then to Sohrabuddin.'[23] This was the beginning of the rise of Modi in Gujarat, enriching Modi's deference in the higher echelons of RSS and BJP.

After the assassination of Indira Gandhi, the support-base of BJP was declining in the Indian polity. In the victory of Ahmedabad Municipal Corporation, the RSS saw a ray of hope of polarisation of Hindu votes. Therefore, it decided to renew the practice of deputing its senior *pracharaks*, that it had stopped in 1980 when Bhartiya Jan Sangh was transformed into Bhartiya Janata Party. In 1987, Lal Krishna Advani specifically asked for Modi to be deputed as one of the two *pracharak*s from RSS.This was the way Modi joined BJP and was appointed as Organising Secretary of Gujarat.

After that there was no looking back.

This was happening when Rajiv Gandhi was proving pusillanimous as his glimmer was fading out mainly because of Shah Bano case and Bofors scam. The new law, Muslim Women (Protection of Rights on Divorce) Act 1986, denied Muslim women even those rights that other Indian women enjoyed. This made even the Congressmen believe that their Party was appeasing the hardcore Muslims. This gave BJP a new tool to become aggressive as Hindu votes began to polarised around it. This also alienated forward-looking sections of the Muslim women. Rajiv wanted to make amends and to pacify Hindus, he allowed regular access to Ram idols, placed by nationalists after the partition, within the Babri Masjid. Earlier access was allowed only once a year. This gave a new bludge on to Vishwa Hindu Parishad (VHP) to demand that the Babri Masjid be replaced by a grand Ram Mandir (temple of Lord Ram). BJP took advantage of the development and began a Ram Janambhomi Campaign (a movement to build a grand temple where Lord Ram was born).

After Modi joined BJP, he gained a new confidence and, it seems, he decided to move upwards in politics by making a strong base at the grassroots. The first thing he did was to make himself visible in the whole of Gujarat state. He planned *Nyay Yatra* (journey for justice) in 1987 and travelled extensively the whole of Gujarat. He organised another Yatra,

Lok Shakti Yatra (journey for empowering people), visiting about 10,000 villages to mobilise people against liquor mafia. During this journey he not only raised funds for BJP but also made a strong base in the tribal areas of the eastern Gujarat.

In 1990, the then BJP President Advani planned his *Ayodhya Rath Yatra*, which eventually brought down the Babri Masjid, from the Somnath Temple in Gujarat to Ayodhya in UP. It was the brainchild of Pramod Mahajan who was also its National Coordinator. Modi was to be in-charge of the firstlag of the *Yatra* and was to accompany it from Somnath to Mumbai. Three aspects of his personality impressed journalists and Advani also, who later became his protector and promoter. First, he had his eye for detail. Every evening, he would provide every journalist covering the yatra a printed sheet with the exact programme for the next day. His planning and organisation of the entire route under his control was certainly precise. Not only that, Modi personally ensured that the accompanying media persons were provided every facility during their travel with the *Yatra*. He made sure that arrangements were made for fax machines at every place, BJP local ofûce bearing all expenses. 'Modi even occasionally suggested the storyline and what could be highlighted! Micromanagement was an obvious skill, one he would use to great effect in later years.'

The second aspect was the clothes he wore. Though he did not wear designer kurtas, he was always flawlessly dressed and his turned-out was perfect. His crisply starched and ironed kurtas made him different from the ordinary RSS–BJP *karyakartas* (workers) who wore crumpled kurta pyjamas.

Third, Modi's expressive eyes, reminded Rajdeep of Kenny Rogers' hit song 'The Gambler': 'Son, I've made a life from readin' people's faces, knowin' what the cards were by the way they held their eyes.' With his wide twinkling eyes, he played the game of life gently, perhaps lacking the killer instinct. 'Modi in those early days smiled and laughed a lot, but his eyes at times glared almost unblinkingly—stern, cold and distant. They were the eyes of someone playing for the highest possible stakes in the gamble of life. His smile could embrace you, the eyes would intimidate.' face.[24]

As a reward, Modi was appointed a member of the 17-member National Election Committee, that brought him to the centre-stage. The following year, Modi was given a major national assignment of organising a 47-day cross-country *Ekta Yatra* (Unity Journey) led by the new BJP President, Murli Manohar Joshi, from Kanyakumari to Srinagar where the national flag was to be hoisted at Lal Chowk.

Modi planned and efficiently executed the entire route and organised all the events along the way. But what annoyed Joshi was his habit of not following Joshi's instructions. For example: Joshi wanted that all travelling BJP leaders and volunteers, should eat together. But Modi often disappeared and went missing with Anant Kumar in Bangalore (now Bengaluru). Joshi was furious, reprimanding him in the presence of all and warned to behave himself as discipline was unbreakable in BJP. Modi, despite that, continued with the *Yatra* and was in the forefront, along with Joshi, and hoisted the flag without wearing a bulletproof jacket, being worn by others.[25]

When Modi returned, Shankersinh Vaghela, Party's Gujarat President was elected to the Lok Sabha. Vaghela was not happy with Modi as he believed that Modi, as Gujarat's General Secretary was trying to outshine him. He believed that Modi was trying to push Keshubhai Patel, his long-time rival, and feared that Patel wanted to be the CM, a position he was eyeing for years. Therefore, to slight him he did not include him in his team and Modi was banished from the party organisation. Modi worked from side-lines in the north-western States for strengthening the party.

Then the historic event of Babri Masjid demolition happened when, within a few hours, thousands of *kar sevaks* (volunteer workers) flattened the Masjid with bare hands or simple tools. It gave new confidence to the BJP as the reticent Hindu middle class became vociferous, widening its base that brought it to power later. Modi, strategically, remained away from the scene, sleeping quietly in Gujarat. He also realised that economic develop-ment, and not hardcore Hindutva, would give it lasting political power.[26] He successfully adopted it in 2014 Election.

When Modi had withdrawn from BJP activities, Gujarat witnessed fateful political developments. In 1990, Chimanbhai Patel became Janata Dal (of which BJP was a partner) CM. This made the Congress leadership edgy and Modi was held responsible for it. The Congress high command from Delhi even pressurised the Gujarat leadership to check, using whatever means were available, Modi's upward movement. BJP, during the early years of 90s, was trying hard to capture power in the next Assembly elections in 1995. But Chimanbhai was holding the Janata Dal alliance 'like a bulwark blocking the BJP's avalanche.'[27] But unfortunately, Patel had a sever cardiac arrest in 1994 and died. His Finance Minister, Chhabildas Mehta and a long-term Congressman who had joined the Janata Dal, became the CM.

Next year, the 1995 Assembly elections were to be held and were significant for the BJP as it was trying for a long desire to acquire power, which it held only for two brief periods of nine and seven months. The Party believed that the time was ripe for it to reap the KHAM dissatisfaction in upper caste Hindus. At that time, three names of Vaghela, Patel and Modi were under consideration for the State leadership. Modi was exiled from Gujarat at the insistence of powerful and ambitious Vaghela. But, to the misfortune of Vaghela, Modi became more powerful during his absence.

Vaghela was so ambitious that he was present by the side of BJP leaders when Babri Masjid was flattened. He was prepared to go to any extent, even leave the BJP or destroy it, to get the coveted post of the CM. Modi was considered Keshubhai's man, whom Vaghela hated as he considered him his strongest rival. Modi's relationship with Vaghela was complicated because of Sanjay Joshi, a creation of Vaghela. Sanjay had worked with Modi when he, along with him, was deputed to work with BJP in 1987. He now became a protégé of Vaghela and a bitter challenger of Modi. Both became opponents and later bitter enemies.[28]

Modi was no less politically powerful as he had a strong leader, Advani, at his back who had sent him to Gujarat in 1994 as Gujarat General Secretary to prepare and strengthen party for the Assembly election. His mandate included training 150,000 party workers to operate in the election next year. It was the task that Modi really loved. With his inclusive political acumen and exhaustive understanding of the caste system in Gujarat, Modi designed a political strategy that gave desired results in the 1995 assembly elections.[29]

The 1995 assembly elections were significant for the BJP as for the first time as it was a straight fight between the Congress and the BJP. In the earlier elections, the BJP did not contest independently. It was either a coalition partner or had seat adjustments with the non-Congress parties. In this election the BJP contested for all the 182 seats.[30]

In the pre-electronic voting machine era, the counting was very slow. The results began to come slowly, everyone was breathing anxiously because expectations were very high at the BJP party head quarters in Khanpur in Ahmedabad. As the evening approached, it was almost sure that the BJP was on its way to a famous victory. The party eventually won a two-thirds majority with 121 of the 182 seats. The assembled huge crowd cheered as leader-after-leader entered the party office. Keshubhai Patel was expected to become the CM. All senior leaders, among them Shankersinh Vaghela and Kashiram Rana, distributed traditional Gujarati sweets and *farsan* (salty Gujarati snack). Modi, the architect of the election strategy for managing the election campaign down to the last detail, was standing in a corner.

The other senior leaders were in the arc lights. Modi saw Rajdeep and emotionally told him on camera that 'this is the happiest moment in my life'. Modi, at that time was an indistinctive and anonymous campaign manager who never claimed any credit and submitted himself to his party with the erce loyalty of the *karyakarta* (ordinary worker).[31]

This spectacular victory by winning 121 of the 182 seats with 52.5 percent votes compared to 27 per cent in the earlier election, made Modi a favourite of BJP high-command and he became very powerful. What made him more powerful was that under his leadership, the BJP won all the panchayat elections later. The two victories were unprecedented and historical that BJP never dreamt. However, success creates enemies and an enmity came from Vaghela. The intensity of his bitterness became hugely intense when Keshubhai Patel was made the CM in March 1995.[32]

Though Keshubhai was sworn in as the first BJP chief minister in March 1995, the whispers in party circles were that Modi would be the real CM and a the 'super-chief minister.' Vaghela took it as a personal offence and considered Modi responsible for all that was happening in Gujarat against him. The rift intensified when Modi began to target Vaghela's supporters from important positions. Vaghela began to plan a coup to show his power and got in touch with Congress who was waiting for an opportunity to pull the government down. Within six months, in September, when the CM was in the USA, he flew his 47 supporters to Khajuraho in Madhya Pradesh as Congress, having 47 MLA, promised to support him. With 94 MLAs in a 182 Assembly, Vaghela could easily become the CM, his cherished desire for a long time. Vajpayee negotiated a deal and Vaghela's protégé Suresh Mehta and a favourite of Vajpayee was made the CM while Vaghela continued in Lok Sabha. But Vaghela agreed on one condition that Modi will have to leave Gujarat. Modi left Gujarat before Vaghela returned with his team. Advani, as in the past, compensated Modi and he was appointed BJP National General Secretary in charge of Haryana and Himachal Pradesh to be based in Delhi.[33]

Modi, during his stay in Delhi, left no opportunity to make the best use of the television. He, in fact, used it to become politically powerful and developed a national prole. It provided him a space in the capital's overcrowded political universe. His significance and popularity increased because, being clear, direct, aggressive, often provocative, he was a chosen party spokesman. Though his space and popularity were increasing in the country, he ensured that he maintained closeness with the RSS by showing strong support to *Hindutva*.[34]

After being exiled once again, Modi came to Delhi in 1996, dejected but with a determination to become stronger because he enjoyed the patronage of Advani, who was the BJP President at that time. A few months later, in 1996, Modi was made in-charge of Haryana, Himachal Pradesh, Chandigarh, Punjab and J&K, where election were to be held soon. Happily, he accepted: 'I was nearer the Himalayas. That was my favourite area, so I used to go to Himalayas again and I enjoyed it.'[35] It was a rare distinction for someone who had joined BJP only eight years back and also a great learning period for him as he said: '...in that period I had a very great opportunity to learn. During that period, I visited so many countries; I had the chance to work with so many stalwart leaders.During that time, I tried to learn computers and technology, which is useful today for me. So, used those days as an opportunity.'[36] And he was true to his words because during his stay in Delhi he travelled extensively in 40 countries and interacted with eminent leaders there. These experiences not only helped him developing a global perspective but also intensified his passion to serve his country better and lead it towards the socio-economic supremacy in the comity of nations. Modi, rather sulking, converted the period of punishment into a phase of erudition. In his words: 'I always turn adversity into opportunity, always. In my present life or my political life, I always do that.'[37] The period he spent in Delhi converted his perception that he was only a regional leader. He now was a leader of the national stature.

During the years in *vanvas* (exile) from Gujarat, he did not, as many political leaders have, go into depress and seclusion. He could have done that, but his ultimate objective was to go to Gujarat as CM one day, but he kept it well concealed. Once installed in Delhi, Modi decided to get into lime-light and speak out on 'national' issues. He decided to expand his public exposure and understand the international situation. Probably he had a long term vision.

Those were the times when television was becoming more important than print media as it gave greater visual visibility to the leadership. Political debates had begun on TV and gave wider and trans-India publicity instantly. Modi was an articulate speaker in Hindi and he took to television rather well. Rajdeep Sardesai in his book, *2014 Election that changed India,* has written about three instances.

The first when he was anchoring 10 p.m. show on Newshour on NDTV with Arnab Goswami. At about 8.30 p.m., the scheduled BJP guest, Vijay Kumar Malhotra, who was to participate in the programme informed that he was not able to come. He did not know how to get a replacement. In sheer desperation he remembered Modi and rang him up. He called him and said in Gujarati: *'Aaveejao, Narendrabhai, tamhari zarrorat chhe'* (Please come, Narendrabhai, we need you). Modi thought for a minute and agreed to appear but told him that there was a problem as he was not having a car. At that time, he was living in 9-Ashoka Road, a bungalow next to the BJP office and allotted to Arun Jaitley. It served as a residence for senior party leaders like J P Mathur and Prakash Javadekar. Rajdeep asked him to hire a taxi and promised reimbursement to him. Arnab and Rajdeep fretted as the countdown began for the show and Modi was nowhere. When only about minutes were left for the programme to go on-air and producers yelling 'stand by' in his ear, Modi appeared on the scene, huffing and puffing, crying out: 'Rajdeep, I have come, I have come!' He knew fully that he was just a last-minute replacement but was not willing to give up a chance of appearing on TV. Had there been any other seasoned leader he would have refused such an offer.

The second incident is when General Musharraf came to India for the Agra Summit in July 1999, Modi again saved Rajdeep from a precarious situation. He was covering the event round-the-clock and needed a BJP guest who would be available for an extended period. Modi again agreed to come without any fuss to Vijay Chowk where OB vans were parked. As soon as Modi arrived, the satellite signal stopped working due to rain. Without any fuss, Modi sat patiently through the rain with an umbrella for almost two hours in the muddy downpour before he was nally put on air.

Third, when 9/11 happened and Twin Towers were destroyed in New York in 2001, Rajdeep was trying to pick up a speaker for his weekly 'Big Fight'on Islamic terror. The BJP leaders in the Government were not agreeing to participate in the programme. But Modi has no such hesitations and participated in the debate effectively. He daringly and strongly said during the debate that Islamic terror was one of the biggest threats to the country: 'It has taken an attack like 9/11 for India's pseudo-secular media to nally use a word like Islamic terrorism and wake up to the reality of how some groups are misusing religion to promote terror.'[38]

Modi, being a shrewd politician, realised that television was the best media to became a known face trans-India. This was a critical period for Modi as he had lost Gujrat and other leaders of his age were becoming close to the power centre. Mahajan was becoming the most powerful leader in the BJP and had emerged as a Man-Friday of Prime Minister Atal Bihari Vajpayee, besides being a powerful minister in the Government. Sushma Swaraj, because of being a powerful orator was a great favourite of BJP leadership. After she contested against Sonia Gandhi in Bellary, Karnataka, she had emerged a fearless political ghter. Arun Jaitley, a highly articulate legal brain was also becoming a *har-fun-maula* (all-rounders), besides being a crisis manager and an effective spokesman on TV.

Being new to 'Delhi Darbar of BJP,' Modi, was trying to make a *niche* and have an identity and space for himself. Things were not easy for him because his opponents accused him of not handling politics properly and supporting his favourites in Himachal Pradesh. Moreover, being a *pracharak*, he was not supposed to play the power game and remain a backroom player. But, the determined and an ambitious politician he decided to take the bull by horns and fight his political quarantine. For an otherwise remarkably self-contident man, he often gave way to a creeping self-doubt over his immediate political future. When in 1999, NDTV conducted a poll on who were the BJP's emerging leaders, Modi was nowhere. Those popular were: Pramod Mahajan, Sushma Swaraj and K. N. Govindacharya. Modi sharply reacted telling Rajdeep: *'Lagta hai aappunditon ne deshme in bhavis hyame inky ahogayehtay kar liyahai!'* (Looks like you political pundits have decided the country's future).[39]

Gujarat after Modi left

Modi's absence in Gujarat was being felt by both, the BJP and the RSS, because the situation began to deteriorate as soon as he left Gujarat. Vaghela was defeated in the Lok Sabha elections of 1996. He rebelled again in 1997 to form his own regional party, Rashtriya Janata Party and become the CM with the support of the Congress only for 370 days. The same year when Vaghela came to power, a new star, Amit Shah, appeared in Gujarat. He was a stock broker and was elected to the Assembly because he was strongly supported by Modi. As it was happening, Sanjoy Joshi developed closeness first with Vaghela and then Keshubhai with the intention of destroying Modi. This was the beginning of hate-relationship between the two and Modi, in fact, destroyed him in the following 17 years.[40]

Situation began to improve for BJP from May 1998 when it won 117 out of 182 in Gujarat Assembly elections of that year. Keshubhai became the CM but in following years he failed to provide an efficient governance to Gujarat because he promoted rampant corruption and nepotism, unknown to Gujarat and BJP. Swapan Dasgupta, a respected academic think-member of BJP in *India Today* accepted that besides promoting corruption and nepotism, he failed in managing the three crises, earning the sobriquet, the "*mahasankatdharak*" Chief Minister (Mr Disaster CM). It may be sheer his misfortune that after he came to power, Gujarat suffered three natural calamities in the following three years. The beginning was with 1998 Kandla cyclone, followed by Ahmedabad floods and four months later a calamitous earthquake in Kutch in 2001. Keshubhai was unable to handle the three crises because 'Relief operations were seen to be tardy. The administration seemed at first paralysed by the natural disaster, and then plain incompetent.'[41]

When Keshubhai was showing his ineptness to rule Gujarat and destroying the party, Modi's stock was rising in Delhi. Almost the same time, in May 1998, Modi was promoted as the General Secretary (Organisation) of BJP with the assignment of revamping the party organisation in several states. He played a key role on several important occasions.

During his six-year *vanvas* (exile) in Delhi Modi developed good connections with journalists, both electronic and print, and also came closer to the BJP leaders who mattered in the national politics. Thus, he became stronger in the RSS as well as its political wing—the BJP. This period, in a way, was the most remunerating period for Modi as he prepared himself for important political positions in Gujarat and India. He did not confine to the Indian politics but also acquainted himself with the international society and politics by visiting 40 countries, including the United States that he visited five times between 1990 and 2000.

In fact, America became a second home for Modi during the 1990s he frequently visited it as *pracharak*. He always enjoyed his stay and rode bikes, went on boat ride, on the beach with a group of friends. He visited White House in a plain *kurta-pyjama*. He was clean-shaven with a lot more hair on his head. An *Indian Express* report quoted Dr Panna Barai, the wife of Dr Bharat Barai who organised the Madison Square Garden rally for PM Modi, recounting Modi's 1993 visit to their home. She told the paper that Modi had come with only two-three sets of cotton *kurta-pyjamas* and would request her to keep one change ready for the next day.'[42]

Suresh Jani, an old RSS friend of Modi with whom he used to stay in New Jersey, from Vadnagar told *The Times of India* that on every visit of Modi India was on his mind.[43] One day Jani took Modi to show the Statue of Liberty in the middle of New York harbour. Modi was so impressed by the Statue that he asked Jani 'why something like that could not be done in India.' It, probably, was the genesis of the Sardar Patel Statue of Unity now taking shape in the Sadhu Bet river island near Vadodara.[44]

He particularly selected and visited those places that were significant for the development and progress of his country. He went to visit NASA in

Houston in 1996 and greatly impressed Kamlesh Lulla, Chief Scientist, who took him around by his scientific mind by asking sharp questions. He again showed his scientific temper at Georgia State University at Atlanta in 1996. Addressing the American and Indian students when a student asked him, "What is the true relevance of Swamiji today?" Modi replied: "Swamiji's mission was to introduce Indian philosophy to the West and bring the message of science and technology to bring prosperity to India." Finding him tech-savvy, Modi's admirers, pooled money to buy him the latest computer. He also visited Massachusetts Institute of Technology in August 1996 to address Indian students and was introduced as the 'future prime minister of India, by Chandan Banerjee, then a student and now a Kolkata businessman. Significantly, MIT president Charles M Vest was also present in the meeting. Surprisingly, Modi gave all his speeches in perfectly comprehensible English, though he spoke haltingly, during his US trips in the 1990s. 'It was English of a working nature but quite easy to understand for both Indian and Americans,' says Banerjee. It's a language he has tended to steer clear of after becoming the Prime Minister.[45]

What most interested Modi during his various US visits was the governance and infrastructure in the country and he made every effort to study them with keenness to understand them. He mainly focused on roads, rivers and urban revitalisation and tried to understand the difference in American and Indian attitudes to these problems.[46]

He travelled far and wide, using New York City as a head quarters, to cities such a Chicago and Boston, and flew to Texas and California to visit and discuss governance and infrastructure — roads and rivers and urban regeneration; how Americans were approaching problems and what India could learn from it—with those who were responsible operating these facilities, told Prakash Swamy to *The Times of India*, one of several Indian scribes who Modi kept in touch within the Big Apple where he stayed weeks at a time. He also travelled, often by road, to and around cities such a Chicago and Boston, and flew to Texas and California.[47]

Modi enjoyed his visits, even going on bikes, for boat ride and, spending time on the beach with a group of friends. He never cared for his dress and visited White House in a plain *kurta-payjama*. He travelled very light and remained pure vegetarian, not eating even onions and garlic, though he had a tough time in following this diet regime. One day he went to the home of Prakash Swamy, a journalist, along with Govindacharya for a meal and drank more *rasam* (thin, very spicy southern Indian soup served with other dishes, typically as a drink.) saying that a 'liquid diet' was better for him. He really made it his second home.[48]

The turning point: 2001 Kutch quack

On the morning of the 51st Republic Day in 2001, most of the VIPs had arrived and the Prime Minister, Atal Bihari Vajpayee was to arrive in a few minutes. The President, R. K. Narayan reached before nine. All the enclosures were fully packed and the crowd was anxiously waiting for the colourful Parade to begin. Narendra Modi was sitting in the sixth row of the VIP enclosure. Just a few minutes after the President had arrived, his cell phone suddenly vibrated. He picked up the mobile and listened to what the person was saying. The person was informing Modi that an earthquake has hit the Bhuj town in the Kutch area at quarter to nine and lasted for more than two minutes. Bhuj is a city in the north-western Gujarat and is situated in the lowlands between the *Rann* (marsh) and the Gulf of Kachchh (Kutch). Modi, instead of going back, rushed to his residence.

Back in his room, he began to organised the rescue work, giving instructions and telling in detail what to do and whom to contact. During his days in Gujarat till he was exiled, Modi had established a wide network of VHP and the RSS workers. Within few minutes after talking and giving instructions, Modi began to organised his departure for Kutch. By the evening he was there.

The first call was made to Premal Nathwani, Group President of Reliance Industries Limited and asked if he could borrow the company jet to fly to Kutch, the hardest-hit district. Modi was sure that Gujarat's then-Chief Minister Keshubhai Patel, who was his rival, would not allow him to use the official aircraft. But he wanted to be the first to reach Kutch to see and analyse what had happened so that he could make a report for the party leadership in Delhi. Nathwani lent him the jet, handing Modi a political victory over his nemesis.[49]

When Modi reached Kutch, his system was already functioning efficiently and effectively. The huge effort was being spearheaded by the VHP's International Secretary-General Pravin Togadia, Modi's good friend at that time. With an initial amount of three lakh rupees, Togadia started placing orders for food and other relief material. By January 30, over 8,000 RSS workers were effective functioning in Kutch district. Floodlights were set up as night fell to help rescuers using crowbars and their bare hands to search through the rubble. Volunteers, friends and neighbours joined them to dig with whatever tools they could find. When he reached Kutch, his volunteers had begun the relief operation. His system was so through that all required resources were mobilize in less than an hour. The entire team was incredibly quick to act and well prepared and provided the suffering people the sort of relief and comfort they needed. They, very efficiently began to organise funeral rites and distributing food that the government machinery entirely failed.[50]

The volunteers were particular in cremating the dead correctly. The management of dead bodies was mostly well ordered, and there was no infection from corpses. Supply of wood was so well managed that it arrived without any delay. The same happened to submerging of ashes in the Ganges. One truck arranged to take the ashes to Haridwar. Muslims were buried by Muslims. Over all the disposal of the dead bodies was correct.[51]

The unprecedented earthquake was of the magnitude of between 6.9 and 7.9. It killed more than 20,000 people (over 1.7 per cent of the city's population), injured 1,66,000 and destroyed nearly 4,00,000 homes. It made hundreds of thousands homeless and destroyed or damaged more than a million buildings. It also ruined a large majority of the crops.The shock waves spread over 700 km; 21 districts were affected and 6,00,000 people left homeless. The epicentre was about nine kilometre south-southwest of the village of Chobari in Bhachau Taluka of Kutch District. The impact was felt as far away as Bangladesh, Nepal and Pondicherry where people fled in panic from a Republic Day parade.[52]

Bhuj is an important city in the economy of Gujarat as it a commercial centre for wheat, barley, cattle, cotton, and salt produced in the hinterland. It is known for its handicrafts and manufacturing of cotton cloth and silver items. Country's first large-scale experiment with solar pond technology (a means of collecting solar energy using brine ponds) was established in this city. It has several educational institutions and is the junction of several state highways and the terminus of a railroad and an airport.

When Modi was busy in organising and trying to reach Kutch as early as possible, Suresh Mehta, then the industrial minister for Gujarat, was present in the city. When he realised the earthquake, he took shelter in a door frame. After the severity of the quack had subsided, he moved by his car to hoist the national flag. Though his car was obstructed by falling houses, he kept on moving and reached the venue. Later he recalled how the air was full of dust, the town was wrecked, and how fallen buildings impeded his passage but he was the lucky one to have survived.[53]

While Modi's team was taking charge of the relief operations, the Government was nowhere to be seen. The Chief Minister, Ministers and the bureaucracy, all were busy in flag hoisting ceremonies. Keshubhai Patel was not aware of the earthquake and he told a journalist later: "I was travelling to a flag-hoisting ceremony. When I reached the venue, my officers told me, 'Sir, the earth shook. The jolt was severe.' I quickly completed the ceremony and rushed home."

His government was not only slow but indifferent also. Officials were stone walling and a reluctant to provide information during the first five days after the earthquake. When Keshubhai finally came on TV to warn of possible after-shocks, his clumsy articulation triggered a panic. In fact, he was sending all the wrong signals to the people looking for solace. His communication skills were zero and his demeanour sluggish and both created a mismatch between society and political leadership. It took few days to go into relief operations whereas RSS and VHP workers who worked along with the army, RAF and gallant fire brigade workers rescued the trapped and arranged for food, medical treatment and care. One case of indifference was narrated by a Swiss team that had landed at the Ahmedabad airport with sniffer dogs. Before leaving their country, they had a 10-hour drill and reached Gujarat after a ten-hour flight. Though they wanted to reach the place immediately, they were asked to 'freshen up' and have a meal so that they can cope up with the rigours of work and may have to sustain themselves on mere fluids. Another example, a team was dispatched from Ahmedabad to Bachchau by bus when every moment counts, especially when 36 hours had already elapsed since the quake. This showed a remarkable lack of appreciation that time is of the essence.

His governance was so poor that there was no coordination between the various departments. Worse, the state Government's responses were affected by lack of departmental coordination. The control room in Gandhinagar learnt of the disaster in Bhuj at 3 p.m. and its first contact with the Kutch collector was after midnight. The crisis zone was thought to be Ahmedabad. The misreading delayed rescue and cost lives.The mis-governance was mainly because of the team of officials around Keshubhai, particularly Chief Secretary L.N.S. Mukundan and Principal Secretary R. K. Lahiri, who had failed in selecting the right officers for the right job. Subba Rao who was sent to Bhuj as relief coordinator proved to be very ineffective and had to return in four days. The reason for the failure of the bureaucracy was that the side-lined officials were sent to handle the relief work. The initial delay and deployment of the wrong personnel led to one lapse after another. On January 30, for example, 120 aircraft with relief material from overseas remained unloaded even as people in as many as 150 villages were short of food and blankets. At the same time, Bhuj, Anjar and Bhachau were faced with a problem of plenty. There was absolutely no coordination.[54]

During the post-earthquake relief operations, the VHP and RSS teams were at the forefront and Modi effectively took over the functions of the government. They distributed aid, opened relief camps, and oversaw rescue and cremation operations. Their well-organised systems of communication and hierarchy, as well as the dedication and discipline of their volunteers, made both organisations popular. Their work was deeply valued by all. Both were one of the first groups to make their presence felt in Bhuj and organised the cremation and ritual services of dead bodies, important to those who survived, was faultless. Either way, the image of Modi in Kutch strengthened and grew thereafter.

On the contrary, the image of Keshubhai was fast worsening and he was becoming a political liability for then BJP. It was certain to the high command that if he continues in the office the BJP is sure to lose the next Assembly election. The collapse and debilitation of 171 buildings that led to nearly 700 deaths in Ahmedabad was being presented by the media because of the Government's indulgence of unscrupulous builders.

The quake was also perceived as an evidence of a politician-business-bureaucrats mafia nexus. BJP legislators complained that wherever they go, they are confronted by angry citizens asked why the Government didn't act against the real-estate sharks. Keshubhai was also being seen as the patron of officials who were inefficient, incompetent and dishonest. Examples were given of the Collector of Kutch who was handpicked by him and the relief work was delayed by 24 hours on January 26 as he lost his nerves. Even the then Chief Secretary L.N.S. Mukundan was not spared as the Comptroller and Auditor-General (CAG) of India had pulled him up in 1999. CAG held him responsible for public investments in the CRB Capital case, but the Chief Minister defended him in the Assembly. By and large, his image was fast plummeting and all the shortcomings of the regime were being pinned on him.

The scenes at the Bhuj collectorate were chaotic on the first four days. Relatives of those trapped alive pleaded with officials for cranes but the callous response was, "Get a crane on your own from anywhere. We'll pay for it." In Gokul Apartment, Bhuj's tallest building, several people died because there was no 30-tonne crane available by January 30.[55] Even in Ahmedabad, for nearly three days the Government struggled to bring in cranes and earth-movers. It was only when Modi suggested that the railways should be asked for assistance, that the government went into action.

It took Keshubhai 48 hours to appeal on Doordarshan for gas cutters for removing those trapped in the debris.

Nothing moved in the officialdom at Ahmedabad and there was allround chaos all around. While numerous agencies from all over landed in Gujarat in a short time and Gujarat was almost flooded with relief supplies—tents, blankets, food packets, noodles and corn flakes, relief agencies, there was no machinery in place to guide them on where to unload the relief.The relief operations were so haphazard from day one that those who needed tents were provided with cornflakes. People in need of food were being given strips of tablets for treatment of diarrhoea and indigestion. Those rendered homeless were provided clothes like jeans, Bermuda and mini-skirts that don't even fit them. And while Kutch people were largely vegetarian, cans of tinned sardines were generously distributed.[56]

It was virtually free for all. "Hundreds of people from the town and adjoining talukas move freely inside the makeshift warehouse and leave with oversized bundles of clothes. Frenzied crowds fight over the prized catches. Men in uniform, sweltering under the sun, relish canned Florida orange juice, full cream milk, brew foreign coffee and sip chicken soup during the cold evenings. 'I heard that many good clothes are lying abandoned in Lalan grounds, so I hired a mini tempo from Gandhidham and came with my wife and other family members to take it away,' says Keshavbhai Solanki, a petty trader who sells old clothes. It's people like him who are muscling in to corner the aid," reported Davinder Kumara in *Outlook*.[57]

Put simply, the Gujarat relief operation was far, far worse than in Latur in 1993. Chief Minister Keshubhai Patel was largely invisible. The collapse of political and moral leadership was complete.

As soon the quake severity had subsided there was a wide demand for Keshubhai to resign. He was initially reluctant to leave the office, but following the defeat of BJP in the by-elections to the Sabarkanta Lok Sabha and Sabarmati assembly seats, he was asked to submit his resignation. He resigned on Tuesday, 2nd October paving the way for Modi to step in his shoes. He had already reached Gujarat on directions from the Prime Minister Atal Bihar Vajpayee.

The die was cast for him to become the Prime Minister thirteen years later after remaining the Chief Minister till then.

****

Chapter Four

Political Training of Indira

Indira was born with a gold-spoon in her mouth in a family of political power-seekers—loyal to, defenders and supporters of the reigning power. In seven generations, the family earned fame, fortune and eminence due to closeness with the ruling power. The founding father of the Nehru family in Delhi, Raj Kaul and his progeny were loyal to the Mughals. When the British power began to rise, his great-grandson, Lakshmi Narayan shifted his loyalty to the British and became their *vakil* (lawyer) and his grandson, Motilal, became a famous advocate and earned fame and money by supporting the British. When Gandhi entered the freedom movement, politically astute Motilal decided to follow him and invited him to stay with him. After his visit, Anand Bhawan was transformed from a British castle to a home of Gandhi's dream. The Nehrus changed their loyalty for the third time and enjoyed power for 60 years.[1]

When Indira was not even three, she travelled to Calcutta (now Kolkata) in September 1920 for a Congress meeting with her grandfather, father and mother. Though she did not understand what political leaders were talking, but she captured in her memory the launch of non-cooperation movement by Mahatma Gandhi. Then onwards she witnessed a radical change in the life and ambiance of Anand Bhawan—from a typical British home it was transformed into a home of Gandhi's dream, all *khadi* (cloth made from home-spun yarn) and Indian vegetarian food. Fifteen months later she was not able to understand why police had come to arrest his grandfather and father. Later she sat in the lap of Motilal who was sitting in the dock. While she did not understand what was going on, the political words against the British rule were assimilated by her mind. She sat amused and dreamy throughout the trial.

A year later, in December 1921, just a few weeks after Motilal and Jawaharlal were jailed in Lucknow she and all the other three ladies of the

Nehru family, Swarup Rani, Kamala and Krishna (known as Betty) went to Sabarmati Ashram to attend the annual Congress meeting in Ahmedabad. They all travelled in a third-class crowded compartment in the harshest, most disgusting, appalling and humiliating conditions. In those days the third-class compartments had hard wooden benches with no fans and no facilities for sleeping. The toilet facilities were primitive. The only redeeming factor during the long exhausting journey was the genuine and undiluted warmth and affection of the crowds that gathered at every station with food, water and flowers. 'By now the Nehrus were almost as famous as Gandhi himself and people felt great solidarity with these women whose son, husband and father had been incarcerated by the British.'[2]

In Ahmedabad, being the daughter of Nehru, everyone adored her thinking that she was representing Nehru who was in jail. After the session, all the four ladies stayed with Gandhiji at his Sabarmati *ashram.* Indira lived a modest life and did not like the unpalatable food she was not accustomed to and she decided to remain hungry. Life has completely changed for all the four after returning from Sabarmati.

Eight years later, she attended Lahore session in which Nehru was to propose *Purna Swaraj* (total independence) resolution. When Nehru was given the copy of the speech, he passed it on to Indira, asking her to read it aloud.'She began haltingly; he interrupted her and told her to 'read it properly.' She read it slowly and deliberately. When she finished it, Nehru said to her, 'Well now you have read it, you are committed to it.'[3]

Back in Allahabad, she realised that Nehru had become a celebrity, a hero and almost a national superstar as the crowds were becoming larger and larger day by day. Her house was filled with people who were showing their love, affection and admiration and asking nothing in return. It was intoxicating for her and probably this all made her aware of the power that politics bestows. This probably intensified on 26 January 1930, which was declared the Independence Day at the Annual Congress session and she hoisted the Congress flag at Anand Bhawan lawns.[4]

She also travelled extensively throughout India to participate in Congress sessions and meetings and witnessed political movement for freedom from very close angles. She also witnessed raids at her house and arrests of her grandfather, father and mother. She also began to nurse patients at Swaraj Bhawan hospital (a wing of Anand Bhawan which was donated to the nation by Motilal), and observed political discussions and strategy meetings at Anand Bhawan in which top leaders participated. Later, Nehru wrote to her when she was in London that he would like her to play a brave part in the public life of India, and "help putting brick by brick in building India of our dreams."

Three weeks before she was 13, Nehru, from Naini jail in Allahabad, decided to educate her for growing politically and began to write her regular letters on world history. This provided her an historical and political education. The letters were published later in *Glimpses of World History,* a compilation of 196 letters in closely-printed 970 pages. Through these letters Nehru made her aware of John of Are, Lenin and Russian Revolution, leadership of Gandhi and, the most important, the power of the people, who make the 'real history.' He also wrote about the political events and educated her about the exploitation of the people by rajas and maharajas and how they lived in luxury while people starved.

Indira learnt real politics because she was at the right place at the right time. Studying at Pupils' Own School in Poona, she had an opportunity to get closer to Mahatma Gandhi whom she visited at Yervada Prison on weekends. In Poona she observed from close-angles the power of strong determination during Gandhiji's famous fast in 1932. Ramsay Macdonald, the British Premier, had announced a separate electorate for *harijans* (untouchable caste in Hindus), as they wanted it. Gandhiji objected and went on indefinite 'fast-unto-death' in Yervada jail. When the British and Gandhi, both did not relent and his condition deteriorated, Ambedkar made Gandhi to agree that *harijans* will be adjusted in the Hindu seats. Gandhiji ended his fast with orange juice which was squeezed and given by the 14-year-old Indira.

Indira, in 1934, joined Santiniketan at the age of sixteen and was happy to be away from intense political activity. Before she joined Santiniketan, she was warned by Jehangir Vakil, the owner of Pupils' Own School that the student hostel, specially the food, will not be good for her. But Nehru vetoed it saying that she should not live like the Prince of Wales but like an ordinary Indian.[5] Though much used to luxuries, she adapted quickly to the simple living at Santiniketan where she shared the room with three girls. The room had no electricity and she slept on the mattress on the floor, took cold bucket baths and used an outdoor latrine.[6] It was in Santiniketan that she became interested in fine arts and classical dance, particularly Manipuri, developed aesthetic sensibility and responsiveness and became obsessed with colours.[7]

Her contentment was short-lived because only a month after joining Santiniketan she got a telegram that her mother was seriously down with pleurisy. She immediately rushed to Allahabad and was pained to see that mother's condition was critical. Nehru, who was released from jail, joined her and realised that she might not survive and 'might leave me.' Though obsessed with this thought, he did not share it with Indira.[8] Miraculously in the following week she improved and Indira returned to Santiniketan. But she was despondent because she feared that in her and Nehru's absence, mother will be neglected by all. She wrote to Nehru, who was in Dehradun jail: 'Do you know anything about what happens when you are absent?...When she was in agony there was no one to help her....It was only when Madan Bhai [Kamala's cousin, a doctor named Madan Atal] came that she got a little comfort and with your release everything changed ... As soon as Mummie is strong enough she should be moved to any place outside Allahabad.'[9] This disturbed Nehru and he wrote to Vijay Laxmi that he was saddened by 'an occasional lack of Harmony, a touch of non-cooperation...in our household...I should like you therefore to remove any discordant notes that might have unwittingly crept in.' But the letter had no effect and Kamala's life remained lonely and discordant.[10]

Lull for Indira was just only for two only months as she had to come back in Allahabad because her mother's condition again became serious and in October, she had to be moved to King Edward VII Sanatorium in Bhowali. She left Allahabad with, Madan Bhai, Feroze Gandhi and Hira Lal, Nehru's personal valet. Nehru was also moved from Dehradun jail to Almora jail so that he visit Kamala once in three weeks.

She stayed there for almost a month during which Feroze became a part of her life and proposed her twice. Though she refused, she drew closer to him as he was devoted to Kamala as she was. 'Inevitably, they drew closer together. For Indira Feroze was a much-needed ally.'[11] Even Nehru was impressed by Feroze's devotion towards Kamala that he wrote in his diary: 'What a brick Feroze has been! Without him it would have been a terrible job...She has few companions now – indeed only Feroze and the nurse.'[12]

While Kamala was in Bhowali, where her condition was deteriorating, Indira at that time 17, was developing an emotional relationship with her French teacher, Frank Oberdorf, a German in Santiniketan who was in mid-thirties. She was also strongly attracted towards him.

In Bhowali, the condition of Kamala was up and down. Though her health was improving, doctors found that the medicine was becoming ineffective and she needed surgery which was possible only in Europe. But the situation was problematic as Nehru was in jail and Indira did not want to leave Santiniketan. But Indira had to leave as the condition of Kamala became so serious that she had to be moved to Europe. Nehru sent a telegram to Rabindranath Tagore telling him to send Indira so that she could accompany her mother to Europe. She did not want to leave Santiniketan and leave for Europe. But there was no choice as her father was in prison and mother had to be taken to Europe for urgent treatment. Having no choice, she left for Bhowali next day, saying good-bye to the 'abode of peace,' which she loved greatly, for ever.

She went to Bhowali. Feroze was already there and they left for Allahabad after a few days. Several days later, she, with Feroze and Madan, left for Bombay and from there on May 23, sailed for Germany. Madan accompanied them. Feroze very much wanted to go with them but could not and joined later. She reached Berlin where Kamala was operated in mid-June. That was the time when Hitler was becoming stronger and was preparing for a war to annex Austria. Indira sensed something dark closing-in.

After the operation, Kamala and She shifted to Badenweiler in the Black Forest region located in southwestern Germany close to French and Swiss borders. The town was known for a spa with hot springs with reputed curative powers. Kamala was in the sanitorium and Indira stayed in a pension with Madan. She visited Kamala twice a day and in between 'she roamed about the town, past hotels and pensions, clinics and sanatoria. She walked in the gardens of the *Kurpark* where a band played daily in the open-air pavilion. And she walked, too, out into the countryside, through farms, orchids and vineyards and into the forests of pine and spruce.'[13]

Kamala was not happy with Indira living in the company of sick people and so she persuaded Nehru to send her to Switzerland. During her stay there she travelled a lot and criss-crossed and met people. She also attended a conference where she met several known professors and discussed joining a Swiss university. But Nehru was opposed to it and wanted her to join Oxford. She was back with her mother in Badenweiler after a month and found her to be very sick and feared that she was dying.[14]

While she was alone in Germany, Feroze was trying to join Kamala and her, unsuccessfully persuading his aunt to send him to London School of Economics. Meanwhile, Oberdorf appeared in Europe and was in touch with her, but could not meet her.

Kamala's condition was deteriorating and Dr Steffan, who was treating Kamala, sent a cable to the Viceroy, the Secretary of State for India and Nehru about her falling health and that Nehru must see her soon as she was dying. Nehru was released from the jail and within five days reached

Badenweiler along with Subhash Chandra Bose who was in Germany. Reaching Badenweiler, Nehru found Kamala in terrible condition and when he discussed her case with Dr Steffan, he got no hope.[15]

In India, Feroze was frantically trying to reach Badenweiler. He was able to reach, to the bewilderment of Kamala and Nehru, by the end of December. But soon left for Wengen, a resort in Jungfrau in Switzerland, where Indira had gone to meet Oberdorf. Feroze, it seems, was aghast to find his rival with Indira and left for Badenweiler the same night. He stayed there till the death of Kamala and did not go to London as he had planned before leaving India.[16]

Kamala was not happy to see Feroze following Indira and she told Nehru that 'she was very worried about Indira's relationship with Feroze and said that she did not want Indira to marry Feroze because she was sure he was unstable. Nor did Kamala think Feroze would enter any profession and be in a good position to support Indira. Nehru tried to sooth Kamala and banish her anxieties, but when he left the room, Kamala turned to Nanu [A.C.N. Nambiar, known as Nanu, a journalist and settled in Europe and good friend of Nehru, being the brother-in-law of Sarojini Naidu] and said, Índu will listen to no one but me. I could have guided Indu gently away from Feroze. But my end is near. Jawahar will give no guidance to Indu. She will…be allowed to commit the mistake of her life.'[17]

Kamala's condition was worsening day-by-day. As she saw sudden deaths in Badenweiler, she expressed a desire to move to Switzerland. Though she was not in a condition to move to another city, she was moved to Lausanne in an ambulance on January 31. Around the same time Nehru was elected the Congress President and at the insistence of Kamala booked a ticket for India for February 28. But he had to cancel the ticket as Kamala died in the morning of the very day Nehru was to fly to India. Besides Nehru, Indira and Feroze at her bedside. Two days later she was cremated in Lausanne. Feroze left for London. Three days later, on March 5, Nehru left for India. Indira stayed back and left for Bex where she was studying in a school.[18]

In March 1937, she was back in India and found her father's robust health falling because of exhaustive travels and meetings during the provincial elections. He was bed-ridden and needed respite. It was decided that he recovered he would have a vacation in Southeast-Asian countries. In early May, he was fit to travel and she travelled to Burma (now Myanmar), Malaya (now Malaysia) and Singapore for one month. Though they were traveling visiting temples and monasteries, much of their time was taken by facing crowds, processions, big functions and people reaching out to meet them.[19] They stayed in Rangoon for two days. Though there was not much political activity, she could observe the pride of being politically important. She became sick, with bad throat and temperature before she left Burma.

Unfortunately, though they met after more than a year after Kamla's death, Nehru and she could not connect with each other. Probably both were aware of each other's secrets. Nehru knew about her affair with Feroze and Indira knew that he loved Padmaja Naidu, daughter of Sarojini Naidu. Indira was not happy because Nehru developed love for Padmaja soon after the death of Kamala, which she thought was a betrayal of her mother's memory. So much was the disconnect between the two that after Indira had returned to Europe Nehru wrote to her: 'Is it not curious that during all these months we hardly had a proper conversation apart from our brief talks about day-to-day activities. I felt the gulf…and could not bridge it. Henceforth it might be best if we meet infrequently. Nehru was aware that Indira was hurt because he told his sister that he did not want to marry Padmaja because 'Indu had been hurt enough.'[20]

She again became politically active, and after that there was no looking back when she joined Oxford and became its most famous student. Being the daughter of Nehru, who was perceived as the most important political leader in India and much respected by the British, she became the centre of attraction. Even the renowned persons in Oxford clamoured to be her friend. She was invited to all important meetings, lectures and almost all social activities. She also joined two politically active groups, University Labour Club and Indian Majlis. The former was to promote democratic socialism and the latter was an association of Indian students in Oxford. She also developed, with the help of Feroze, connections with leftist activists in London. She also came in close contact with a group of leftist youngsters, who became important after India got independence and worked closely with Nehru and Indira. These were: Nikhil Chakravarthy, a veteran journalist, Mohan Kumaramangalam, one of the Indira Gandhi's cabinet ministers, and P N Haksar, her Principal Secretary and main political advisor. She also joined India League in London and helped V K Krishna Menon in actively supporting Spanish Civil War (1936-39) by mobilising volunteers for certain events.[21]

As an active member of the League she collaborated with the Communist Party of Great Britain and other Leftist organisations. In London, she held public meetings and protest marches against Neville Chamberlain's appeasement policies and supported the republican cause in Spain. She helped League's Indian Committee for Food for Spain, of which Feroze Gandhi was the organising secretary, in sending food to the starving and entrenched republicans. She also boycotted Japanese goods at Oxford when Japan attacked China, organised a fund-raising performance by Uday Shankar to raise money for medical aid in China and even auctioned one of her bracelets to raise money for the Republicans in the Spanish Civil War. Indira also often helped The Spain-India Committee to organise cultural events to raise funds and donated an ambulance to the Spanish democrats.[22]

In June 1937, Indira decided to drop out of Oxford as she did not want to fail in the third and the final attempt to Mod exam for admission to graduation course. Almost at the same time, Nehru wrote to her that he would be visiting London for important meetings. She began to plan his meetings with the help of Menon and Agatha Harrison, a Quaker social worker and close to Nehru. By this time, she has become politically strong-minded and opposed Nehru's meeting with Lord Lothian, a close friend of Nehru but supported Fascists and Hitler, who had invited Nehru to spend a weekend with him at his country home. Indira strongly opposed Nehru's meeting with him, telling him that 'Lothian is against all that you stand for and believe in and the people that you are likely to meet in is house will be the same—die-hard Tories and Fascists.'[23] But Nehru was equally adamant to go and stay with Lord Lothian because he claimed that he was strong enough to withstand people like him.

During Nehru's stay in the UK, Indira travelled with him and met all the stalwarts in politics, academics and society. She met persons like Palme Dutt, Harold Laski, Clement Atlee, Sidney and Beatrice Webb, and Labour MP, Stafford Cripps. She even, despite her strong abhorrence for Lord Lothian, went with her father to stay at his country home for the weekend. There she met Conservative MP Nancy Astor, Oxford MP Sir Arthur Salter and Principal Advisor to the Prime Minister, Stanley Baldwin. From Britain she went to France, Czechoslovakia and Hungry, attending World Peace Conference at Paris. These were the times when the clouds of the Second World War were intensifying over Europe. Hitler had already annexed Austria and took over Sudetenland region of Czechoslovakia after the Munich Conference and Agreement two weeks after Nehru and Indira returned to London. Nehru flew back to India in mid-September. Nehru was much impressed by Indira's political maturity and understanding and, when back in India, wrote to her: 'I used to dream that when you grew up, you would play a brave part in what is called public life in India, to shoulder this heavy burden, to help putting brick upon brick in the building of India of our dreams.'[24]

In early March 1941, Indira again fell sick and left for India with Feroze; stopping at Cape of Good Hope and Durban. She reached India mid-April. At Cape of Good Hope, though the stay was only for one day, she went to watch the debate in the Parliament. In Durban, she and Feroze stayed for a week where she was treated with great respect and reverence. The Indian community organised a public reception in her honour and was taken around the city before she attended the reception. By the time she reached the reception venue, she was shocked by the pathetic and wretched life that the blacks were living in shanty towns worse that the foulest slums of Calcutta. The overflowing auditorium was expecting a political speech, but she, to the utter shock to Indians, condemned the servile attitude of Indians towards the white showing utter apathy on the plight of the black majority. The audience showed their annoyance by shocked silence and not a thunderous ovation as she and Feroze expected. To add insult to the injury, she was avoided by the Indians during the rest of her stay in Durban.[25] Nevertheless, Indira showed her nerve and boldness to speak what she felt. Strangely, only three years back, when Krishna Menon had asked her to speak at an India League meeting, words suddenly failed him. Frozen with nervousness she did not know how to begin, and with great difficulty, could only say a few incoherent words in short shrill sound, only to be ridiculed by the audience.[26]

She began her political activities from the moment she landed at Bombay. Her coming back was widely covered in the media and Gandhiji wanted her to come to *Sevagram Ashram*, Wardha near Nagpur to see him. She did not want to go there but a message from Nehru made her to change her mind. She went to spend a few days with him. When she reached Allahabad from *Sevagram*, the *National Herald*, founded by Nehru four years back, interviewed her which was reproduced by most of the national newspapers all over India. When she met her father in Dehra Dun jail, four weeks after her arrival in Allahabad, he knew that his daughter is already a national figure. She, meeting him after almost two years, shocked him telling that she wanted to marry Feroze. The disturbed Nehru had 'restless nights' for a long time.[27]

Obstinate Indira, as she had become over the years, married Feroze on 26 March 1942 despite widespread family and public protest. The marriage, besides being historic, was the greatest political event of the year because Anand Bhawan continued to be the venue of political activity even on the wedding day.[28] Congress leaders, who had come to attend the marriage deliberated on the strategy for the Cripps Mission, only a few hours before the dinner. The Mission was sent by the U.K. Premier Winston Churchill to enlist Congress' support for the Second World War. It had arrived just four days before their marriage.

After two months, she and Feroze had belated honeymoon as guests of Sheikh Abdullah in Srinagar. Coming back, both went to attend the AICC meeting at Bombay, where 'Quit India' resolution was passed. Early morning, next day, Indira woke up Nehru as police had come to arrest him. A few weeks later she and Feroze were also arrested when Indira was to speak at a flag-raising ceremony.[29] Both were imprisoned for 13 months for organising and participating in nationalist political demonstrations against British rule. In the jail she celebrated *nauroz (*Iranian new year that Parses in India celebrate) by wearing a new sari.[30] She was released on 13 May 1943, but was to be rearrested when she refused to accept the internment order to go to Khali near Almora. But her ill health rescued her.

Just one year before independence, cracks began to appear in her marriage. It was happening because of Feroze's involvement with a number of other women even when Indira was in Lucknow where he was working as Director of the *National Herald.* She was particularly disturbed by his affairs with her cousin, Lekha Pandit, who was a junior reporter in the same newspaper. Feroze was also involved with a young Muslim girl, daughter of a Congress Minister in UP, whom he wanted to marry after divorcing Indira. He even told his decision to Nehru. But Indira did not want to get a divorce from him and, to restrain Feroze, Nehru asked Rafi Ahmad Kidwai to intervene. He ultimately resolved the problem and Feroze agreed to stop the affair and Miss Zahir was married.[31]

Though Feroze's problem was resolved, distance between the two deepened. An additional cause was that Nehru, as he became the interim Prime Minister in September 1946, needed an official hostess and someone to manage the house. He asked Indira to manage his house. She moved to Delhi and Feroze lived alone in Lucknow for the next five years, making their marriage 'neither married nor separated.'[32]

India was divided in August 1947 and a massive number of refugees from Punjab began to enter Delhi. These people had become exasperated as they had reached Delhi after a long suffering. They were allocated in different camps. Indira, spent long hours in these camps taking care of their various problems. She fearlessly talked to people who were on the edge and took quick decision with confidence, without being emotional. She worked with Subhadra Datta (later Joshi after her marriage and became a member of Parliament).[33]

Nehru, for security reasons after Gandhi's assassination, moved to Teen-Murti House, a huge 30-acre palatial house of the British Commander-in-Chief, who resided in the true British style. Managing an opulent house that had high ceilings and spacious rooms, long corridors, a huge ballroom, large drawing and dining rooms, reception rooms and a number of bedroom suits was not an easy task, particularly when the Prime Minister did not have an elaborate establishment as at present. Even the refurbishment, like replacing vestiges of the British aristocracy such as paintings of royalties and heavy curtains needed a sophisticated mind oriented towards Indian culture. Also, now that Nehru was the Prime Minister of an independent country, he needed a fulltime official hostess to manage complicated establishment and a large staff as he was to receive and officially and formally entertain a number of foreign dignitaries and heads of the Governments.[34]

She was not enthusiastic to work as PM's hostess for two reasons: Mostly she was in Lucknow with Feroze and two children and she did not want him to leave alone to flirt with other girls; and, she was 'simply terrified of social duties and parties.' But she had no option as Nehru would send her telegrams: 'Important guests coming, return at once.'[35] So, she decided to move into PM's house rather shuttling between Lucknow and Delhi. In October 1949, despite a miscarriage and strong advice of doctors, she went with Nehru as his hostess to the United States. This was her first official assignment, but the end of a short-unsettled marriage. She also began a new phase of her political life, though bitter because aunt Nan, India's Ambassador, excluded her from all official functions. But she attended a few unofficial functions and in one of the functions she met Dorothy Norman, a left-wing Jewish, who became her 'sole mate' and the only lady with whom she was in constant touch, through correspondence, till her death.[36]

On her return, she went to Lucknow and was appalled by the corruption and Chief Minister G B Pant's efforts to control *National Herald.* She immediately asked Nehru to check Pant. This was her first effort to control her father for better functioning. Later, she did not approve Nehru dismissing Sheikh Abdullah as the Prime Minister of J&K (as the J&K CM was known at that time). Much later, in 1955, when the decoy plane of Chou En-lai, going for Bandung Conference at Jakarta, was blown up after refuelling in Hong Kong, Nehru thought it to be the handiwork of the British intelligence and wanted to send a stinker-telegram to the British PM, Anthony Eden, but stopped when Indira strongly advised him not to act in hurry.[37] Nehru, during the same conference, exploded when the Prime Minster of Ceylon (now Sri Lanka) introduced a resolution condemning 'neo-imperialism of the communist block' and wanted to walk out. Only Indira could calm him down and she did.

The Congress party wanted her to contest for the Parliament in the first general election of 1952. But she refused on the pretext that the children were too young. But in fact, she refrained from contest because her father and husband both were contesting. She relentlessly canvassed for both and Nehru was much impressed by her hard canvassing for 12 to 15 hours a day.

As India moved on, Nehru became more and more busy, often working for 18 hours a day with small breaks. Indira, therefore, was involved more in her father's affairs. Her official status was giving her better positioning than her husband. It further worsened her deteriorating marriage. Besides involved in managing PM's house and Nehru's affairs, she was also engaged in various social activities and managed and established a few organisations for the welfare of the children and women like *Bal Bhawan* and promoting arts and crafts. In 1955, she was elected a member of the Congress Working Committee (CWC), the highest policy-making body of the Party, at the initiative of U N Dhebar, the Congress President and Lal Bahadur Shastri, who later succeeded Nehru as PM. She became more and more confident as more and more important persons began to come to her for advice and get their work done by Nehru. Despite enormous political importance and clout, she admitted to Dorothy that she was 'deeply unhappy in her domestic life…I am sorry…to have missed the most wonderful things in life.'[38]

As Indira was becoming politically stronger and powerful, Feroze intensified his political attacks on Nehru, may be to embarrass her. After remaining backbencher for two years, he suddenly became vocal and began to expose business tycoons in the Parliament. He also humiliated Nehru by raising the issue that he, despite being an MP, was not allowed entry to VIP enclosure while Indira sat on the dais. Nehru had to apologise. He also began to pass snide remarks on Nehru, inside the Parliament and in Party meetings. He also began to openly flirt with other women, including Tarakeshwari Sinha, Mahmuna Sultana, and Subhadra Joshi. In 1958, he exposed 'the Mundhra Scandal' in which the Life Insurance Corporation was forced to buy 15 million shares of Haridas Mundra's company. Mundra was a businessman who was liberally contributing to Congress. After an inquiry by a Commission, T. T. Krishnamachari, the then Finance Minister, had to resign, much to the chagrin of Nehru. He became a popular opposition leader to Nehru and MPs collected around him in the Central Hall of the

Parliament.[39] Indira began to feel unsettled and found solace in Yoga. This was time when Dhirendra Brahmachari (the one who is celibate), a tall, handsome Bihari, entered her life and became her closest confident and politically most powerful. He taught her yoga for an hour and so was with Indira behind closed doors every morning.

Brahmachari, a pauper at that time had come to Delhi in 1958 when he was asked to leave Kashmir for making sexual advances towards female students who were learning yoga from him. Mathai had written in his book that after he fascinated Indira, Nehru also began to take yoga lessons from him. This gave great following to him as many influential political leaders soon fell in Brahmachari's camp. Lal Bahadur Shastri, Jayaprakash Narayan, Morarji Desai and Rajendra Prasad, the then President of India, were a few prominent persons who began to learn yoga from him. This made him politically powerful in Delhi Durbar.[40]

When she was nearing forty, she was politically more matured and outspoken, even with Nehru, who had begun to depend on her in political affairs. He began to send her to States to gather information and talk to leaders on his behalf. But he never sought her advice when she was back. He also did not discuss with her the issues in detail. So, she, and rightly, began to think that her father considered her as his assistant and not confidant. She even complained to M O Mathai, her father's personal assistant but his man Friday, that his father never discussed political issues with her at meals.[41] She also told a number of people that she expected Nehru to have more confidence in her. Though Nehru never sought her advice, she kept on advising him whenever she thought that he was not being open-minded. As early as 1956, she cautioned Nehru not to rely too much on Morarji Desai and Kamaraj, both powerful political leaders in Maharashtra and Tamil Naidu respectively. Her argument was that it 'creates dissatisfaction in many and cuts your contacts with all those who hold different views. Sorry to inflict this on you but I just had to get it off my chest.'[42]

Though she was politically involved in the functioning of the government, she did not contest the Lok Sabha election till she became the Prime Minister. In the second Lok Sabha elections of 1957, the Congress President U. N. Dhebar and many other Congress leaders wanted her to contest and had spread a rumour that she would be persuaded to accept a seat. But neither she nor Nehru agreed for it. Interestingly, she was involved, in the selection of Congress candidates, as a member of Central Election Committee (CEC), but never became a candidate herself during Nehru's time. In 1957, she canvassed intensively, much more than she had done in 1952 election. Besides she worked very hard in the Phulpur constituency of Nehru and visited all the 1,100 villages and talked to people who waited for her for hours.[43] She also went to Gujarat and the Punjab, getting up early morning and returning late night. Her tour to Punjab was tiring, as she wrote to Nehru that 'Punjab was strenuous but most exhilarating too. I had 100,000 people in Rohtak just for me—imagine that.'[44]

As months rolled on, she began to gather more power. In 1958, she became a member of the Central Parliamentary Board. Acquisition of more political power, further increased her status among the political leaders and it began to reflect in her appearance. She was realising that from a sick girl she was becoming a healthy and fit woman when she wrote to Norman that people tell her that she looked 'lit up from inside' with a new vitality. This made her politically more active, dynamic and influential.[45]

By the time Nehru reached the age of 69, he had become tired and was unhappy with politics and politicking. He wanted to resign and had a long conversation with Indira on this subject. She, rather talking to him one-to-one, wrote him a letter in which she strongly suggested him to resign because 'some very ugly things are happening around you.'[46] She also wrote that: 'So much is rotten in our politics that everybody sees things through avaricious myopic eyes and is quite unable to understand nobility and greatness. There will therefore be a feeling that you had no intention of giving up the Prime Ministership and were only bluffing. If you are outside, it may at least reassure the general public that you were not responsible for all the wrongdoings.'[47] But Nehru, as long as he was alive, never resigned.

The year 1959 proved to be a landmark in her life when U. N. Dhebar, the Congress President wanted to retire eleven months before the end of his two-year term. He and Govind Ballabh Pant, a powerful leader from Uttar Pradesh, decided to make her the President. She was not willing to accept the onerous responsibility and told Pant, that it would not be possible for her to handle it. But Pant over-ruled her saying that it was not the question of what she decided. 'We have decided and you have to do it,' said he, adding that it was her duty. Pant also discussed the issue with Nehru, who was also not in favour of Indira becoming the Congress President. But when Indira sought his advice, he merely said that she had to take the call and decide and he was not going to enter into it. In fact, Pant and Dhebar stage-managed the whole plan of trapping her. When she refused and Nehru also was not willing, Pant and Dhebar, leaked the news to the media that she would be the next Congress President. The media reacted negatively and wrote editorials that she was not fit for the job. Both went to her and asked her if she would let the press 'to get away with this.' She had no option but to agree.[48]

On February 2, despite her and Nehru's unwillingness, she was elected the Congress President to succeed Dhebar for eleven months. It seems she was not very happy with this new assignment as she wrote to Norman: 'A veritable sea of trouble is engulfing me. On the domestic front, Feroze] ...has always resented my very existence, but since I have become President, he exudes such hostility that it seems to poison the air. Just to make things difficult for me, he is leaning more and more towards the communists and is sabotaging my efforts to strengthen the Congress. Unfortunately, he and his friends are friendly with some of our ministers and an impossible situation is being created.'[49] Thus, her becoming the Congress President further deteriorated her weakening marriage.

She took charge after six days at Congress headquarters in Delhi and became the third generation Nehru to be the Party President after 1928, when Motilal was elected the first Nehru to this position and was taken through the streets of Calcutta in a majestic cavalcade. Jawaharlal was taken through the streets of Lahore on a white stallion in 1929.[50]

Soon after becoming the Congress President, she faced two critical problems. The first problem that she faced, was a critical political development in Kerala which was a unique state. Kerala had a strong Communist Party that came in power after the 1957 elections with E. M. S. Namboodiripad as the Chief Minister. The New government passed radical agricultural reforms and legislation to control private educational institutions annoying the religious interest groups. All joined together to agitate against the Namboodiripad Government. Congress also jumped into the agitation jointly with the Muslim League, whom it strongly opposed because it held the League responsible for the country's partition in 1947.

When Indira was fighting the communists in Kerala, Feroze agitated in Delhi to oppose her efforts against the communist government in Kerala. At a Congress meeting he asked: 'Where are the principles of the Congress? ...Has the Congress...fallen so low that we are going to be dictated [to] by communal elements, by leaders of a caste?...in Kerala you have forged the instrument of your own destruction.'[51]

Three months later, Nehru dismissed the Kerala government and imposed President's rule. This was the first dismissal of a State government in independent India. In the elections later the Congress, aligned with Muslim League and other right-wing parties, came to power.

Nehru's decision to dismiss the communist government in Kerala was his own as he himself was not in favour of this government continuing. This was based on advice from various persons in whom he had deep faith. Krishnan Menon, Nehru's trusted advisor, had warned him as early as January 1958 that 'sinister trends' were developing in Kerala and may get worse with the passage of time. In May, Nehru had given a hint to the reporter of *Daily Telegraph* (London) that communists will not be able to stay in power for long in Kerala.[52] In fact, Nehru was becoming alienated from Communists, in general, because of the Soviet policies in Hungry and Yugoslavia. He was getting convinced that communists were turning Kerala into an anarchic and violent State. This was proved by the second report by Krishnan Menon, nine months after his first one, that things were becoming gloomier. He, therefore, asked the Home Minister to collect more infor-mation from Kerala. He, at that time, was even thinking of sending army to control violence. To verify the various negative report, he himself went to the State's capital, Trivandrum (now Thiruvananthapuram) in June 1959, and was aghast by the situation prevailing there which were 'near hysteria with thick walls of group hatred.'[53] He advised the CM Namboodiripad to call fresh elections which he refused. Five weeks later, Nehru dismissed the Kerala Government.[54]

Though the decision of dismissing the Kerala Government was independently taken by Nehru, Indira was criticised widely for being responsible for it. It was said that she had shown her ruthlessness for the first time and indicates her despotic inclinations and indifference to democratic practises. It is true that she was not in favour of the communist government continuing in Kerala, but she never forced Nehru to dismiss the Kerala government.[55]

The second critical situation developed in Bombay State (now Maharashtra) where an agitation had developed for the bifurcation of the state on linguistic basis in two states: Gujarat and Maharashtra. Though all the states were reorganised three years back, Punjab and Bombay remained bilingual. But after the 1957 elections, the agitation began for two separate states out of the Bombay state. The agitation that Indira faced was on the issue of the city of Bombay as both the states wanted to have this city. Nehru was against the separation of Maharashtra and Gujarat but, Indira after visiting Bombay was convinced that the partition of Bombay State was the best solution of the problem as unless it was done there would be perpetual law and order problem in that region. To solve the problem in a practical way she appointed a committee to study the problem. The committee suggested that Bombay be bifurcated in two states, Maharashtra and Gujarat and Bombay be given to Maharashtra. Though Nehru was against it, she persuaded Nehru to agree and the State of Gujarat was created out of Bombay State and the city of, Bombay remained with Maharashtra.[56]

As her 11-month term was coming to an end, she was becoming frustrated with the reproach that she was receiving after the Kerala episode. She began to think of getting rid of this exhausting position. She wrote her frustration to Norman in October: 'I have gained tremendously in self-confidence. But I do not wish to continue for many reasons. The routine part of the work takes too much time and is too confining. I have felt like a bird in a too-small a cage.'[57] She was so restless that she could not sleep on the night of October 30 and got up at 3:45 a.m. to write a letter to her father stating that her girlhood was not easy and 'I have felt like a bird in a very small cage, my wings hitting against the bars whichever way I moved. The time has come for me to live my own life. I just want to be free and find my own direction. The experience of being the President of the Congress has been exhilarating at times, depressing at times, but certainly worthwhile. But … I can only be warped and unhappy if I have to continue.'[58] Making it known to her father that she was resigning, she made it public also. But instead of getting a feeling of relief, she became depressed. She wanted to make herself happy with the help of music and poetry.[59] But despite of this, she was spending sleepless nights, not much because of depression but the pain caused by stones in the kidney.

During her presidency, Indira developed stones in her bladder and was operated after her term ended in February. This brought Feroze closer to her, who was with her in the hospital and moved back to PM's house to take care of her after the operation. She was fully recovered after four months and the whole family, Feroze, Rajiv, Sanjay and she, like a happy family, spend days together in Srinagar. With this she thought that the family has united and even discussed of building a house of their own. But destiny was written differently, and two months after returning from Srinagar, Feroze had a massive heart attack and died just four days before his 48th birthday on September 8, 1960. Indira was truly grieved and missed Feroze, despite all the bitterness in their marriage. She wrote to 16-year-old Rajiv at Doon School: 'However much one loves one's father, it is not as close as that of a husband and wife.'[60]

The death of Feroze wounded her materially and emotionally. 'It was not just a mental shock, but it was as though someone has cut me in two,' she accepted. And she wore only white sarees for a long time, because as she accepted later that after Feroze died 'all the colour drained out of my life.'[61]

It took four months for her to come out of the blankness and her normal self after she came back from a two-month tour of Africa, South America, Mexico and the United States in January 1961. Though she still felt depressed, she began to participate in political affairs of the Congress. She again became a member of CWC and CEC and was soon busy in selecting candidates for the 1962 general election. She came in her real form after the miserable humiliation by the Chinese in October 1962 and supported those who wanted Menon's resignation, telling a friend that 'it does not matter who they are, if people do not function, they must go. No one is indispensable.' It proved that she was capable of taking cold-blooded decisions with no emotions. In fact, she wanted to avert the blame away from Nehru.[62]

Things were moving differently after the Chinese humiliation and as Nehru was becoming depressed and politically weaker some powerful and important leaders began to think of his successor. K. Kamaraj, a former Congress President and Madras Chief Minister and a powerful Congress leader formed a syndicate of five, including himself. The other four were: Atulya Ghosh of West Bengal, S K Patil from Bombay, Sanjiva Reddy, Chief Minister of Andhra Pradesh and S Nijalingappa, the Chief Minister of Mysore. They had a secret meeting in October 1963 in Tirupati, a temple town in Andhra, where they decided that a collective leadership, headed by Lal Bahadur Shastri, and not Morarji Desai, should succeed Nehru. This stymied Morarji's chances of becoming Nehru's successor.

The falling health of Nehru made him politically weak and mentally exhausted. It drained him of all power and strength, physical and emotional, causing a stroke early January 1964. He was partially paralysed on the left side while rising to speak at the Congress session. Though Biju Patnaik, a former Chief Minister of Orrisa (now Odisha) and a powerful Congress leader wanted Indira to become the Deputy Prime Minster to ease Nehru's work pressure, she refused. She was thinking of leaving politics after the Chinese War so that Nehru would not depend on her. She even selected a small house in London as she wanted to be close to Rajiv, who was studying at Cambridge and Sanjay, who was readying to go to UK. But she could not buy the house because she did not have adequate money to purchase it.[63]

Nehru died in the afternoon of 27 May 1964 and Indira again was in deep depression after taking care of all the post-death formalities. During the past 18 years she was wholly devoted to Nehru and involved in his work. Now she felt lonely and isolated as he was no more there in her life. It seems she had some premonition of the coming events and had written, only two months earlier to Norman that she wanted to leave India and politics. She did not know what she should do as she was homeless and penniless. But her daze was broken when Shastri called her three days after the death of Nehru and requested her to accept prime ministership saying: '*ab aapmulk ko sambhalleejiye*' (now you take over the responsibility of the country). Thereafter, a number of important Congress leaders approached her to accept the offer. But that seemed to be just to ascertain if she were interested? If she were, then all the plan of the syndicate would have jeopardised and there would not have been any succession war. After her final refusal, the syndicate manoeuvred a unanimous election, though Desai did not give up easily, of Shastri as the Party leader and the new PM.

After becoming the PM, Shastri offered her a cabinet post; though she showed her reluctance, she accepted it. The main reason might have been revival of her political life of which she had become accustomed, a home and a regular income. But she was not happy with the portfolio of Information and Broadcasting with fourth ranking in the Cabinet as she was thinking an important ministry like foreign affairs. She was nominated to the Rajya Sabha as she did not want to contest an election. One Safdarjung Road was allotted to her where she lived till she was assassinated in 1984, except 1977 to 1979, the post-emergency gap in her prime ministership.[64]

Indira Gandhi did not want to live a life of anonymity as she was always treated someone very important. She became the most powerful person when Nehru became the Prime Minister, as his hostess. Only eight months before the death of Nehru, she had written to Norman that 'privacy, unfortunately, is not possible for me even in the remotest corner of this continent. I have had people presenting their cards and their problems even at the foot of the Kolahoi glacier (16,000 feet high)! It is not just meeting people but that they come only to get or ask something.'[65]

Even though she declined to head the Government and accepted a low importance ministry, she clamoured for importance and expected Shastri to consult her before taking important decisions. So, she began to flout Shastri. The first indication of that was when Shastri appointed Swaran Singh Foreign Minister, she complained late Inder Malhotra, a senior journalist and a former Resident Editor of *TheTimes of India* in Delhi that she expected to be consulted before the decision was finalised. Soon, she began to feel restless as she was out of the power-orbit and began to throw her weight around. The first opportunity came within ten months when in March 1965, anti-Hindi violent agitation began in Madras State (now Tamil Nadu) against declaring Hindi as the official language. Though Shastri and Kamraj wanted to wait before announcing a decision, she, without taking the permission of or even informing the PM flew to Madras and gave assurance of not imposing Hindi. The violence stopped thereafter. When told by Inder Malhotra that this was against the protocol, she bluntly said that she was not just a minister but an important leader as well and the Government would fall if she resigned. And if need be, it will be repeated.[66]

She did not have to wait for long to repeat her deed. In August 1965, she had gone to Kashmir for a holiday. When she was there, she came to know that Pakistani soldiers dressed as civilians were preparing to capture Srinagar and incite a pro-Pakistani movement. She visited forward areas and talked to soldiers. She again flew to Kashmir when war broke-out in September and addressed a large crowd in Srinagar promising not to give an inch of Indian territory to the aggressor. She also visited several war-affected areas and addressed big crowds. This time also Shastri's permission was neither sought not he was informed. Shastri, also a sharp and shrewd politician had decided to send her to UK as Indian High Commissioner after his return from Tashkent. But destiny was written differently.

Indira, besides taking liberty in taking bold political decisions, formed a cabal who strongly backed her. It included: Dinesh Singh, who was made a minister when she became PM, Ashok Mehta, Deputy Chairman of Planning Commission, Inder Gujral, who became her trusted fellow and minister, Satish Gujral, a painter who had painted a portrait of her and Romesh Thapar, a prominent journalist of his times. Dinesh and Inder were always at her command.[67]

Shastri died in Tashkent after a fatal heart attack on January 11, 1966. Her secretary N K Seshan, informed her and also told that Home Minister, Gulzarilal Nanda had gone to meet the President. She rushed to the Rashtrapati Bhawan where the President, S Radhakrishnan swore Nanda as the acting PM. Only two persons were present—Finance Minister, Sachindra Chaudhuri and she.

Among those present to receive Shastri's body 'was a well-known astrologer, clad, despite the extreme cold, in thin white *khadi* and *chapplas* [slippers]. He was a holy man who was most popular among political and bureaucratic circles being close to Jawaharlal and Indira Gandhi. A high-ranking Congress leader spotted him and hastily moved up to him and asked: 'What do the stars foretell?' 'A hat trick' was the reply.'

Both Nehru and Shastri were from Allahabad and his prediction, that proved correct, was that the next Prime Minister of India would also be from there.[68]

****

Chapter Five

Modi Becoming PM

After almost extinction of the Bharatiya Janata Party in 1984, it began to emerge an emerging political force. What made it stronger was the *Ram Janmabhoomi* (birth place) movement aimed at building a *mandir* (temple) at the site of the Babri *Masjid* (Mosque) in Ayodhya, Uttar Pradesh. The BJP claimed that it was a temple that Mughal Emperor Babur demolished and constructed a mosque on its remains. Modi was the main organiser of the first stretch of the then BJP President L.K. Advani's famous cross-country *Rath Yatra* (chariot procession) to Ayodhya that prompted the RSS and BJP volunteers to demolish the Babri *Masjid* in 1992.The demolition incited nationwide Hindu-Muslim riots causing the death of more than 1,000 people. Modi also organised another successful *Rath Yatra* for senior BJP leader Murli Manohar Joshi in 1991. It further consolidated his position bringing him closer to the BJP's national leadership. Thereafter, Modi was shifted to Delhi to work as National Secretary in 1995. His assignment was to monitor the party's activities in Haryana and Himachal Pradesh.[1]

Though Gujarat was BJP's stronghold much before Modi appeared on the scene as a strong political leader, the BJP became weaker because of mismanaged relief works during and after the 2001 Bhuj earthquake. As much needed relief did not reach to the suffering people, BJP began to lose its grip on the State. It was mainly because Keshubhai Patel miserably failed to manage the post-quake relief operations due to his corrupt practices and poor governance. The corrupt practices by CM's supporters were so widespread that goods meant to provide relief did not reach to the people and were openly sold at market places. All this put BJP on the spot.[2]

The dissatisfaction of the people was soon reflected in BJP losing two by-elections: Sabarmati Assembly and Sabarkantha Lok Sabha. The Sabarmati constituency fell in L.K. Advani's parliamentary constituency of Gandhinagar. As Advani was the Union Home Minter at that time, a defeat in his constituency was a double shock to the Party. The distressed BJP and the High Command felt that Gujarat would be lost forever if Keshubhai was not replaced. In fact, his dismissal was being discussed in the BJP, as well as in the RSS,since the Kutch quake and they were waiting for an opportune time to get rid of him. Losing two important seats gave them the right opportunity to show red flag to him.[3]

After having decided to replace him, Keshubhai was summoned to Delhi by the then Prime Minister Atal Bihari Vajpayee to discuss the deteriorating situation in Gujarat. On meeting the Prime Minister, he, instead of discussing the situation, asked for a grant of 41 lakh crore rupees for the rehabilitation of the quack sufferers. The flabbergasted Vajpayee admonished him for the poor relief operation and the relief material being openly sold in the market. He asked him to first utilise the existing resources judiciously before asking for more money. The money is not to be wasted like it was being blown in Gujarat. He curtly dismissed him saying that he should meet Advani.[4]

The crestfallen Keshubhai met Advani and BJP General Secretary Madanlal Khurana and other senior BJP leaders. All suggested him to resign lest Gujarat may go to Congress in the following elections. After meeting all, the depressed Keshubhai realised that he had reached the end of the road and now there was no possibility of his continuing the CM. He had escaped dismissal on two earlier occasions in his controversial tenure of just a little more than three years, but now it was tough to hold on to the job.[5]

The BJP High Command finally decided that Keshubhai had to go. To get the decision sealed, President K Jana Krishnamurthy met the PM in the evening and told the reporters that the new CM in Gujarat will be decided in a day or two.

Keshubhai, before returning to Ahmedabad, objected to the 'insulting' and authoritarian manner in which he was being asked to go. He also asked his supporters to send a memorandum underlining their support to him. Around 30 MLAs, mainly from the politically dominant Patel community, sent a communiqué stating that Keshubhai Patel was doing fine work in Gujarat and was not to be blamed for the byelection defeats. However, if he were to be replaced, the new Chief Minister should be appointed after consulting the BJP's State unit. But the entire Gujarat was alive with the rumour that Modi might be coming as CM.[6]

In the morning of October 2, before returning to Ahmedabad, Keshubhai gave his resignation to the BJP President Jana Krishnamurthy. In Ahmedabad, when he got down from the plane, Keshubhai was in an iconoclastic mood and said that he had not yet been asked to submit his resignation to the Governor and that it was up to the legislature party to elect a new leader. The rival of Keshubhai, former Chief Minister Suresh Mehta, who had sensed that Modi might be sent to Ahmedabad as the next CM, publicly announced that he would not join Narendra Modi's Government as he was much junior to hm.

But by overnight all became quite and next morning, a sullen and subdued Keshubhai Patel held his last press conference as Chief Minister and said that in a few hours, he would submit his resignation to the Governor. This changed the entire situation suddenly and all those who were opposing Modi becoming the CM, affirming compliance of High Command's decision.

In the evening of 30th September, Advani and Jana Krishnamurthy assembled at 7, Race Course Road. A few minutes later, Prime Minister Vajpayee joined them. He posed a question to Advani asking what was to be done for Gujarat. Advani replied that both were discussing the same issue and suggested a few names for the CM. All the names were discussed for almost an hour and it was unanimously decided that Modi will be the only one who can bring Gujarat back to BJP. Advani particularly narrated an incident to tell how popular was Modi in Gujarat. In 2000, a reunion of those who were detained during the Emergency was organised in Ahmedabad on June 28. At that time Modi's entry in Gujarat was banned. But his presence could not be prevented because being an official function he was respectfully invited. Nevertheless, he was seated at the far end of the dais to show that he was the least important of the awardees. But to their consternation, he received a full five-minute standing ovation by the crowd when he was called by the National President to receive a shawl and citation for his underground work during the Emergency. Keshubhai and BJP State President Rajendrasinh Rana were crestfallen and dumbstruck.[7]

After listening to all this, Vajpayee agreed for Modi to be the next CM of Gujarat because besides being the most popular BJP leader, he was also disciplined, experienced and had strong organisational ability. It was, finally decided that Narendra Modi will replace Keshubhai Patel as Chief Minister of Gujarat.

****

On September 30, 2001, Madhavrao Scindia died in a plane crash. Along with him four journalists, who were accompanying him, were also killed. He was going to Kanpur to address a Congress rally, part of the series of pre-election meetings planned by the Congress, and named *Parivartan Yatra* (travel for change). Next day, Modi was attending the cremation of a journalist friend who had died in the crash when his mobile began to buzz. It was a call from the Prime Minister who asked him: 'Where are you?' He told him that he was at the cremation grounds attending the last rights of a journalist friend who had died in the crash along with Scindia. The PM asked Modi to reach his residence, 7, Race Course Road (now 7, Lok Kalyan Marg) as soon as he could. A perplexed Narendra Modi reached PM's residence in the evening. As Modi was taking his seat and making himself comfortable, Vajpayee told him impassively: 'You must leave Delhi and go away from here.' The PM also told him that he was becoming overweight because he had been eating all that 'Punjabi food' for three years.

Modi was shocked and asked: 'Where would I go?' The PM replied in one-word: 'Gujarat.' Modi thought that being the All-India Organisation Secretary, he would also be overseeing Gujarat and asked if he would be losing other states that he was looking after. The PM told hm that he would be taking over from Keshubhai as the CM and contesting an Assembly by-election later.[8]

Modi's took no time in declining the offer saying that he was out of touch with the affairs in Gujarat as he was away from the state for six long years and now, he did not know many people there. Also, he had no administrative experience, had not been even an MLA. But Vajpayee knew very well that he was speaking a lie because he knew almost everyone there. Therefore, he insisted and told Modi that Keshubhai Patel's administration had incurred public wrath over the last one year. Also, he was not doing well in the aftermath of the 2001 earthquake in Gujarat which killed 20,000 people. Modi was told that some members of the Keshubhai Administration were colluding with unscrupulous builders who did shoddy construction that led to many deaths due to felling structures. Modi still did not agree and offered to spend ten days every month in Gujarat and keep on doing his usual work. Vajpayee kept on persuading Modi to accept the offer but Modi keep on refusing. Ultimately, Vajpayee told him that it was an order to move to Gujarat and leave Delhi. Modi got up without giving any commitment.

As soon as Modi entered his room, he got a call from Advani enquiring about his meeting with the Prime Minister. Modi told him all the conversation he had at PM's house and that he didn't want to move in Gujarat. Advani brusquelytold him that in view of Keshubhai Patel's falling health and BJP becoming unpopular because of his alleged abuse of power, corruption and poor administration, BJP national leadership had decided to change the CM and Modi has been chosen as a replacement. Now he had no other option but go to Gujarat as the next CM of Gujarat. Advani, realising Modi's lack of experience in government, suggested him to be Patel's Deputy Chief Minister. But Modi refused and told Advani that he was 'either going to be fully responsible for Gujarat or not at all.'[9] Modi still didn't agree but gave his consent on the morning of Tuesday October 2. Realising that his destiny has been finalised by the top BJP and RSS leadership, he collected his few possessions and settled his affairs to leave for Ahmedabad next day. He flew to Ahmedabad early on Wednesday October 3 to prepare for taking charge as the new CM of Gujarat. He was sworn in the new Chief Minister on October 7.

Modi created a history when a *pracharak* (preacher), for the first time, became the Chief Minister of a major State. He was administered the oath of the 14th Chief Minister of Gujarat amidst a lot of fanfare and gate-crashing by unruly party workers during the forty-minute ceremony that was held under a huge specially-erected pandal at the Gandhinagar helipad ground. The swearing-in was a show of great mass support of Modi in Gujarat as it was attended by 50,000 party workers and a large number of BJP stalwarts from the Centre and some other States, besides leaders of some partners in the National Democratic Alliance. It was the day when the United States and its allies, in less than a month after attacks on the World Trade Center in New York, dropped their first bombs on Kabul, Kandahar and Jalalabad.[10]

The oath-taking ceremony was witnessed by the Chief Ministers of three States, Rajnath Singh of Uttar Pradesh, Om Prakash Chautala of Haryana and Prem Kumar Dhumal of Himachal Pradesh, besides a large number of Union Ministers including L.K. Advani, Murli Manohar Joshi, Ram Vilas Paswan, Arun Jaitley, Jayawanti Mehta, Ved Prakash Goel, Suresh Prabhu, Kashiram Rana and Vallabh Kathiriya. The party's national president, Jana Krishnamurthi, the former party president, Bangaru Laxman, the vice-president and in-charge of Gujarat affairs, Madanlal Khurana, Secretary, Sunil Shastri, the party chiefs in Uttar Pradesh and Rajasthan, Kalraj Mishra and Ramdas Agarwal, the former Rajasthan Chief Minister, Bhairon Singh Shekhawat, and the NDA convener, George Fernandes, were also present.[11]

The Congress, besides certain leaders from BJP, boycotted the ceremony saying that such extravagance was not needed when the victims of the January 26 earthquake were still passing their days without a roof over their heads. But so much was the popularity of Modi that when the function ended, party workers tried to climb on to the dais to greet him. When this hula-bulla was going on, Modi was calm and later went in an open jeep along with the State Party chief, Rajendrasinh Rana, to accept the greetings of his large fans. Before taking over charge, he drove to visit his aged mother. It was a great day for him as he came from a lower-middle class family from Ghanchi community, an OBC caste involved in oil extraction. More so, as the state was ruled by the dominating landowning Patels, an upper caste.[12]

After taking charge of the State, Modi began to reorganise the governance to improve things. His first priority was to focus all his energies on learning the skills of governance because he had never held any political office and to remain CM had to contest an election within six months. In most of the briefings with the officers, he was silent and allowed them to talk. This way he learnt how administration worked. During the meetings and presentations, he was very attentive, as if he was sketching every word, every intonation, everything. But while he was trying to learn the functioning of the governance, he was facing resistance from senior state BJP leaders who were displeased by his ascendance.[13]

After settling down in the office, he earnestly began work on his election from Rajkot-II constituency. He won the election by 14,728 votes, defeating the Congress candidate Ashwin Mehta and entered the State legislature on February, 24.[14]

While he was finalising strategies and plans, a major incident jeopardised his entire process of reorganisation because a major happening in Godhra became a defining moment in Modi's life.

****

In early February 2002, Anika, a twelve-year-old girl, the daughter of a senior engineer at Larsen and Toubro in Surat, was told that she would be giving a dance performance at her school's annual day on March 1. It was to be her first dance in costume, and Anika insisted that her grandparents, who lived in Ahmedabad, should come to Surat to see her on the stage. Her grandfather assured Anika that they would certainly be there to see her perform. But only two days before her performance, on February 27, she was traumatised because the programme was cancelled due to a tragedy in Godhra (meaning 'land of cows').[15]

On February 27, Godhara was windless and the day temperature was rising when at 7:42 in the morning Sabarmati Express (Sabarmati is the river that flows through Ahmedabad), with 2,300 passengers, steamed into the station. Godhra, a city near the border with Madhya Pradesh and 155 km away from Ahmedabad, is the administrative headquarters of the Panchmahal district. The railway station is situated in a densely populated Muslim neighbourhood and is dominated by garages and auto workshops. Poverty and illiteracy rates are very high in this area.[16]

The train was five-hour late and most of the passengers were mainly *karsewaks* (volunteers to work at temple site), who had gone to Ayodhya. They were returning back to Ahmedabad after participating in the *Poorna Ahuti Yagya* (complete offering worship), a ritual at the traditional birthplace of Rama.

After a stop of five minutes, the train pulled out of the station. It had hardly moved 100 meters, when someone pulled the emergency chain and the train came to a halt. As soon as the train stopped, a large crowd of Muslims surrounded the train and begin to shower stones and bricks. It created a panic in the train which was full of exhausted passengers tired from a long journey. Passengers from several bogeys were forced to shut the windows of their bougies to protect themselves. The railway police were unable to disperse the crowd. The train, after some time, resumed its journey, but within a few minutes, the emergency chain was pulled again, this time simultaneously from several coaches. It halted at about 700 meters away from the station.

A crowd of around 2,000 local Muslims, who lived in the nearby areas, gathered and surrounded the train. As soon as the train stopped, they began shelling it with bricks, stones, burning missiles and even acid bulbs, crying '*Maro, kapo, badhanejalavi do*' (burn them all) and '*Hinduoko maar daloaurjala*' (Hindus should be cut and burnt). Their targets were especially coaches—S-5, S-6 and S-7. These war like cries were not made by the crowd only but were relayed over a public address system and from the nearby mosque. These were heard far and near. Not only that, the guard of the train was not allowed to go and reset the emergency chain because the crown showered stoned on him and he was forced to withdraw into his van. This prevented the driver to move the train. The crowd also cut the vacuum pipe between coaches S-6 and S-7, preventing any further movement of the train. They also locked the doors of these two coaches from outside. The passengers in these two bogies (S-6 and S-7) were completely closed in their compartments.[17]

A fire started in coach S-7 and the passengers quickly extinguished it. The attack intensified after that and coach S-6 was in flames within a few minutes. A few passengers were able to get out of the burning compartment but were stoned and attacked with sharp weapons, receiving serious injuries, some were even killed. Others got out through the windows and took shelter below the coach. But fifty-eight passengers were burned alive, including twenty-seven women and ten children. The whole attack lasted 20-25 minutes.[18]

The police were helpless as it was outnumbered by the crowd. The fire brigade was also obstructed by the crowd to reach the burning train by throwing stones at it, smashing its windscreen and windows. Somehow or the other it could reach the burning train in twenty minutes. But, by that time, all persons in the bogey were burnt alive.[19]

****

When all this was happening, Modi, after getting up as usual at five in the morning, was eating his breakfast after going through his routine. He was completely unaware about the happenings in Godhra. The first confused news reached to him around nine. Though he wanted to reach there immediately, he could not because it was the Budget day and Budget was to be introduced. As soon as the budget process was over, he called a Cabinet meeting and issued a state-wide alert. He flew to Vadodara and took the ONGC helicopter and reached Godhra around four in the afternoon. The situation was far worse than he had expected. He immediately ordered to impose curfew in Godhra and 28 other cities from the next morning. Later it was extended to all urban areas in Gujarat.[20]

Back in Gandhinagar, he realised the gravity of the situation and realised that a backlash of the Godhra burning may follow any time. With a view to check it, he directed all the available police force to be deployed in all sensitive cities and requested for assistance from the Army. But he was told that the Army was deployed at the Pakistan border and, therefore, cannot be made available. He told them: 'Yes I can understand that the Army is not available at this moment, but they must have some juniors. Just as long as they have uniforms, that will help us.' After the blank refusal he made an official request to Advani through a fax next day conveying him the enormity of the situation and asked for the Army help.[21]

But the Hindus were determined to take revenge and their number was increasing every hour and soon it became more than the number of security forces. Realising the seriousness of the situation, Modi requested the neighbouring States of Maharashtra, Madhya Pradesh, Rajasthan and Punjab to provide him their security forces, but none agreed to help him.[22] The situation changed when George Fernandes, the Union Defence Minister, flew in Ahmedabad on February 28 and met Modi at 10:30 in the night.

Soon after the meeting, the Army reached Gujarat by midnight. By the next day, thirteen companies of the Army were deployed in Ahmedabad.

While Modi was taking steps to ensure that the Hindu reaction did not blow up, VHP volunteers were telling Hindus in different cities on what had happened at Godhra. By the next morning, around ten in the morning, a huge crowd of armed Hindus came out on streets setting Muslim property to fire and killing them. Crowds of enraged Hindus, led by extremist Hindu leaders, attacked Muslims, killing them and setting fire to their houses and other properties. The situation became worse when some Muslims leaders retaliated. In Chamanpura area where nearly forty persons, including former Congress MP Ehsaan Jafri and his family members were killed, there were just a few armed guards when the crowd began assembling. Reinforcements did arrive but by that time the mob had swelled to 10,000. Even after police firing, killing at least five persons on the spot and forty in Ahmedabad alone, the carnage went on unabated.The situation was aggravated further when Jafri fired from his revolver on the mob injuring seven. Others in the housing complex also threw acid bulbs on the crowd.[23]

With the passing time, situation kept on deteriorating. According to Ahmedabad Police Commissioner P.C. Pande: 'In my 32-year career I have never seen something like this. It was an upsurge, unstoppable and unprecedented. A stage came when it became physically impossible for the police to tackle mobs running into thousands.' The fire brigade which had the capacity to handle 100 fire calls received 400 calls on February 28.[24] By now Modi had realised that when the dead bodies would reach to their families, the emotional reaction would be too strong and would be difficult to control. So, he wanted the bodies of the victims to be cremated near the Sola Civil Hospital where they were brought for post-mortem on February 28 from Godhra. The hospital is on the western outskirts of Ahmedabad with negligible Muslim population. Cremation there, Modi thought, would help containing the anger. Some VHP leaders present at the spot were also under instructions to convince the relatives of the victims to agree to the proposal. But the moment the proposal was floated, the families of those killed, flared up and accused the BJP 'of acting in a manner worse than the Congress.'[25]

Modi's thinking was correct; as soon as the bodies reached their homes, retaliatory violence began. The burning of fifty-eight, mostly women and children, in the most heinous and barbarous way, traumatised the people and the reaction was instantons. There was no reaction in the beginning and the situation was calm till the afternoon of that day. But when the charred bodies began to arrive and there was no comforting voice from the

Government and the media did not condemn this barbaric act, the Gujarati people, known for their non-violent exceptional patience, were so angry that the whole Gujarat burnt. For three days, tens of thousands of infuriated Hindus came out on streets and set fire to Muslim shops, houses, vehicles and killed a large number of Muslims. It, in fact, was the whole Hindu community that came out from all sides. They were from all parties, all classes and were uncontrollable. Nine-hundred-and-seventy persons—720 Muslims and 250 Hindus—were killed when the uprising subsided. This was the official figure; the real figure might be even higher.

The Gujarat Riots were the first riots that were shown on live television across India. Hundreds of thousands of people watched Gujaratis running amok on the streets, calling for revenge and demanding that all Muslims leave the country. It created a nation-wide abhorrence for the BJP in general and Modi in particular. Not only that, the vicious Gujarat bloodshed developed a wide division within the party. Modi was backed by the hardcore RSS followers, while the broadminded feared that the riots would alienate liberal Hindus who looked at the BJP as 'the party with a difference' by the resurgent face of militant Hindutva.[26]

Shanta Kumar, the former Chief Minister of Himachal Pradesh and a Cabinet minister in the Vajpayee Government was the first person to hold Modi guilty for promoting riots. He demanded action against the VHP and Bajrang Dal, declaring that 'those counting votes on dead bodies are not Hindus'. He also said that 'he was pained and disgusted by the events in Gujarat. Those who think of consolidating Hindutva by shedding blood in Gujarat are the enemies of Hindus.'[27]

The RSS did not agree with those who accused Modi for the riots. It fully supported Modi because Shanta Kumar's remarks came only a few days before the scheduled meeting of the BJP national executive in Goa and the Sangh leaders did not want Modi to leave the battle half-way. So much was the reaction against Shanta Kumar that he had to give two written apologies: one to Krishnamurthy, and another to the RSS in-charge for the VHP, retracting his statement that the actions of the VHP had sullied the entire Hindu community. Moderates who were in power worried because they feared that parties supporting the BJP-led coalition Government may withdrew their support. But RSS did not buy this argument and decided that Modi would have to be defended, even at the cost of the Vajpayee Government.[28]

RSS was emboldened because many of the secular regional parties including the Janata Dal (United) in Bihar, the Dravida Munnetra Kazhagam in Tamil Nadu, the Telugu Desam Party in Andhra Pradesh and the Trinamool Congress in West Bengal, who were supporting BJP did not threaten to walk out of the Government.

Vajpayee was not convinced about the innocence of Modi and was certain that Modi had not judiciously handled the situation after the Godhra train burning. He was so annoyed with Modi that he did not visit Gujarat till April 4. But after the visit and before leaving Gujarat, he held a joint press conference with Modi in Ahmedabad. As the conference was going on, a reporter asked what his message for the Chief Minister would be. Vajpayee took a few moments to answer the question and said that Modi should follow '*raj dharma*' (the duty of the king). He further said: '*Raja keliye, shasakkeliye, prajapraja main bhednahin ho saktahai. Na janamkeaadhaar par, najaatikeaadhaar par, nasampradaykeadhaar par* (A king, a ruler, should not discriminate against the subjects. Not on the basis of birth, not on the basis of caste, not on the basis of religion).' Modi was sitting next to him and his expression changed from a smile to a mild laugh, then a frown and became pokerfaced when Vajpayee was speaking. He then turned towards him and said, 'Hum *bhiwohi kar rahehai sahib* (that's what I am doing sir).' Vajpayee took a few seconds to respond after that and said, without turning to look at Modi, 'I trust that Narendra bhai is doing the same.' Modi's smile returned briefly after that.[29]

On April 7, Vajpayee left for Singapore and Cambodia on a five-day official tour. After the plane had taken off, Ranjan Bhattacharya, Vajpayee's son-in-law, went to Arun Shourie, the Union Disinvestment Minister and said: 'Shourieji, please go and meet him. *Baapji* (respected father) is terribly upset.' Shourie got up and moved to the PM's cabin. He found Vajpayee sitting ashen face with head down and not looking up. He seemed to be depressed and deeply dejected. Soon, Shourie realised that the PM was upset for one major reason: Gujarat. He suggested that he should speak to Advani about the possibilities of salvaging the situation, and may be Modi has to be replaced. But the 'pep talk' did not cheer Vajpayee. He told Shourie that he would talk to Advani about it.

In Singapore the Gujarat issue came up in an interview on the third and final day of their stay. The journalist who interviewed Vajpayee first stated that Singaporeans were wary of communal disturbances, clearly indicating that he was referring to the recent riots in Gujarat, under the BJP rule. Then he shot off his question: 'And in India such disturbances have happened not once, but several times. In this regard what can Singapore learn from India's experience and what can you share?'

Vajpayee paused and rubbed his forehead with his right hand before answering, revealing a level of discomfiture in answering questions related to the Gujarat riots. Then, weighing his words to make it as official as it could get, he said: 'Whatever happened in India was very unfortunate. The riots have been brought under control. If at the Godhra station, the passengers of the Sabarmati Express were not been burnt alive, then perhaps the Gujarat tragedy could have been averted. It is clear there was some conspiracy behind this incident. It is also a matter of concern that there was no prior intelligence available on this conspiracy. Alertness is essential in a democracy. We have been cautious. And if one does not ignore even small incidents like one used to in the past, then one will certainly not be successful in fighting terrorism.'[30]

****

The National Executive of the BJP met on April 12 in Goa. It was the first meeting after the Gujarat riots. Vajpayee, had returned from Cambodia the previous day and was flying with Advani and Jaswant Singh, the External Affairs Minister in his Cabinet. He had asked Brijesh Mishra, his Principal Secretary and National Security Adviser, to tell Shourie to be with him in his plane. When Shourie entered the plane, Vajpayee was seating next to the window and Advani sat facing him. Jaswant Singh was also there. A few minutes after the plane took off, Vajpayee picked up a newspaper and opened it so widely that he didn't have to face Advani at all. A little while later, Advani also picked up a newspaper and began to read. Shourie and Singh looked at each other and moaned.

Shourie, seeing that the two were avoiding to talk each other, took the newspaper from Vajpayee's hands and said:'Vajpayeeji, newspapers can be read later also. Why don't you tell Advaniji what you wanted to tell him?'Vajpayee kept the newspapers away, and muttered in his usual style that Modi must go. By the time they landed in Goa, the decision was taken: 'Modi would go.'Jaswant Singh had narrated the version of this episode differently. According to him, though Advani didn't protest when Vajpayee insisted that Modi had to go, the home minister added:'There will be chaos in the State.'[31]

The Goa meeting was a momentous gathering of BJP leadership from all over the country. Vajpayee had come with a determined mind that Modi must go; Advani, on instructions from RSS was well-prepared to defend Modi. He had properly briefed three persons of how they would act when the question of the removal of Modi would come up. Modi, in the first session, declared that he would like to sit as a general executive member and not as the CM. It was almost indicating his willingness to resign. The

BJP President, Jana Krishnamurthi, in his presidential speech condemned those who demanded the resignation of Modi. Modi stood up when Krishnamurthi had finished and said: 'From the Party's point of view this is a grave issue. There is a need for a free and frank discussion. To enable this, I wish to place my resignation before this body.'

Vajpayee suggested that it would be better if the issue is discussed the next day. Before a discussion could begin Pramod Mahajan, the Parliamentary Affairs Minister, stood up and said that a decision should be taken up today only and need not be postponed. He had the backing of Sanjay Joshi, who despised Modi from the older days. Now the issue was before the National Executive for discussion and decision.

Immediately, as was planned, three members, Balbir Punj, Dina Nath Mishra, both newspaper journalists and Arun Jaitley, Finance, Corporate Affairs, Commerce and Industry and Law and Justice Minister in Vajpayee's Cabinet got up. The three said in one voice: 'Why Modi should resign? It was natural for Gujarat to react to the Godhra burning of Hindus.' Most of those present immediately got up and said that there was no need for Modi to resign. Vajpayee felt humiliated and realised that it was almost a rebellion against him. Shourie, realising that things were not moving as decided on the plane, got up and narrated the discussion between Vajpayee and Advani on the plane and the decision taken by them. But people were not in a mood to listen and voices from all sides kept on repeating: 'It cannot be done! Modi cannot be allowed to go!'[32]

Vajpayee took no time to understand the situation, and said, "Let's decide on it later." But someone from the delegates shouted: "It can't be decided later, it has to be decided now." And as if this was a cue, the audience in one clear voice supported the suggestion. When this was happening, Advani didn't speak a word, knowing very well that that Vajpayee wanted Modi to be out. Seeing that things were taking a different turn and Advani was not supporting him, Vajpayee decided not to have a confrontation and challenge the strength of the pro-Modi forces.The moderate Prime Minister, who had wished for Modi's removal a month earlier, now surrendered to the RSS and pro-Modi forces. Later, in his speech Vajpayee took up the flag of the hardliners and spoke in Modi's language saying that 'In Indonesia, Malaysia, wherever Muslims are living they don't want to live in harmony. They don't mix with the society. They are not interested in living in peace...We don't need lessons in secularism from anyone. India was secular even before the Muslims and Christians came.'[33]

And Modi stayed for good Twelve years.

****

After the Goa's meeting Modi became stronger not only in Gujarat but also in the BJP. To further strengthen his position, he wanted to prove that the people of Gujarat were with him. Therefore, he decided to dissolve the assembly in July 2002, eight months before the expiry of its term. The opposition parties were stunned because of his popularity, Modi was sure to win in Gujarat. The Congress wanted the elections to be postponed for as long as possible. The Election Commission was not sure if in the prevailing environment Gujarat would be ready for free and unbiased elections. Therefore, a team headed by the Chief Election Commissioner (CEC), James Michael Lyngdoh visited Gujarat to assess the situation and suggest if elections could be held. On its return, without revealing how it had reached to the decision, it declared that elections were not possible under the prevailing conditions at that time. It probably, was based on the assertion that minorities, that formed ten percent of the population of Gujarat, were not likely to vote because they were still traumatised. Interestingly, the opposition, particularly the Congress, was asking for Modi's resignation, and when he did, they did not know where to look.[34]

Modi's reaction was aggressive and he became belligerent and hostile towards the Election Commission, particularly the CEC whom he began to call by his full name, James Michael Lyngdoh, during public speeches.This caused hardened attitudes on both sides. CEC was firm that it was not possible to hold elections in Gujarat and Modi began to say that Lyngdoh was an outsider and should not be allowed to order local Gujaratis in such a way. He called CEC's attitude as 'elitist and disdainful.' Lyngdoh's reaction was that Modi was speaking 'the gossip of menials.' Lyngdoh went to the extent of calling Modi's Government as a 'discredited government' and the call for elections was from 'a few mad people who were saying it without authority.' He went to the extent of calling Gujarat officers 'a bunch of jockers.'[35] Ultimately the Supreme Court (SC) came to the help of Modi when its bench observed that as there was no breach of mandate to hold elections within six months of the last sitting of the Assembly, the application of Article 356 of the Constitution did not arise. The bench also said that Article 324 casts a responsibility and duty on the Election Commission to hold elections at the earliest. CEC, under the pressure of SC ruling and support to Modi by certain sections of the media, announced elections in Gujarat on December 12.[36]

Modi had begun to plan the strategy for the elections much before these were announced. Being a *yatra* veteran he knew that *yatras* (organised travels) have 'powerful political effect such multi-location, many-staged journeys could have, with their opportunities for remote voters to feel a close proximity to their leaders, and be assured that their concerns were being listened to.'[37] The first was the annual 35 km Jagannath *Rath Yatra,* the 125th edition was to set off on 12 June. The second, a *Shobha Yatra*, was organised on the *Janmashtami* day (Lord Krishna's birthday) on August 31. The theme of the *Yatra* was 'Fight against Terrorism.'

The third, *Gujarat Gaurav* (pride) *Yatra*, was to be the biggest and grandest before the elections. It was to travel throughout Gujarat covering all the 25 districts and 182 Assembly constituencies. But Shankersinh Vaghela opposed the *yatra* saying that he was planning to organise his own *Yatra* from the Bhathiji Maharaj temple in the village of Fagvel, from where Modi's Yatra was to start. Modi had to postpone the Yatra because BJP did not want to annoy Vaghela, from whose constituency it was to start. The Congress was also opposed to it. Modi had to succumb to the pressure from Prime Minister Vajpayee and postposed it. It was postponed second time when Vaghela joined Congress and was nominated Gujarat's party President and said he would hold his own *Yatra*. Modi, in a respectful letter to him wrote: 'Please, after you…' Finally, he announced September 8 the date for the commencement of the *Gaurav Yatra*. The response of the people was tremendous as thousands of people attended it and moved along with it.

While the *Gaurav Yatra* was moving on, the terrorists attacked the Akshardham Temple and the *Yatra* was stopped for ten days. The attack was aimed at spreading widespread communal riots all over Gujarat, Akshardham Temple being the most venerable temple in Gujarat. But Gujarat remained peaceful and no violence happened anywhere and the *Yatra* was better attended after that. 'Even at the tiniest of hamlets large crowds waited long hours to receive the latest "Hindutva" icon. The best indicator of the public mood was perhaps the way women and the youth have been responding to Modi. Setting aside the tradition of greeting a male with a "namaste" women even in rural areas wave out to Modi who is selling himself as a "brother" or "son," reported Uday Mahuhrkar in *India Today*.[38]

Nadiad town was the high point of the sixth leg where one lakh people turned up to hear Modi sharpening his knives against the Congress, secularists and Muslim fundamentalists over the Godhra episode and its aftermath.Modi's Yatra got a boost in the last week of October when Deputy Prime Minister L.K. Advani and BJP President M. Venkaiah Naidu, who had maintained a distance following Modi's intemperate remarks against Muslims, arrived in Gandhinagar to announce that the roadshow was a great success.[39] Since its beginning, the response to the yatra every where surpassed all expectations. The Yatra passed through 3,000 km, touching

100 of the 182 assembly constituencies accounting for nearly 1.5 crore of the total 3.4 crore voters in the state.[40]

During the *Yatra,* the Congress and the media were claiming that *Yatra* was a flop and Modi would lose the election. On December 6, six days before the pooling, an opinion poll predicted that BJP and Congress were likely to win between 85 and 90 seats out of 182 total seats. A research by Rediff showed that *Yatra* was a'flop,' having no impact on 34 per cent of the people.[41] But Modi was confident that BJP would win with good majority, saying only a day before pooling: 'On the ground I see no battle; we remain unchallenged. Rather, I saw a frenzy in favour of the BJP wherever I campaigned.'[42] He was, as the results proved, hundred per cent correct because the general animosity towards Modi triggered a voting sweep for Modi.

When the pooling ended, 61.5 percent of the voters had voted and the exit pool predicted between 93 and 109 seats to the BJP. But, to the surprise of all, when the results were declared, BJP begged 126 seats and the Congress was almost wiped out, securing only 51 seats. Modi was again swornin the CM on December 22, at Sardar Patel Stadium. This time, the ceremony was attended by one lakh people and even the Prime Minister, who wanted to dismiss him after the riots, came to attend the swearing-in. It was the first time in Indian's political history that a Prime Minister attended the swearing-in of the Chief Minister of a State.[43]

Modi after the election

After winning the election and having been cleared by the people for riots, Modi began to work on improving his reputation maligned by the opposition parties, media and even some sections of the BJP. After that, Modi just forgot riots and completely focused on the development of Gujarat. Wrote Swapan Dasgupta, a BJP political analyst: 'What he has done is change the narrative and go for (economic) development. From 2002 onwards, he does not mention the riots any more. It does not come into his speeches. This focus on development was backed up by a very powerful publicity machine.'[44]

The astounding victory in the 2002 elections strengthened Modi's position in the BJP in general and Gujarat in particular. With both of his detractors, Vaghela and Keshubhai, becoming minimal force and Sanjay Joshi being away in Delhi, Modi had all Gujarat by himself. He decided to focus on a peaceful development of Gujarat and with a team of capable, devoted and loyal bureaucrats he began to carry it out.

The development strategy

The first priority in the strategy was peaceful governance and establishing law and order in the State. It needed big changes in his Government. He began to do that. The first change was dismissing Gordhan Zadaphia, Minister of State for Home Affairs because he was responsible for police inaction during the riots for which the entire blame was put on Modi. Being very close to Togadia, Zadaphia gave him a free hand in encouraging riots. By dismissing Zadaphia, Modi sent a message to Togadia that his days in Gujarat were numbered. He pushed him out and stopped consulting him and VHP on matters of governance. Along with Togadia, he side-lined all those who were remotely responsible for the riots. Even the Additional Chief Secretary of the Home Department, Ashok Narayan, was overlooked for promotion because, Modi thought, he was unable to do a complete job of controlling riots.[45] Modi also began to remove temples that were illegally built haphazardly all over Ahmedabad and were against the rules of city planning. He also demolished a Sufi dargah that was illegally constructed.[46]

Secondly, Modi began to improve governance and planned to make the administration sleek and efficient, without reducing its size, though he knew that half a million bureaucracy was oversized for a population of 50 million. His strategy was to reform the administration by making it functional, transparent, technology-enabled, decisive and largely corruption-free. His modus operandi to reduce corruption was e-governance. This was widely praised because his administration became transparent and largely corruption-free. A U.S. Congress's Report '*India: Domestic Issues, Strategic Dynamics, and U.S. Relations,*' noted that: 'Chief Minister Narendra Modi has streamlined economic processes, removing red tape and curtailing corruption in ways that have made the state a key driver of national economic growth.'[47] In India also, Gujarat under Modi was known for its corruption-free administration. In fact, the Rajiv Gandhi Foundation placed Gujarat among the least corrupt states in India, for which its Director, Bibek Debroy, was dismissed by Sonia Gandhi.

He was able to do this by considering the bureaucracy as a resource and worked out a plan to improve its operational productivity by giving them more freedom to work. He organised meetings, named it *chintan-shibirs* (brain-storming sessions), where all his top officials from various departments would meet regularly. In a *Chintan Shibir* one head of the department would present the progress made in his department to the other heads of the department. This gave all departments a holistic understanding of the issues that the State was facing and promoted healthy sense of competition among bureaucrats, thus leading to higher efficiency and faster implementation of key initiatives. He told them that he wanted everyone to give his/her best to the Government and the people and no one would not be punished if any bona-fide mistake was committed when doing his/her duty honestly. He clearly told them: 'Don't bother about the punishment; in my office there will be no punishment. You have to take risk, you have to perform. If any problem arises, I am responsible.'[48] It was a drastic and untried step and had an amazing impact on the work culture in the State.

The bureaucrats had never heard a CM speaking in this language. In no time all felt involved and began to take utmost interest in their work. Now they willingly opted for training programmes thinking that by doing this, they would be doing their job better. He also empowered them to take decisions. An Albright Stonebridge Group (headed by former U.S. Secretary of State Madeline Albright) Report mentioned that Modi had virtually done away with the process of frequent transfers of bureaucrats, thus giving the administration the stability needed to provide good governance. He also allowed officers to select a work in which they were intensely interested. His thinking was that if an officer was allowed to work on a project of his interest, he would be more passionate and would give in his best to it. He told them: 'You choose any project you like, which gives you satisfaction, and implement it in your way. Don't worry about the resources, I will give you all.'[49] This had a very positive effect on the bureaucracy as everyone was very satisfied with the work he decided to do and this improved his overall performance.

Another step was to introduce e-governance and digitize most of the government services. His administration made intensive use of technology for reducing corruption. He focused on digitizing a large part of the procurement process which allowed persons and companies to submit bids online. It gave transparency to government contracts. E-governance was made available to every village in Gujarat by providing internet connectivity and making it a part of the Gujarat State Wide Area Network (GSWAN). All basic services such as death, birth and income certificates, applications for government schemes and tax payments were available at e-Panchayats. The extended computerisation of Gujarat reduced the scope for giving or receiving bribes. Corruption, naturally, came down drastically.[50]

Further, he reduced red-tape functioning which was responsible for slow-moving governance. High and junior officers in the Gujarat administration became alert about the work they were expected to carry out. May be that there was not much significant behavioural transformation in bureaucratic tradition, but everyone knew that if files were not disposed of expeditiously, or tardiness was noticed, the officer responsible for non-action would be transferred to an inhospitable position or would face some penal action.[51] Thus, Modi was able to change the fossilised mindset of the bureaucracy which began to realise that the satisfaction of citizens was most important.

Another focus of Modi's governance was to end the wide spread corruption in the State. His slogan was: '*Hoon khaato nathi khaava deto nathi*' (I don't take bribes and don't allow anyone else to take bribe either). He also told all bureaucrats that anyone accepting bribes will be immediately fired. This went down to the lowest level as it was known to everyone that Modi never accepts bribe. This set forth a new culture of integrity and honesty down the corridor. Modi also ended the culture of promoting the favoured bureaucrats; it became performance-based, those who were best-performers were promoted fast and given the best postings; the dullards and dishonest were relegated to oblivion.

Modi gave top priority to communication as he realised that the major problem in the government was lack of interaction. He told his biographer, Andy Marino that: 'One person who is sitting at the table thinks that no one should know what he is doing. All is compartmentalised thinking and in watertight compartments, psychologically and physically. I wanted to change this environment.'[52] And he changed it with a new approach for having better communication with officers. The first thing he did was to tell Secretaries of all Departments: 'Think you are the chief minister of this department' and plan what you are going to do in five years?'

An innovative step was that he would assemble all senior officers for a workshop in the evening continuing even till late night. In each workshop, one officer would give an exhaustive presentation before the top 250 members of his government along with representatives from agriculture and industry. It was followed by a prolonged discussion.This exercise went on for months together. The effect was that every Department of the Government knew about the plans of all other Departments, ending in better coordination between them. The maximum benefit was to the Finance Department (FD) against which everyone complained of not providing adequate resources. The maximum beneficiary of these meetings was the Finance Department because after its presentation, in which it conveyed its problems and limitations, everyone began to realise how difficult it was for the FD to meet every demand of other Departments. Then onwards all

Departments stopped quelling with it and began to cooperate. In Modi's words: 'So self-discipline came out of it. And because of that the thinking process was in a single direction. And they were all feeling, 'Yes, I am the chief minister of my Department. I have been given all the authority.' This had a very positive effect on the bureaucracy as everyone was very satisfied with the work he decided to do and this improved his overall performance.[53]

Lastly, he comprehended the importance of improving relations with Muslims in Gujarat and took various steps to do this. First, he increased the participation of Muslims in Government. M J Akbar, a senior newspaper editor wrote in an article in *The Times of India*, that 'ten years after the riots Modi's Government had more Muslims on its payroll than Bengal. It had more Muslim constables in every police station than any Congress State, or even Mulayam's UP.'[54] Within a decade, Modi helped Muslims to have successfully rebuild their businesses with his investor-friendly economic development model.

Zakir Hussain, a Gujarati businessman had made up his mind to wind up and look for a place where he could safely do his business. But his mother refused to leave and the family stayed back. Eleven years later he was able to establish eight restaurants and two low budget hotels, including one of Ahmedabad's most popular Mughlai food restaurant, called WoW, a stone's throw from the city's heritage Ellis Bridge. It became the finest dining place with a terrace barbeque and began to have roaring business.[55] Hussain had a special word for Modi for the improved law and order situation and corruption-free environment in Gujarat since Modi became the CM. He told *India Today:*'Law and order is under control, people move freely, I no longer have to pay *hafta* [weekly protection money] to anyone. Things related to government have become simpler and transparent. I can freely concentrate on my business.'[56]

Zafar Sareshwala, CEO of Parsoli Motors, which sells the largest BMW cars in Gujarat, is another example of how Muslims changed their opinion about Modi. Sareshwala had lost his business after the rioters ambushed his office in 2002. He filed cases against Modi and the then Home Minister, L.K. Advani, in the International Court of Justice. He also lobbied the UK Government and later the US Administration to deny a visa to Modi. But today he is Modi's 'man-Friday' because Modi helped him to rebuilt his business after 2002.[57]

After the tumult over riots had subsided, Modi began to work on the economic development of Gujarat. He realised that economic development was not possible without the support of the corporate sector. For this he redesigned himself as a business-savvy, investor-friendly administrator and lured major foreign and Indian companies to invest in his sprawling coastal state, known for its spirit of entrepreneurship.

With a view to attract big corporate houses he formulated the Industrial Policy of 2003 and exempted a large number of industries from obtaining no-objection certificates from the Pollution Control Board. He also made it easier to get agricultural land for industrial use. Next year, in 2004, he introduced the Gujarat Special Economic Zones Act making land acquisition easier and labour laws less strict. Five years later, he enacted the Gujarat Special Investment Region Act to promote "mega projects". Gujarat's Industrial Policy of 2009 made Gujarat the most attractive investment destination not only in India but also in the world.

He realised that the major problem of the corporate was getting land for setting up industries. He set up the Gujarat Industrial Development Corporation (GIDC) to provide land to industrial units on 99-year lease and created more Special Economic Zones. During 1990-2001, GIDC acquired 4,620 hectares (ha) land and the acquisition rose to 21,308 ha between 2001 and 2013. Land was usually sold to industrialists at less than the market price. Modi also wanted to attract big investors and gave them significant concessions in terms of fiscal subsidies. Sales tax incentives and deferment, Rs. 1,253.56 crore per year between 1990-1991 and 1999-2000, increased by almost five times during the period 2000-2001 to 2006-2007 to Rs. 5,966.72 crore per year. Tata Motors' Nano plant benefited from such tax incentives, in addition to a soft loan and land at a price lower than the market value.[58]

As a result, Gujarat became very popular among Indian businessmen in the early years of the 2000s. The Adani Port and SEZ was developed on 3,585 ha of land in Mundra, it became India's number one private port. Reliance developed a petroleum refinery with a capacity of 27 million metric tons per annum, which over the years expanded to 62 million tons per annum. Essar also set up a steel plant of 11 million tons per annum capacity.[59]

Five pillars of development

In a post-election announcement Modi outlined, water, energy, people, education and security, five pillars of his development strategy. His development agenda included the concept of 'inclusive growth' in which 'Gujarat first' was the guiding principle. The five pillars were named as '*Shakti* (sacred force),' which is the originating energy and perpetual dynamism of the universe in the Indian ancient philosophy. The concept of '*shakti*' is a feminine force and is personified by goddess Kali and is responsible for all change and liberation in the universe. This force was the central point of all changes that Modi was trying to bring about in Gujarat. His emphasis was more on women as he more often underlined that it was unfortunate that half of India's talent was being wasted by not fully utilising the women force for development.[60]

Water resources: Modi realised that water was the basic resource to any development model, because 'water is life.' He named it *'Jal Shakthi* (Water Power).Though India is criss-crossed by rivers, unfortunately, a visionless, arbitrary approach to development has polluted most of the rivers and other water bodies. But because of increasing population and lack of localised water conservation programmes, these rivers were facing ever increasing pressure to supply water for irrigation and drinking. Modi decided to treat each and every drop of water preciously. His strategy was to converse local water by enabling construction of lakhs of check dams while at the same time creating a water grid by interlinking small rivers and streams. Water from Sardar Sarovar project now flows through Sabarmathi in Ahmedabad. His integrated approach resulted in the rise of ground water level in a dry State like Gujarat. Modi also assertively encouraged drip irrigation to save each drop of water. In ten years, Modi brought more than five lakh hectares under drip irrigation.

Modi's efforts on water and soil conservation resulted in unfailing ten percent growth in agriculture, against national average of just three per cent. His administration also provided drinking water through mobile tanks to majority of the people living in small towns and villages and had to walk miles to fetch water. Modi also realised that water was required for the development of the industry and so with the help of a Japanese company, began to make efforts to desalinate sea water for industrial use for Dahej SEZ from solar powered desalination plants.[61]

Energy:*Urja shakti* was the name Modi gave to energy resources. It was basic to Gujarat's economy as food was to a household. It was really unfortunate that India, an emerging economy in the world, could not supply adequate electricity to its citizens, particularly in rural areas. The industrial development was suffering because of frequent power cuts round the year, particularly during summers. He was clear in his mind that the power and energy sectors were the biggest constituents of the infrastructure sector. The past administrations ignored it and consequently development hampered. He admitted to Amol Sharma of *The Wall Street Journal* that frequent power cuts embarrassed him because these cuts resulted in a great loss for India.[62]

Modi was particularly disturbed because in the absence of electricity rural people suffered the most. He told Amol that 'Villages (in Gujarat) didn't use to get power at dinner time. They'd eat in the dark. Kids didn't have light to study for exams; if mother was sick, there was no electricity…It disturbed me. Then I got involved. God helped me. He gave me a technical solution: separating the network so there are different power lines for agriculture and for domestic use. It became a huge success story – we completed it in 1,000 days. All the states of India felt that this should be replicated in their States too.'[63] Modi's determination gave results and within the next few years after becoming the CM the whole of Gujarat had 24x7 power supply around the year and Gujarat became a power-surplus state.

Modi did it by reforming the Gujarat State Electricity Board (GSEB) which was in a mess when he became the CM. Power supply was erratic, power thefts were rampant and the state electricity board used to bleed money. Modi decided to reform it by appointing Manjula Subramaniam, a bureaucrat known for her efficiency, the Chairperson of the GSEB. She gave the best results by splitting GSEB into seven different companies, each having a different non-overlapping mandate. While she provided efficient management, Modi ensured that there was no political interference. Soon GSEB became profitable and supplied power round-the-clock to the whole of Gujarat.[64]

Modi took a unique step to improve the power supply in the rural areas; he introduced the *Jyoti Gram Yojana* and separated the feeder line supplying power to rural areas from those supplying power to residential and industrial uses. In 2005, under a Rural Feeder Segregation Programme, he bifurcated its transmission lines catering to rural areas into those serving the households and those meant for use on the farm. This was done to identify the heavily subsidised farm sector consumers and provide them cheaper power on a single-phase line for a fixed number of hours each day. Residential consumers were supplied costlier power on a three-phase line throughout the day. This eliminated the diversion of subsidised power for household use—a key reason for losses historically.[65]

In this way, power was supplied to two different sectors resulting in balanced load. Also, the GSEB was able to measure the exact amount of electricity used for agriculture, thus minimizing the abuse of the differential pricing mechanism. It also allowed the Board to supply electricity to domestic users for 24 hours a day while providing high quality (voltage) supply to the agricultural sector for 8-10 hours a day. The Jyoti Gram Yojana was so successful in Gujarat that the Planning Commission suggested that the programme of feeder separation should becarried across the country.[66] Modi adopted a programme of large-scale rural electrification and all villages in Gujarat had electricity by 2006. Gujarat became the first State in the country where all the 18,065 villages were electrified and had access to three-phase uninterrupted electric supply.[67]

Modi's emphasis on rural electrification resulted in booming rural economy with growth in agriculture, agro-processing and small manufacturing in the country side. Rural migration to urban areas also declined.

With a view to improve the power situation in Gujarat, Modi took effective steps to curtail power thefts, that ranged from 20 per cent in urban to 70 per cent in rural areas, by passing a law to curb power thefts. He also established five special police stations to clamp down on power thefts and started disconnecting the power connections of those with large unpaid dues.[68] Along with reducing power thefts, Modi instituted mechanisms to minimize transmission losses by strengthening sub-transmission and distribution systems.[69] This was also made possible by a combination of investments in infrastructure, separation of feeder lines, strict monitoring of ground level data and the administrative will to ensure that T&D losses came down.[70]

Modi also developed a gas grid to supply gas to industries and homes and laid emphasis on hydro carbon exploration in India and overseas. His was a conscious attempt to convert Gujarat into a gas-based economy. His comprehensive energy policy focuses not only on abundant energy but also to make it clean. Steps were also taken to encourage wind, solar and other renewable energy generation. Gujarat built a 2800 MW capacity from wind-based energy sources alone.'An analysis of the key sectoral growth indicators - including capacity addition, power deficit and the health of power distribution companies - reveals Gujarat's breath-taking rise from a power deficit to a surplus state within a decade after 2004 on the back of strong implementation of reform measures.[71]

Human Resource: *Jan Shakti* was the name given to human resource. Modi rightfully thought that development was not possible without robust and educated people. Though Gujarat was ahead of other States in India in industrialisation, human development indices were weaker compared to the southern States. The CMs in the past ignored developing human power, but Modi was clear in his mind that this should get the topmost priority. Right from the beginning, he made mindful efforts to correct this glitch in the social sector. The first step he took was to check students dropping-out from schools. He also encouraged education for girls and personally contributed money for it from his auctioned gifts. He gave high priority to quality education through *'Gunotsav'* (quality enhancement initiative) campaign and designed *'Vanche Gujarat'*(reads Gujarat) campaign to improve reading habits among school going children and general population.[72]

Modi initiated all round efforts to improve the quality of human resources across the social spectrum so that Gujarat could achieve higher benchmarks in human development and social sector. With a view to achieve this he made efforts on improving public health by adopting initiatives like '*Chiranjeevi Yojana*,' (Long-life Plan) and "108" emergency services to decrease infant mortality rate. He also provided emergency medical help. Cleanliness and tree plantation drive under '*Nirmal Gujarat'* (clean Gujarat), did achieve good success. Gujarat had one major problem that its large population was anaemic. Modi started a programme to supply fortified flour with micro nutrients through Public Distribution System and also started a mid-day meal scheme to check mal-nutrition among children to encourage physical activity and sports.[73]

Since Gujarat had huge tribal population, that was neglected in the past, he introduced a special '*vanabandhu kalyan yojana' (forest brothers welfare plan)* to achieve an all-round development of tribal areas. It achieved spectacular success within five years. For the welfare of women, a programme named *'Mission Mangalam,'*(Happiness mission), an integrated poverty alleviation approach was introduced to empower rural women in 2010. It was based on the belief that if overall prosperity of the community is the objective, then its every segment must flourish. He set-up '*Sakhi Mandals*' (friends' self-help groups) which were combined into the corporate value chain benefitting the stakeholders. *Mission Mangalam* was to help women to earn their livelihood to become independent.[74]

Knowledge and security: Knowledge and security were named *Gyan and Raksha Shakthi* which were fundamental to success in a highly competitive world of today. Modi had a remarkable vision to enhance the knowledge and skills of the population of Gujarat. To achieve the two fundamentals for development, Modi established Pandit Deendayal Petroleum University for research in energy including nuclear and solar, specialised universities like Children's University, Indian Institute of Teacher Training, Forensic Science University, *Rakshashakthi* University, Kamdhenu University, Law University. Since technical education was a neglected area in Gujarat, Modi focused heavily on providing quality technical education to cater to the needs of growing manufacturing sector. His efforts included upgradation and increase in number of ITIs, Polytechnics and Engineering colleges. He also initiated skill development programmes to train manpower in different skills separate from conventional education route to achieve synergy between Industry and technical education. He started '*Karmayogi Yojana*' (Hard-workers'programme) to train bureaucracy.[75]

Modi effectively used technology to improve knowledge in Gujaratis. Almost all villages in Gujarat were connected with broadband network. Though national defence didn't come under Modi's jurisdiction he took measures to secure Gujarat coast to avoid any unwarranted infiltration. To check terrorism, he made it very clear that he would not tolerate any inadvertence in policy towards terrorism. He also showed great interest in making Gujarat a hub in defence related manufacturing for India's overall self-reliance in defence readiness.[76]

Focus on agriculture

Agriculture in Gujarat is the vital sector of State's economy. It provides food-grains to the people and raw materials for agro-based industries. Therefore, Modi gave top-most priority to the development of agriculture by adopting several measures for its transformation. In fact, he made Gujarat a role model for other States. Modi was appreciated by ASSOCHAM and Anna Hazare for transforming Gujarat a success model of agriculture. The then President of India, Dr A. P. J. Abdul Kalam wanted all states to follow Gujarat's model for developing the agricultural sector. Modi's efforts increased Gujarat's agricultural income from Rs 9,000 crore to Rs. 34,000 crore during his tenure of chief ministership. Also, between 2000-01 and 2007-08 agricultural value added grew at an annual rate of 9.6 per cent (despite a major drought in 2002). This was more than double of India's agricultural growth rate, and much faster than Punjab's farm growth during the green revolution heydays. Indeed, 9.6 per cent agricultural growth was among the fastest rates recorded anywhere in the world during that period.[77] This happened when more than half of Gujarat is desert and 70 per cent is arid and semi-arid. The majority population of Gujarat being rural, this phenomenal boost in agriculture created millions of satisfied voters. Modi did manage it as he took several steps during his twelve-year period as Chief Minister.

First, giving top priority to irrigation, he developed a 'river grid' system by linking two dozen rivers in Gujarat. Besides, he implemented micro-irrigation projects on a massive scale and built micro-irrigation infrastructure in the State. Secondly, supporting check dams, he constructed more than one lakh such dams, more than ten times the number constructed in the 1990s. These dams not only helped conserving water but irrigated the vast, arid regions of Saurashtra and Kutch. Thirdly, he encouraged drip irrigation that was widely used in Israel and was badly needed for water conservation in semi-arid Gujarat. He provided fast-tracked subsidies and loans for purchasing drip-irrigation equipment to farmers, who paid just five per cent of the total cost of the equipment. The State Government gave a subsidy of 50 per cent and banks, through loans, provided the remaining 45 per cent. This upbeat approach encouraged farmers to quickly adopt drip irrigation and the area under it grew from 10,000 hectare to five lakh hect are as during the 10-year period.[78]

Fourthly, he implemented two-tier rural electrification. Under Jyoti Gram Yojana high-quality power supply was ensured to farmers' tube wells and pump sets. The quality power supply to agriculture caused phenomenal agricultural growth in the State. Fifthly, he facilitated diversification of land to high value cash crops. Farmers were able to switch over to high-value crops like mango, banana, wheat, fennel and non-food crops like cotton with the availability of regular electricity and water supply. Farmers were also encouraged to adopt BT cotton that produced higher yields per acre than the traditional cotton, giving high income to them.[79]

Sixthly, Modi was the first CM to introduce soil-health cards (SHC) in 2003. Under this scheme, 1.8 lakh farmers were issued SHCs which were made after the scientific testing of soil for properties such as mineral composition, water-retaining capacity and productivity. The cards were custom-tailored to each farmer's land and contained information such as the right crops suited to the farmers' land and the right amounts of fertilizer, pesticide and water to be used on it. This information helped farmers to increase productivity and crop quality.[80]

Seventhly, Modi promoted alternate methods of farming and marketing like contract farming. This attracted corporate entities, such as Reliance Fresh, Food Bazaar and Spencer, to the agricultural sector in Gujarat as they were allowed to deal directly with farmers. Eighthly, *Krishimahotsavs* (annual farmers' events), annual events, were started in 2005 to enable farmers to interact with Government officials and agricultural experts. Farmers, during these events, brain stormed and learnt the news ways to augment agricultural productivity. They were able to learn the best practices in agriculture and use them on their farms. Government officials were also able to get a better understanding of the problems faced by the farmers on their farms.[81]

Ninthly, animal husbandry was given high priority and the State Government actively promoted it. Intensive animal vaccination drives to improve the quality of animals were conducted at Krishi Mahotsavs. Animal health camps were also organised throughout Gujarat where animals were given over-all health and dental check-ups. Lastly, as discussed earlier, Modi implemented large-scale rural electrification programme providing electricity to every village in Gujarat. In fact, it became the first State in the country to achieve 100 per cent rural electrification.[82]

Industrial development

During his exile from Gujarat, Modi travelled 41 countries and realised that only economic development could make a country great and respectable and key to economic prosperity and development was investment in industries.

Therefore, on becoming the Chief Minister, he decided to develop Gujarat industrially to make it the most developed State in the country. He thought widely and realised that the only possible way to do it was by attracting businessmen and industrialists to Gujarat. For this he designed the concept of business summits to convince them that their businesses will prosper there. He began organising biennial Vibrant Gujarat Global Investors Summit (VGGIS) from 2003 onwards to demonstrate that the State could be their major investment destination. VGGIS brought business leaders, investors, corporations, thought leaders, policy and opinion makers to Gujarat to see themselves the opportunities that exist there. The summits were to be advertised as a platform to understand and explore business opportunities in Gujarat. These were to be marathon matchmaking ceremonies of investment pledges and signing proposals for investing in Gujarat.[83]

The first Vibrant Gujarat Global Investors Summit was organised in 2003 by the Industrial Extension Bureau of Gujarat in association with the Government of India, United Nations Industrial Development Organisation (UNIDO) and the Federation of Indian Chambers of Commerce & Industry (FICCI) and Confederation of India Industry (CII), from 28 September to 2 October 2003, during the Navratri festival at Ahmedabad and Surat.The event had a large presence from China. It focused on: Industrial Investment, Agro-Processing, Biotech- Pharma, Natural Gas and Oil, Infrastructure, Mining, Tourism, Apparels and Gems-Jewellery at Ahmedabad and sectoral sessions on Garment, Textiles and Gems and Jewellery at Surat. There were also exhibitions to provide a platform for exhibiting products and services. One-to-one discussions were organised between the prospective investors, government officers and the project promoters. At the end of the event, 76 Memoranda of Understandings (MoU) promising investments worth US $14 billion were signed.[84]

Sixth Vibrant Gujarat 2013 was the last during the Modi-regime and was held on 11-13 January 2013 and became a platform for various States of India and other countries for business collaborations, knowledge discussions and experience sharing. Key areas for development, including innovation, sustainability, youth and skill development, knowledge sharing and net-working were discussed during the Summit which displayed the strength, progressive stand, investor's initiatives and art and culture of Gujarat. It was attended by 2,100 delegates from 121 countries and ended in 2,670 strategic partnership intentions.[85]

Modi successfully marketed Vibrant Gujarat as a major global business event. The six summits that Modi organised in Gujarat during his tenure generated investment pledges worth $920 billion. This made Vibrant Gujarat Summit a big step towards improving the image of Modi after the riots. It was needed as Modi realised that as a hardliner, he would have limited acceptability in the political spectrum. These Summits helped in shaping his image.[86]

Modi converted these Summits into 'mini-Davos,' with Japan and Canada as partner countries, and 'turned the act of investing in what has long been one of India's most business-friendly and industrialised states into a high-profile spectacle—and amplified the disclosure of annual investment inflows into singular triumphant announcements. In other words, Modi has successfully deployed the ancient mercantile and entrepreneurial energy of Gujarat to overhaul his own image.'[87] Modi's idea of investment summits was adopted by many other States in the country.

This happened despite the fact that the large number of prominent businessmen were opposed to Modi because of 2002 riots. In 2003, after his resounding victory in Gujarat Assembly elections, he managed an invitation from the CII, country's biggest and most powerful business trade association. It organised a special session "Meeting with Narendra Modi, the New Chief Minister of Gujarat" on February 6. The CII community, by and large, was jittery as the industry in Gujarat had lost Rs. 20 billion ($409 million) in the riots. Even international investors were afraid of investing in Gujarat as long as Modi was the CM as they feared further chaos in Gujarat. 'Two of Bangalore's biggest IT chieftains, N. R. Narayana Murthy of Infosys and Azim Premji of Wipro, issued strong public condemnations. At a CII national meeting in April 2002, the Chairwoman of the energy major Thermax, Anu Aga, had received a standing ovation after delivering an impassioned speech about the suffering of Muslims in Gujarat'.[88] But Modi knew Gujarat was of critical importance to the overlords of Indian business. He came to Delhi to mend his image with the captains of the industry, but he would do so, as always, on his own terms.

Modi was on the dais with two business luminaries—Jamshyd Godrej and Rahul Bajaj along with Tarun Das, the Director-General of the CII. Modi expected a friendly welcome from CII but it was denied to him, rather he was ridiculed. Godrej, instead saying good words, suggested Modi to use the mandate from his victory to ensure the safety and security of all Gujaratis. Bajaj was even more blunt when he said that 2002 had been a 'lost year' for Gujarat. Looking at Modi, he asked, 'Why don't we get investment in Kashmir, the Northeast, or Uttar Pradesh and Bihar? It is not just the lack of infrastructure, but also the sense of insecurity. I hope this won't happen in Gujarat—all this comes to mind because of the unfortunate events last year.' Turning to Modi Bajaj added: 'We would like to know what you believe in, what you stand for, because leadership is important. You are today the undisputed leader of your Party and Government in Gujarat and we want to know you better...We are prepared to work with governments of all hues, but we also have our own views on what is good for our society and what works for it.' Modi patiently listened to outpouring criticism but when his turn to speak came he expressed his ferocity: 'You and your pseudo-secular friends, can come to Gujarat if you want an answer. Talk to my people. Gujarat is the most peaceful State in the country,' and turning to Godrej and Bajaj, he said: "Others have vested interest in maligning Gujarat. What is your interest?'[89]

Modi, being Modi, showed his fury when, within a few days after his return from Delhi, a group of Gujarati businessmen, who were close to Modi—Gautam Adani of Adani Group, Indravadan Modi of Cadila Pharmaceuticals, Karsan Patel of Nirma Group, and Anil Bakeri of Bakeri Engineers— established a rival organisation, the Resurgent Group of Gujarat (RGG). All members of RGG threatened to withdraw from the CII because it humiliated and snubbed Modi and, therefore, all Gujaratis. The RGG asked the Gujarat Chapter of the CII, which had more than 100 members, to leave CII as it had failed to protect the interests of the State. Since the BJP was in power in Delhi, the Government of India ministers began to maintain distance from CII. This became a cause of worry to CII, because being a lobbying organisation, it wanted to be effective but it began to lose its effectiveness.[90]

Das was edgy and wanted to meet Modi to ask for forgiveness. He contacted Arun Jaitley, then the Union Law Minister and a close friend of Modi and had a discussion with him for more than two hours at his residence. Jaitley promised to Das that he would discuss the issue with Modi, who was likely to come home for dinner at his house. A few days later, Jaitley told Das that if he wants the issue to be resolved, CII must formally apologise him. A few days later Das personally delivered to Modi a mild letter of apology in Ahmedabad. It read:'We, in the CII, are very sorry for the hurt and pain you have felt, and I regret very much the misunderstanding that has developed since the 6th of February, the day of our meeting in New Delhi.'All those who had spoked wildly about Modi in the CII meeting realised the importance of Modi and Gujarat. Three months later, in a further gesture of reconciliation, the CII helped Modi organise his first international meeting with investors, in Zurich, under the aegis of the World Economic Forum.[91]

This was the beginning of winning those who were annoyed with him and over the years, one by one, Modi, being smart, shrewd, and playing his cards slowly, won everyone in the business community. His best came in 2008 when Ratan Tata announced that he would shut down the factory of manufacturing people's car, Nano, in Singur, West Bengal. He took this step because of two-years of severe and violent agitation over the compensation of land by farmers. The agitation was led by opposition leader Mamta Banerjee who was then trying to acquire power from the ruling Communist Party. West Bengal's loss was Modi's benefit as four days after withdrawing from West Bengal, Tata declared that he would shift the Nano plant to Gujarat, investing Rs. 2,000 crores.

Immediately after Tata had announced the withdrawal, Modi sent Tata an SMS: 'Welcome to Gujarat.' Tata had also received messages from four states to set up the factory in their states. But none moved as fast as Modi who offered the most generous terms and the agreement between Modi and Tata was signed within 10 days. This attracted worldwide attention of investors and within weeks of the plant's inauguration in June 2010, both Ford and Peugeot approached Gujarat, seeking plots to build their own factories. The GIDC had acquired a total of 2,200 acres, and handed over sizable plots to Ford and Peugeot (along with a substantial package of financial incentives, similar to what Tata was offered). The initial resistance from the farmers around Sanand quickly crumbled as the proposed compensation grew. Landholders were paid more than ten-times the market value for their property. Before Tata arrived, the price for one acre was only Rs. 300,000; the GIDC paid at least thirty lakhs per acre, and issued cheques to the sellers within a week.[92] With the success story of Sanand, Modi's reputation as a 'development Guru'increased hundred times and he used it the major theme of his speeches to both voters and businessmen.

Special Economic Zones: Modi realised that he needed to implement a growth engine to generate large employment, encourage manufacturing and boost exports. To achieve this objective, he introduced the scheme of Special Economic Zones (SEZs) which were also to provide a trouble-free functioning system and highly developed setup and support services. He was the first CM to enact the Special Economic Zone (SEZ) Act in 2004 which specifically delineated duty-free enclaves and made it his special theme when addressing the people of Gujarat. This made him the darling of businesspersons. Pharma giant Wockhardt's Habil Khorakiwala, the FICCI President in 2007 called Modi a 'dynamic visionary,' and Ratan Tata said: "You are a fool if you are not in Gujarat."[93]

Modi introduced the SEZ policy when it was being criticised in many other State. But Modi intelligently avoided the denunciation by not promising land and thus, was out of the politics of acquiring land. He offered wasteland or told industrialists to negotiate directly with farmers, because, he told them that his job was to make the business easy and not to get in the business of business. As to make SEZ more saleable, in a bold move a month before the VGGIS, Modi relaxed prohibition in the SEZs.[94]

Infrastructure development: Modi had learnt from his foreign visits that infrastructure was basic for faster economic development and poverty alleviation. Therefore, he decided to provide the best infrastructure in the form of road and railway transport system, ports, power, airports and ensured their efficient working. His first priority was roads. Though Gujarat had one of the best road-networks in India, with 74,000 km roads and 98.83 per cent of Gujarat's villages were connected by *'pucca'*(all-weather) roads, Modi decided to improve the quality of roads. He gave top-most priority to highways, improved the quality of roads hugely and made them of international standards. A top Planning Commission study, supported by the World Bank, mentioned in its Report that Gujarat offers an example of international best practice in roads management. It also stated that the International Roughness Index (IRI), a measure of the quality of roads, of highways in Gujarat was better than internationally desirable levels. It also specified that the IRI of Gujarat's highways ranged from six metres per km to 20 metres per km in the year 2000 and improved to less than four metres per km in 2007.[95]

Secondly, he constructed new roads and highways on a massive scale and widened and upgraded existing roads. It reduced travel time and also give an enormous enhancement to agriculture and industry as goods and agricultural products reached markets, ports and warehouses faster. For example, 551 km of urban roads were modernised and upgraded under the

Vikas Path Yojana (development road plan) and 3,281 km rural roads were upgraded under the *Kisan Path Yojana* (farmer's road plan). After the Bhuj earthquake struck Gujarat, the government promptly reconstructed 4,095 km roads.

Next priority were ports. Modi adopted Public-Private-Partnership (PPP) model for port development to get rid of red-tapism. It allowed private players to build greenfield ports under the Build-Own-Operate-Transfer (BOOT) charter. Private players were given the power to determine pricing and tariffs at ports and even allowed complete operational freedom. This encouraged massive private investment in the ports. The Mundra port, the Dahej port, the Hazira port and the Pipavav port are all private ports build under this model. They have a combined capacity of over 100 million tonnes p.a.[96] The PPP model doubled the cargo-handling capability of ports in Gujarat from 135 million tonnes in 2001 to 284 million tonnes in 2011, handling three-fourth of the entire cargo handled by Indian ports. The PPP-port development model of Gujarat was so successful that Odisha (earlier Orissa), Karnataka and even Kerala governments adopted it.[97]

Lastly, Modi, provided several attractions to the industrialists in general and manufacturing in particular resulting in Tata Motors, General Motors, Ford and Maruti Suzuki setting up large manufacturing plants in Gujarat. They established the core-industrial factories which provided backward and forward linkages, developing a large number of ancillary industries like spare parts, components and dealership giving rise to large employment among the unskilled, skilled and professional workers. This also raised land prices around the industrial areas. Modi not only provided attractions to the industry but personally won over industrialists to setup their factories in Gujarat.

Modi realised that the two problems that industrialists faced was land acquisition and clearances. So, he designed an equitable land acquisition policy and facilitated super-fast clearances ensuring that acquiring land for factories was easy and beneficial to both farmers and industrialists. He assured farmers that they would not only get the market price for their land but would also be paid an additional ten per cent of the price paid by the acquirer. In addition, land owners were also promised one developed commercial plot to the extent of one per cent of their acquired land at a token price of one rupee per square meter. This is how he made the land-giver a part of the entire development process so that he too could reap the benefits of development on his land. The policy also outlined that any landowner whose entire landholding in the village was acquired would be entitled to one-time financial assistance equivalent to 750 days of minimum agricultural wages, amounting to Rs. 75,000 for the loss of livelihood. Similarly, any landowner who became a marginal farmer as a result of the land acquisition would get one-time financial assistance equivalent to 500 days of minimum agricultural wages. The policy gave one more attractive offer to farmers: The Gujarat Government would sponsor one person from farmer's family, between the age of 18 and 45, for an ITI training course up to two years. And GIDC will also provide employment to one member of each affected family. Additionally, three per cent of the difference between the allotment price and price at which land was purchased would be deposited into a separate bank account for building schools, hospitals and internal roads in the adjoining area.[98] This made farmers to celebrate selling land to industries instead of agitating whenever a new industrial project was announced in their area.

The Modi Administration also took a pro-active role in facilitating all the required clearances for the setting up of all factories and plants. The administration also gave special concessions to industries to make Gujarat attractive to them.[99]

Finally, Modi ensured reliable electricity and water supply to industries and Gujarat became a preferred option to industries in India and abroad and this attracted industries because factories cannot run without continuous and stable supply of electricity and water. Modi made Gujarat's electricity situation excellent and provided plentiful water supply.

During his twelve-year regime in Gujarat, Modi made the State richer, enjoying faster GDP growth, more jobs and better industrial development than India as a whole. When he left Gujarat in 2014, its population was just five per cent of India's population occupying six per cent of India's land mass but it accounted for 7.6 per cent of India's GDP. The success of Modi was summarised by *The Economist*: 'The state has moved from a deficit in electricity generation in 2002, to a surplus, despite the energy demands of a booming economy. Its 18,000 rural villages are connected to the grid. Water supply is abundant….his emphasis on basic infrastructure, a hallmark of the Gujarat model, extends to making land easily available for commercial development….India sits a lowly 142nd out of 189 countries in the World Bank's "ease of doing business" rankings. But in Gujarat factories spring up more readily because permits, licences and environmental clearances are granted quickly. This predates Mr Modi's time in office. A focus on basic infrastructure and public goods; a drive to make civil servants honest and accountable; a penchant for IT; a flair for marketing to business investors. The elements of Mr Modi's brand of economics are not obviously those of Margaret Thatcher or Ronald Reagan, to whom he has been compared by some commentators. Thatcher wanted a small state. Reagan also said that "the nine most terrifying words in the English language are: 'I'm from the government and I'm here to help.' Mr Modi, by contrast, believes government can be made to work better.'[100]

'The Gujarat model is more about ideologically-neutral good governance than the sort of big-bang reforms seen in 1980s America and Britain. What sets Mr Modi apart from many of his predecessors is his ability to make a decision and be held accountable for it. But his record suggests those hoping for big privatisations or bold labour reforms are likely to be disappointed,' says Vivek Dehejia, Resident Senior Fellow, IDFC Institute, Mumbai.[101] While inaugurating the Uttarakhand Investors Summit in Dehradun, Modi said that when he became the Chief Minister of Gujarat for the first time in 2001, he wanted to turn the state into South Korea.[102]

And he almost did it.

****

The general elections of 1998 were extremely significant for the BJP as for the first time it emerged as the single largest party with 182 seats, leaving Congress behind with 141 seats. It formed the Government, with Vajpayee as the Prime Minster with the help of other regional parties. Atal Bihari Vajpayee was sworn in as the Prime Minister for the second time. But he could not continue for more than 3 months as the AIADMK withdrew support. Vajpayee resigned but won again in 1999 elections in the backdrop of the Kargil war. The BJP again emerged as the single largest party with 182 seats while the Congress could win only 114. Vajpayee was able to form a more stable NDA this time around and this was the first time that a non-Congress alliance lasted a full five-year term. Atal Bihari Vajpayee was sworn in as the Prime Minister for the third time.

The BJP went in for early elections alongside launching an 'India Shining' campaign. Though it could win the middle class vote, the poorer sections voted for the Congress and other regional parties resulting in the defeat of the NDA. The BJP could win only 138 seats while the Congress improved its tally to 145. The regional parties again ruled the roost with 159 seats. The BJP conceded defeat and the Congress then formed the United Progressive Alliance (UPA) with support from other parties and outside support from the left parties. Sonia Gandhi refused to become the Prime Minister amidst the controversy about her foreign origin. Manmohan Singh was chosen as the Prime Minister.

Election 2009

The BJP went in for early elections and launched 'India Shining' as the principal theme of the campaign. But that did not present the true picture of the achievements of the BJP during Vajpayee regime because the development and prosperity was confined to urban India only, rural India remained deprived. Therefore, it could win the urban votes and the poorer sections in the rural areas, which formed the bulk of the voter supported the Congress and other regional parties resulting in the defeat of the NDA. The BJP could win only 138 seats while the Congress improved its tally to 145 and regional parties with 159 became the largest group. The BJP conceded defeat and the Congress formed the United Progressive Alliance (UPA) with support from other parties. The Congress led UPA implemented a lot of programmes for deprived sections of the society like Right to Information (RTI) and the National Rural Employment Guarantee Scheme (NREGS). It also waived off farm loans in 2008. Elections in 2009 were announced against this background.

The BJP was in a dilemma as two persons claimed to be the Prime Ministerial candidate, Bhairon Singh Shekhawat and Lal Krishan Advani. But BJP, ignored the claim of Shekhawat and decided Advani to be their PM candidate saying that any person who had held a higher constitutional position would not contest any other election. Shekhawat was the Vice President and had contested the election for the President. 'It will be like taking a bath near a well after having a holy dip in the sacred Ganga River if he does so,' said Rajnath Singh announcing the candidature of Adani early January 2009. Unfortunately, BJP under the leadership of Advani, only condemned Manmohan Singh, a highly regarded and honest person, and did not present a constructive plan for development and rural prosperity in the country. Consequently, BJP lost heavily winning only 116 seats, bringing gloom in the Party. The Congress won 206 seats, a huge improvement from 2004 and formed the Government again. This was a great shock to the BJP and a titanic fall of Advani.

Advani PM's Candidate in 2009

L. K. Advani, 82, had been an important front-rank leader of the BJP since its inception as Jan Sangh. Born and brought up in Karachi, he had his early schooling and college education in Karachi and Hyderabad in Sindh (now in Pakistan). After the Partition, his family migrated to India and settled down in Bombay (now Mumbai) where he graduated in Law. While in Pakistan, he joined the RSS at the age of fourteen. He became a *pracharak* of the Karachi branch. From Bombay, he was sent to Matsya-

Alwar in Rajasthan and worked in Alwar, Bharatpur, Kota, Bundi and Jhalawar districts until 1952.

In 1951, he joined the Bhartiya Jana Sangh (aka. Jana Sangh), when it was founded by Syama Prasad Mookerjee as a political wing of the RSS and became Secretary to S. S. Bhandari, then General Secretary of the Jana Sangh in Rajasthan. In 1957, he came to Delhi to look after the Parliamentary affairs of the Jan Sangh and soon became its General Secretary and, later, President of the Delhi wing of the Jana Sangh. In 1967, he became the leader of the city's Metropolitan Council and also assisted K. R. Malkani in editing the RSS weekly *Organiser.* He became a member of the national executive in 1966 and joined Rajya Sabha from Delhi in 1970 and from Gujarat in 1976. In 1977, he became a part of Janata Party as Jan Sangh was merged into it after the Lok Sabha elections of 1977. But soon, because of internal rifts in the Janata Party, erstwhile Jan Sangh members quit the Janata Party and formed the new Bhartiya Janata Party.[103]

After the assassination of Indira Gandhi in October the 1984, BJP fell in bad days and Advani became its President. He focused on Ram Janmabhoomi campaign and supported the Vishwa Hindu Parishad (VHP) for the construction of a Ram Janmabhoomi temple at the site of the Babri Masjid in Ayodhya. It provided rich dividends in the general elections of 1989 as BJP won 86 seats, a substantial increase from two in 1984. Advani became the most popular BJP leader after his Ram Rath Yatra from Somnath in Gujarat to Ayodhya in U.P., but it was stopped by the Chief Minister of Bihar, Lalu Prasad Yadav, saying that it was leading to communal violence. In the following 1991 general elections, the BJP benefited from the Ram Temple movement and became the second largest Party in Lok Sabha after the Congress. In 1992, the Babri Masjid was demolished.[104]

Advani decided to resign as an MP in 1996 following allegations of his involvement in the infamous Hawala scam and declared that he would not hold any political office till his name was cleared by the court. He was acquitted by the Supreme Court on March 2, 1998 and was consequently re-elected the same year.

He became the Deputy Prime Minister and Home Minister in Vajpayee Cabinet the same year and continued till the BJP Government lost 2004 elections. After losing the 2004 elections, Vajpayee retired from politics and Advani became Leader of Opposition from 2004 to 2009. During this period, Advani had to deal with rebellion from within the party.[105]

His low point began when on a visit to the Jinnah Mausoleum at Karachi, described Mohammad Ali Jinnah a 'secular' leader and was asked to resign as BJP President. However, he withdrew the resignation a few days later, but continued till December 2005 when at the Silver Jubilee celebrations of the BJP in Mumbai Rajnath Singh was elected in his place.[106]

The story of Advani visiting Pakistan and praising Jinnah is interesting and has been vividly described in Karan Thapar's *Devil's Advocate: The Untold Story.*

The Pakistan Government in 1998 asked its High Commissioner in India, Ashraf Qazi to develop friendship with Advani. He was a close friend of Karan Thapar, a journalist and TV interviewer, and requested him to help developing a rapport with Advani. Karan requested George Fernandes, Defence Minister and Karan's good friend, to help him in this endeavour. George invited Qazi at dinner at his house and soon both became good friends and developed a trust in each other, Qazi in early 2000 asked George to arrange a meeting with Advani. George fixed a meeting and Karan drove him to Advani's Pandara Road house at ten in the night. The meeting was clandestine as no one else knew about it and lasted for 90 minutes. Twenty such meetings were held secretly during the next one year, mostly at night. When, in late May 2001, Musharraf, was invited to India, Advani gave the entire credit to Qazi.

The last Advani-Qazi meeting was held when Musharraf visited India. After the Rashtrapati Bhawan banquet, before the Agra Summit next morning, Qazi, went home after the banquet, changed from his formal dress into casual clothes and went to Advani's house. Though the summit failed, Advani and Qazi remained best friends.

A few months later, a day after the attack on Parliament on December 13, 2001, *The Pioneer,* a BJP supported paper, was hoisting a dinner to celebrate its 10th anniversary. Both Qazi and Advani were present at the dinner. Qazi was avoiding Advani but when Mrs. Advani saw him, she insisted that he must meet her husband. Qazi was hesitant as he thought it would be embarrassing. But when he met him, Advani gave him a Punjabi 'double shake hand' and greeted him warmly. Qazi told Karan later: 'What an amazing man, he is!'

Five months later, on May 14, 2002, three Pak-terrorists attacked a tourist bus from Himachal Pradesh near the town of Kaluchak in J&K killing seven people. After doing that they entered the family quarter of the Army and fired indiscriminately at the inmates, killing 23 persons, including 10 children, eight women and five Army men. The furious Government asked Qazi to leave India within a week. One day before he was to leave India, Advani invited him for a personal farewell.

'When it was time to leave, Ashraf started to shake hands.

'*Galey lago,*' Mrs Advani intervened. Both men were taken aback. They stared at her. '*Galey lago,*' she repeated. And then, almost as if this was what they both wanted, Advani and Ashraf embraced.[107]

'I was standing behind Ashraf, so I could clearly see Advani's face. Tears had welled up in his eyes,' wrote Thapar in his book, *Devil's Advocate: The Untold Story.*

The way things happened it appeared apparent that Advani had a soft corner for Pakistan that was ignited by Qazi who became his bosom friend by the time he left India. Tears in his eyes when he bade farewell to Qazi substantiated it. But Pakistan, it looks, was having ulterior motives in developing friendship with Advani. The first definite evidence came when Pakistan's Foreign Minister at that time, Khurshid Kasuri, visited Delhi in 2005. Kasuri called on him as he was the leader of the opposition and also BJP President. Probably when Advani was nostalgically recalling his days in Pakistan, Kasuri extended him an invitation to visit Pakistan with his family. Advani gave no reply to Kasuri.

Karan was to interview Kasuri the same night. Suddenly in the afternoon his telephone began ringing and surprisingly Advani was on the line, asking him to meet him early evening. Neither he told nor Karan asked the purpose of this unexpected meeting. Karan went to Advani's house, who told him about the meeting he had with Kasuri and his invitation to him to visit Pakistan with the entire family. He requested Karan to tell Kasuri that he would be delighted to visit Pakistan and would like to do so with his wife, daughter, son and daughter-in-law. Karan dutifully passed on the message to Kasuri, who seemed to be extremely pleased as things were happening the way they were planned. He was sure that legendary hospitality of Pakistan and exposure to the country would change Advani's attitude and soften his attitude towards Pakistan. Kasuri immediately asked for a paper and asked Karan to write down the names of Advani's family members.

Things moved fast and an official invitation was sent by Pakistani Government to him to visit Pakistan with his family. Advani most gladly accepted it and visited Pakistan a few weeks later.[108]

Advani arrived in Pakistan on a week's visit on Monday, May 30, 2005. Pakistan went out of its way to make his visit not only high profile but also efficacious. During his eight-day tour, he was given the welcome of a visiting head of the State: official red-carpet welcomes, meetings with President Pervez Musharraf, Prime Minister Shaukat Aziz and other notables, addressing at several institutions, a grand tour of the archaeological remains of *Takshasila*, laying the foundation stone for the project to restore the historic Hindu temples at Katas Raj. But the critical moment came when he visited the mausoleum of Mohammed Ali Jinnah in Karachi. As he walked in accompanied by his family and the Chief Secretary, Home Secretary and Inspector-General of Karachi police the national anthem, Pakistan '*sarzameen shad bad,'* was played. A guard of honour was given by the Pakistan Navy, in whose jurisdiction the mausoleum fell and the local TV channels gave live coverage to his visit. Advani laid a wreath of roses and tube-lilies on the tomb after a prayer from the Quran was recited by Moulvi Liaqat.[109]

Standing before Jinnah's tomb, Advani described him as 'secular' and an 'ambassador of Hindu-Muslim unity,' and 'a great man' who had espoused the cause of secular Pakistan in an address to his country's Constituent Assembly. He also said that Jinnah's August 11, 1947 address was really 'classic, a forceful espousal of a secular state in which while every citizen would be free to pursue his own religion, the state should make no distinction between one citizen and another on grounds of faith. My respectful homage to this great man.'

Before leaving, he wrote in the Visitor's Book: 'There are many people who leave an inerasable stamp on history, but there are very few who actually create history. Quaid-e-Azam Mohammed Ali Jinnah was one such rare individual. In his early years, Sarojini Naidu, a leading luminary of India's freedom struggle, described Mr Jinnah as an 'ambassador of Hindu- Muslim unity.' His address to the Constituent Assembly of Pakistan on August 11, 1947, is really a classic, a forceful espousal of a secular state in which, while every citizen would be free to practise his own religion, the state shall make no distinction between one citizen and another on grounds of faith. My respectful homage to this great man.'[110]

More interesting was the brochure on the mausoleum that was given to Advani by the caretaker. It read: "The necessity of a separate homeland became all the more vital as the Hindu majority made it increasingly difficult for the Muslims in India to live a free and unfettered life according to the tenets of Islam? So, within the short span of a few years, the Quaid rallied the Indian Muslims under the green flag of the Muslim League and gave the Pakistani movement a momentum which neither the British Government nor the Indian Congress could contain.[111]

Another interesting, but serious, fact was that all through his trip, he was asked to comment on a case dating back to 1948, in which he was named a conspirator in a plot to assassinate Jinnah. The BJP leader had laughed it off, but Pakistani officials said the FIR, naming Advani, had still not been quashed.[112]

Unfortunately, what he wrote in the visitors' book at the Jinnah mausoleum in Karachi made him to lose his BJP presidency because he earned the wrath of the RSS, and the whole nation, as it undermined the widely-believed doctrine that Jinnah was responsible for the painful Partition of the country. On his return, RSS expected him to issue a contradiction, but he refused to do so. So, he was asked by the RSS to resign and he stepped down by the end of 2006. Later, Advani and the RSS patched up and he was named the BJP's Prime Ministerial candidate for the general elections in May 2009 as no other national leader of his stature was available. On 10 December 2007, the Parliamentary Board of BJP formally announced that L. K. Advani would be its prime ministerial candidate for the general elections due in 2009. However, he was informally but firmly told that the 2009 general election would be his last chance for power and after his defeat, the gerontocracy was politely but firmly side lined.[113]

After being named the prime ministerial candidate, Advani entered into a strenuous and intensive campaign. He travelled more than 60,000-odd km, braving the sweltering heat with temperatures hovering around 40 degrees Celsius to reach out to every nook and corner of the country. The 82-year old Advani even lifted weights and pitched himself in cyberspace. His backroom boys worked round the clock, while the BJP leader also found time to interact with young and first-time voters on his website. Advani made a strong case for himself by his continuous tirade against Prime Minister Manmohan Singh, calling him weak and subservient to Congress President Sonia Gandhi.[114] But it didn't work and with this Advani lost the hope of becoming the prime minister of India for ever. He was even asked not to become the leader of the opposition and Sushma Swaraj became the Leader of Opposition in the 15th Lok Sabha.[115]

Modi: PM's Candidate

BJP was in dilemma about announcing the prime ministerial candidate before the 2014 elections as Advani had brought quite a gloom in 2009 when BJP lost heavily. He again expected to be named the future PM of India as the chances of forming the Government were high. But two things happened: Mohan Bhagwat, became the *Sarsanghchalak* (Chief) of the RSS at the young age of 59. He was one of the youngest leaders to head the

RSS after K. B. Hedgewar and M. S. Golwalkar. He was not in favour of Advani contesting the 2009 election as the future Prime Minister. But since he had taken over the control of the organisation just a few months back and, therefore, did not want to oppose the senior-most leader of the BJP. Also, at that time there was no other powerful leader of national repute. But by 2014, Bhagwat had become the most powerful chief of the RSS and was determined to have his say in the selection of BJP's prime ministerial candidate. Moreover, he was of the same age as Modi (both were born in September 1950, Bhagwat being only six days older than Modi) and had worked together at various positions in the RSS. Bhagwat had also deep roots in Gujarat as his father Madhukarrao was a *pracharak* in Gujarat and was Modi's guide and mentor as a young recruit into the RSS in Gujarat.[116]

Secondly, Modi had become the most successful and powerful leader in Gujarat. He had developed the image of an achiever and a development-oriented Chief Minister. His reputation had become that of a doer not only in India but abroad also. That was the reason that Modi, despite stiff opposition from Advani and few of his cohorts, was unanimously nominated to be the prime ministerial candidate for the BJP in the 2014 election.

Rajnath Singh, the then BJP President, after the12-member BJP Parliamentary Board meeting on Friday, September 13, 2013, announced at a press gathering that Narendra Modi would be prime ministerial candidate for the 2014 Lok Sabha. He also said that it was done as per the Party's tradition where Parliamentary Board, the highest decision-making body of the Party, takes the decision. He also said that the decision was unanimous and was taken keeping in view the mood and aspirations of the people. On Advani's protest, he said 'he is a respected leader and will continue to be respected. We will keep seeking his guidance.' Advani, as he was opposed to Modi's nomination, did not attend the Parliamentary Board meeting. However, Murli Manohar Joshi, former BJP President and Sushma Swaraj, Leader of Opposition in the Lok Sabha, who were also opposed to Modi's candidature, attended the meeting and agreed to the majority decision. Rajnath Singh had frenetic meetings with these two important senior leaders to make sure that they go with the majority so that the decision was unanimous. Thus, ended weeks' back-room manoeuvrings at the behest of the RSS chief Mohan Bhagwat who played a significant role in Modi's nomination and had made it loud and clear that he wanted Modi's name to be announced before the commencement of the 'inauspicious' fortnight on September 20.[117]

Before the Parliamentary Board meeting, Gadkari had met Advani to persuade him on Modi's name. Swaraj and Ananth Kumar were also present in the meeting. Advani had laid down a few conditions for supporting Modi's candidature. These were that: Modi should resign as Gujarat Chief Minister and also Campaign Committee chief's position should be given to Sushma Swaraj. Rajnath Singh gave no definite assurance but said that the Party would consider all his suggestions. Despite this Advani refused to attend the Parliamentary Board meeting.[118]

Advani had his own reasons to oppose announcing Modi's name at this juncture. He wanted the BJP Chief Ministers to be consulted on the issue and that the decision should be made after the forthcoming Assembly elections in Madhya Pradesh, Chhattisgarh, Rajasthan and Delhi. Advani also argued that making Modi the prime ministerial candidate would relegate issues like price rise and corruption, on which the BJP had attacked the Congress, and Modi, being a controversial leader will become the only issue. Joshi and Sushma Swaraj were also opposed to Modi's projection at this juncture. Though Advani stood by his decision, Joshi and Sushma changed their stand to join the majority.[119]

Advani, not only did not attend the meeting, but also sent an angry letter to Rajnath Singh almost at the same time when announcement about Modi was made. He wrote in the letter that: 'This afternoon when you had come to my residence to inform me about the Parliamentary Board meeting, I had said something about my anguish as also my disappointment over your style of functioning. I had told you that I will think whether I should share my thoughts with other Board members or not. Now I have decided that it is better that I do not attend today's meeting.' [120]

As soon as the Board meeting was over, Modi, accompanied by other members, except Advani and the former Prime Minister Atal Bihari Vajpayee, who was bed-ridden, walked to the Media Conference Room. Rajnath Singh, amid sound of conch shells, announced the Board's decision. It was followed by brief media statement by him. Modi, while accepting the nomination, thanked Vajpayee and Advani for their valued contribution to the Party. He also assured the Party that he would do his best to bring the BJP to power in 2014. He gave a slogan '*nayisoch, nayiummeed*' (new thinking, new hope) and said the BJP would go the 2014 polls promising good governance and development while fighting against corruption and price rise. He said the country was going through a 'crisis' and BJP would require blessings of people from Kashmir to Kanyakumari and Attock (it was rhythmic only as Attock is in Pakistan) to Cuttack so that this situation ends. Thanking Party leaders and NDA allies for their support, Modi committed himself to work tirelessly to ensure BJP's victory in the 2014 elections.[121] Soon after the announcement, Modi went to meet Advani to seek his blessings. During the 30-minute meeting, Advani obliged him but also asked him about the letter written by suspended IPS officer D G Vanzara who had quit service while attacking Modi.[122]

Modi was nominated as BJP's Prime Ministerial candidate because of several reasons. First his image of a dynamic and no-nonsense Chief Minister of Gujarat. His successful record of Gujarat's CM was unprecedented as Gujarat was never as peaceful and developing as during his regime. Secondly, stubborn L K Advani's dismal performance as a Prime Ministerial candidate in the 2009 Lok Sabha elections. Thirdly, Mohan Bhagwat becoming the *Sarsanghchalak* (Chief) of the RSS who stressed that the country should be led by young leaders.

Modi 2014 Campaign Strategy

After the BJP finally decided to bet all its chips on Modi in 2014 Lok Sabha elections, he decided to present himself as a teamster of change and worked on a new political strategyto mobilize voters' support. In fact, Modi took the command of the election campaign, from planning to execution, right from the beginning and decided to rewrite the rules of the game and redefined Indian politics to capture popular imagination around himself. Modi, in the past ten years, had transformed himself from a regional, right-wing politician to a decisive leader with a clear development agenda. He used this to tell people that he was the only and the best to take India forward. The first thing he did was to form a task force to handle his election campaign. Piyush Goyal and Ajay Singh were given the responsibility to handle the overall media strategy and a team was constituted to handle his campaign in Varanasi. He also decided to use the skills of advertising legends such as Ogilvy & Mather's Piyush Pandey and McCann Worldgroup's Prasoon Joshi. He convinced Sam Balsara of Madison World to help him at various levels. Advertising agency Soho Square, part of the WPP Group, was asked to handle television, radio and print campaigns who came up with catchy slogans such as '*ab ki Baar Modi Sarkar* (Modi Government this time).'[123]

BJP decided to go full-throttle with a Narendra Modi-centric strategy, setting a target of reaching out to at least 25 crore people through rallies and other public interactions of Modi across the country. The main stress was on rallies to directly reach out to over 25 crore people.The party also decided to focus on States like West Bengal, Kerala, Odisha and in the northeast where its presence was almost zero.[124]

BJP's 2014 strategy was a carefully scripted communication and public relations strategy that used social media effectively to communicate its message. It was a very good mix of all technologies. It wasn't just social media but all digital platforms, including mobile and Internet and was combined with advanced use of analytics to decide how, where and when to communicate, the campaign targeted 810 million voters in 543 constituencies across 11.36 lakh (1.13 million) polling booths. Modi motivated his team to realise the potential of social media which he had used effectively in his election campaigns in Gujarat to spread the message about his government's achievements.[125]

Developing Winnable Platform

After a brainstorming session, the Information, Communications and Campaign Committee headed by Piyush Goel, Rajya Sabha Member, was given, a target of 272 seats in the Lok Sabha election. It was named 'Mission 272 Plus,' and he was asked to drow the road map for this ambitious target. While giving details about 'Mission 272 Plus,' Goyal told media: 'There are at least seven crore young voters who are not registered. Our Mission 272 Plus aims to get them registered as voters, educate them about what the BJP stands for and persuade them to cast their vote on that crucial day.' He also said: "The BJP plans to tap into growing anger among the youth with regards to corruption and poor governance. The young are yearning and aspiring for a new India and our effort is to become a platform for their voice." It was also decided to raise an army of volunteers in the coming months who will be trained to use various digital platforms to increase the Party's nationwide outreach. Its strategy was to use the latest communication technologies to approach the youth, who have shown a marked preference for Modi as PM.[126]

The BJP decided to enlist 10,000 volunteers and another one-lakh online volunteers by the end of August. This figure was to increase as the elections were to draw closer and the BJP campaign picked pace. Special training sessions were organised to teach the volunteers about the contents of their message and the use of technology in reaching out to potential voters. The BJP already had technology to reach to target voters. For instance, it had the software enabling it to access details of each voter and his family members. This was to help volunteers to persuade those who have not registered as voters and then track them physically till the election.[127]

Next step was to formulate astratagem for achieving this Mission. The task was given to Amit Sheth, a Professor at Wright State University's Knowledge Computing Center in Ohio. He, with a team of over 100 young techies and consultants, developed big data of election information for designing the election strategy and campaigning. It helped in raising funds, work and rework on advertisements, and create detailed models for voter engagement in swing states as well as gender and minority voter clusters to increase the power of their micro-targeted strategy. This was modeled on the election management of Barak Obama, though it was somewhat smaller in size, scale and perhaps style. In the words of Arvind Gupta, the BJP master strategist behind Modi's 3.67 million followers on Twitter, 12 million 'likes' on Facebook and the party's 68 million page-views on Google Plus: 'We have developed our own customized digital tools based on both commissioned and open source data that puts us in direct touch with voters.'[128]

Sheth was fast to change the tools of the strategy to help Modi, perhaps one of the most tech-savvy politicians in India. An example was the unique digital event like *'Chai pe Charcha'* (Talk over tea), an unprecedented election event that put the BJP leaders directly in touch with people at tea stalls in villages at publicized localities through a combination of satellite, DTH, internet and mobile. It was inspired by a comment made by a senior Congress leader, Mani Shankar Aiyar, in the AICC meeting at Delhi in January, 2014 that Modi was only a '*chaiwala*' (tea seller). He mocked Modi's Prime Ministerial ambitions and said: 'I promise you in 21st Century Narendra Modi will never become the Prime Minister of the country. …But if he wants to distribute tea here, we will find a place for him to distribute tea here.'[129] *Chai Pe Charcha* became an innovative break as it was held in over 4,000 locations across India. During these *Charchas*, Modi heard the views of the people and then answered their questions on a wide range of issues and in the process trying to connect with the entire cross-section of society.

Chia pe Charcha connected Modi with people as *Chai* is one drink that most Indians start their mornings with. BJP strategists were clever enough to understand that it is *chai* that connects India and it was used to bind audience and promote content among people with the *Chai Pe Charcha* and this campaign naturally had a mass appeal. But it worked specifically for two reasons: It talked to people in their terms and became one rare time when a PM candidate invited people to have a discussion over tea. It tried to establish a conversation with common people. BJP members left no stone unturned to make it a success. People gathered on streets and market corners with NaMo tea cups in their hands and looking at the camera. It was a nationwide tea carnival.[130]

A new era in campaigning was brought in when Sheth retrieved real-time data on ongoing elections, which included voter sentiments, emotions and concerns in different constituencies and states. The data was used to drive donations, enroll volunteers, and organise resources on the ground to improve the effectiveness of everything from door-to-door contacts and phone calls to micro-messaging and social media. Technology and data analysis played a crucial role in Modi's election which involved more than 930,000 polling booths and 1.7 million voting machines, with 11 million personnel managing the election. This was the beginning of a new phase in electioneering by changing the way elections were fought. Modi's strategy team ousted the old-time political strategists who relied more on hunches and intuitions to gauge complex demographics of caste, religion, community and localities. Modi replaced them with quantitative analysts, programmers and data scientists. Sheth brought data analytics from research labs to real-time monitoring of people's reaction to politics, policy and rapid responses to crisis situations. It played a significant role in changing many political outcomes in 2014 election.[131]

Modi's strategy team developed Twitter into an effective campaign instrument and BJP tweeted like never before. Later, a study of the 2014 general elections indicated that the more one tweeted, the brighter were the chances to win. Twitter, in fact, became an important platform for the BJP to reach out to a certain section. Congress joined Twitter quite late, only in March 2014, and therefore, it was greatly outpaced by BJP in the race for tweets. According to the University of California study, the BJP posted 80,981 tweets during the 2014 elections, far ahead of any other political parties. It used it as a broadcasting medium tweeting Party messages as shareable content, such as images, which users shared in their personal networks. It helped in changing the mindset and perception of the urban population which had never voted for BJP in the past.[132]

Modi's innovative implementation of the strategy emphasized using the modern information system at the grassroot level. With the objective of getting an edge over other parties, extensive use of information and communication technology (ICT) was made by each State unit and was controlled by a core team. All this was done with high level of precision and the use of modern techniques: DTH channel for *Chai Pe Charcha*, 3D rallies for youth and extensive use of social media for reaching to all sections of the society. The implementation was under the supervision of top management which kept a tab on the situation and sorted out problems at the ground level which helped in increasing motivation of cadres.

A very innovative way of reaching a very large audience was the 'Bharat Vijay 3D rallies' using 3D holographic technology helping Modi to address multiple public meetings at the same time. All the event locations were equipped with a technical setup including 40x40x35 feet projection cubes used for delivering Modi's speech in a 3D form which was telecasted from a central location. Before the start of his speech, *nukkad natak* (street plays) and *Kavi Sammelans* (poetry recitation sessions)were organised to entertain crowds. This technology projected his life-like presence at all meeting locations. Modi had successfully experimented with this technology during 2012 Gujarat Assembly election campaigns. However, it was used for the first time in India in a general election. This mechanism enabled people in far-off places to experience a real connect with him. Using this technology, BJP, in association with Citizens of Accountable Governance (CAG), reached out to 1000-plus locations across the country by organizing multiple rounds of 'Bharat Vijay 3D rallies.' These 3D rallies were in addition to the 185 Bharat Vijay rallies addressed by Modi.[133]

During the election, Modi addressed 12 rounds of 3D rallies covering 1,350 locations and the response was phenomenal because a large number of youngsters wrote to Modi on mail and social media after the rally. The missed call strategy also worked as ten million missed calls were logged on the designated numbers. The call center then used to do the follow up by getting the e-mail ID, residential address and voter ID. All this helped BJP to track voters which was helpful on the polling day. The local units were asked to inform the voter about his booth number and location thereby ensuring that the person comes out and votes.[134]

BJP decided to contest the 2014 election on the plank of '*vikas*' (development) which created first-time exultation and expectations, especially among the youth and the middle class who expected more jobs, better infrastructural facilities and more growth opportunities. This expectation was fanned by using social media and was effectively utilised by the BJP's electoral strategists to make it the central plank of the party's campaign. It also won some support and acceptability for the BJP from sections of liberal intelligentsia and the business community who were otherwise averse to BJP's saffron agenda.[135]

When the results of the 2014 elections were announced, the BJP won a landslide victory to form the largest majority government since the 1984 elections, first time since then that a single political party won majority to form its Government without the support from other regional parties. It was the result of a carefully drawn communication and public relations strategy using effectively and widely social media for communicating its messages. Arvind Gupta, BJP's National Technology Head explained that

'It wasn't just social media but all digital platforms, including mobile and mobile Internet. Combined with advanced use of analytics to decide how, where and when to communicate, the campaign targeted 810 million voters in 543 constituencies across 11.36 lakh (1.13 million) polling booths.'[136] It was specifically focused on converting the 'floating [unsure] voter, who had not decided which party he would vote.

The digital campaign was planned after long diligence including four years of meticulous data collection, collating information in a scientific manner and making timely actionable analysis. The team had organised data on each of the 543 constituencies and exactly knew how many voters were using mobile, social media and Internet in each constituency. Besides, analytics was used to understand which polling booths had voted for the BJP in the previous elections. For each polling booth data analytics was used to segregate voters into blocks to determine who were favouring, unsure or against the BJP.[137]

The BJP's 2014 election campaign was developed around the perceived failures of the Manmohan Singh Government and widespread corruption in its second term. Modi was presented as a Chief Minister leading an honest government in Gujarat and was presented as the corrective medicine to Singh as a weak and ineffective PM heading a corrupt and ineffective Government. He was portrayed as a strong and honest leader who would bring *Acche Din* (the good times) in India using the slogan, '*sabkasaath, sabkavikaas*' (with the support of all, development of all).

What made Modi win?

Modi's strategy team not only designed a winnable platform, but implemented it perceptively. The five major themes of his agenda were:

Making India a strong economy: India, after major economic reforms in 1991, managed by the then Finance Minister, Manmohan Singh, had brought inspiring economic growth, averaging above eight per cent per year in the following years. But it slowed down during the ten-year rule of Sonia Gandhi-controlled Manmohan Singh's Government. Narendra Modi sharply focused on developing a strong economy during the course of his campaign. He battered the Singh's Government for stalling development projects while in Gujarat projects were cleared and implemented at a fast rate. Leading business houses of the country supported Modi's claim and said that he was a decisive administrator who could bring economic growth during his regime.[138]

Controlling corruption: During the Singh's rule, a large number of corruption scandals involving public funds and resources came out of the cupboard which tattered the UPA Government. Anna Hazara, backed by the BJP, came on the street with anti-graft protests that created a forceful anti-incumbency wave across the country leading to the launching of the Aam Aadmi Party (AAP), having strong backing from the masses. Modi, during his campaign, cashed on this animosity among the people. Modi, all throughout the campaign, strongly announced that he would act as a '*chowkidaar*' (watchman) and ensure that corruption was totally removed from the society.[139]

Youth-oriented development: India's electorate was progressively becoming young and half the country's 81 crore voters were under 35 years of age. For them employment leading to prosperous life was the first priority. Modi promised to create jobs for them to provide secure employment.[140]

Using technology in the campaign: Modi and his competent team formulated and operated a high-pitched and tech-savvy campaign. Being used for first time in India it overwhelmed and engrossed voters directly through social media. Modi snapped campaign selfies that went viral and even appeared as a holograph at campaign events. He also tweeted daily for months. The Congress party, particularly its chief campaigner, Rahul Gandhi, eschewed Twitter.[141]

Infrastructure: Modi made a specific mention of the lack of infrastructure— roads, ports, railway lines and air connections—for low economic development. Besides, the existing infrastructure was also in bad shape. Roads were shabby, ports were without modern facilities and there was a huge shortage of adequate electricity supply. He told the audiences that infrastructure development and its maintenance would be high on the list of problems that he would tackle with. He always gave the example of Gujarat where because of infrastructure improvements—priority to building thousands of kilometers of highways and attracting investment to build up the country's largest modern port—gave a boost to investment leading to better employment. He promised to bring the same focus if elected Prime Minister.[142]

Modi's marketing strategy: The main reason behind Modi's grand success, according to Professor S. Bharadwaj, Chair Professor of Marketing, Great Lakes Institute of Management,was the formulation of an intelligent and workable strategy which had very innovative six elements that were used for the first time in any political election. These elements gave him high visibility and powerful muscle to his election campaign. The six elements were:

Understanding voter perceptions: Any election has to keep in mind the voters' perceptions. It is like understanding consumer insights which is always based on consumers' research. Modi's team also conducted voters' survey and found that Narendra Modi had a much higher brand value than that of the BJP. Therefore, it was decided that Modi and not BJP would be projected in all election campaigns. After the results, it looked obvious, but six months before the results it was not believed at least by the senior BJP leaders. In fact, it was the foresight of the RSS that BJP was forced to take the decision in favour of Modi.

Engaged the best brains in advertising: He hired the best-known names, Sam Balsara, Prasoon Joshi and Piyush Pandey who were widely known in the advertising circle because of their successful record. They also had vast and rich experience from managing hundreds of successful campaigns with blue-chip companies. They treated BJP as a client and took sentimentality out of the picture and looked at only business. The media management by the experienced trio was one of the strong reasons for the better than expected victory.

Captivating slogan: Since slogans are strongest tool in the marketing of a product, BJP gave utmost importance to captivating slogan like '*Ab ki Bar, Modi Sarkar*' (This time, Modi Government) during the campaign. It proved to be tremendously haunting as it was easy on the tongue and everyone could speak it. It was designed keeping in view the limitations of the non-Hindi people as they could easily articulate it as they understood its meaning, and therefore, it reverberated with everybody.

Unified communications campaign: BJP ensured that the campaign managers used multiple modes of communication messages, intensely and intensively. All messages that were used were unified to popularise Brand Modi and what he stood for. It was communicated through TV, print and radio advertisements. Besides, YouTube, Facebook and Twitter were also used widely. Uniqueness of different audiences and segments of the society were taken into consideration when deciding the modes of communications to be used. TV was used to reach the average man, Internet to reach out to the youngsters who were online most of the time and roadshows and rallies to reach rural people. Narendra Modi addressed hundreds of rallies throughout the country and communicated people in a most intimate way, using Bill Clinton's technique of connecting with the audience in a natural way.

Word of Mouth: Person-to-person is the most powerful and effective way of communication. They took a lesson from 'Kolaveri Di,' a song from the soundtrack of the 2012 Tamil psychological thriller film, which did not use any marketing technique. But within a week of the official release of the video, it received more than 3.5 million views on YouTube, more than one million shares on Facebook, while trending in India on Twitter the whole time. The song became the top downloaded song on mobile with 4,100,000 downloads within the first 18 days of release.

The campaign managers realised that a sizeable migrant labour from Bihar and Uttar Pradesh was working in Gujarat and when they would go back their homes, they would canvass for Modi in their villages and towns. Therefore, BJP workers were asked to create a clear perception among this groups that Modi was a doer who gets things done. They were also trained to create a perception that Manmohan Singh's Government was suffering from policy paralysis. This was to create an image of Modi as a person who makes team to work and delivers results.

Database Marketing: The campaign managers, particularly in important States like Uttar Pradesh and Bihar, collected huge database which was used to reach out directly to the people. The Congress and other political parties failed to do this exercise and, therefore, their campaign was unexciting.[143]

Men behind Modi's election campaign: The success of a political campaign ultimately depends on the brains of the capability and astuteness of persons who formulate and implement the campaign strategy. Modi chose rely on party machinery and did not deliberate with senior party leaders. Instead, he selected his own team persons who worked closely with Modi. They were carefully selected and borrowed from the RSS. He also picked up three of his trusted ministers from Gujarat.

The major-domo behind Modi's election campaign strategy was thirty-five-year old Prashant Kishor, a native of Bihar. He was with the UN as health expert for eight years in Africa and was heading the United Nations Aid Mission in Chad, West Africa. He had prepared a paper documenting economic prosperity and malnutrition in India. He came to Gujarat in 2011 and caught the attention of Modi who invited him for a coffee meeting which ended with Prashant Kishor joining Modi's team. Much influenced by his strategic thinking, Modi asked for his help in the coming 2012 Gujarat Assembly election because Modi was afraid that third term victory may be difficult. He accepted the challenge and hard-sold Modi's election strategy in Assembly polls in Gujarat. Much impressed by his innovative ideas and out-of-box-thinking, Modi retained him for the 2014 General Elections and he became one of the most important persons in Modi's team designing strategies for months before 2014 elections. He introduced many clutter-busting techniques and innovations in Modi's campaign including the employment of 3-D holograms at public rallies and the "*Chai pe Charcha*" outreach, which turned a barb by Congress leader Mani Shankar Aiyar about Modi's days as a young tea-seller on trains into a point of public connect. He only consulted and reported to Modi and BJP had no influence and control on him.[144]

As the May 2014 general election approached, Kishor created Citizens for Accountable Governance (CAG) in 2013, which was joined by nearly 200 young Indian professionals from top schools and companies. Many of them were alumni of IITs and IIMs and all were dressed in smart casuals and carried iPhones and looked like they were at a corporate offsite. They diligently carried out Modi's marketing and advertising campaign to take Modi 'to the dark zones of the country, where the party and the man himself are unknown.' All had quit comfortable banking and consultancy jobs to be part of CAG. They all put together a wildly successful social media plan to project Mr Modi as the face of good governance for the Gujarat elections in 2012 and then the 2014 election.Their work played a big role in making Modi popular.[145]

Prashant helped Modi in selecting a team of professionals to manage his election. The team had four divisions. The first was that of back-room boys who handled administration and coordination with different Modi teams. It consisted of three of Modi's secretaries operating out of Gandhinagar: Chief Principal Secretary K Kailashnathan, Additional Principal Secretary A K Sharma and Principal Secretary G C Murmu and the Resident Commissioner in Delhi Bharat Lal. Campaign strategy team was drawn from CAG that prepared the blueprint of Modi's marketing and communication strategies that were drawn by CAG, having 200 full-time employees and more than 1,000 part-time volunteers. The third was that of communication manager. Modi's former OSD Hiren Joshi, a former RSS man managed Modi's digital strategy, including his social media campaign. The main stream campaign, TV, print and radio ads, was handled by Manoj Ladwa, a London-based merger-and-acquisitions lawyer. He played a crucial role in getting the UK to open its doors to Modi. Media planning was handled by marketing communications agency Madison and advertising veterans such as Piyush Pande and Prasoon Joshi provided creative inputs for the campaign. Ladwa supervised the whole process from an office in New Delhi's Lodhi Road.[146]

The last Day

Modi wrapped up his campaign on May 10, by addressing his last rally in Ballia in eastern Uttar Pradesh. Ending his campaign at a rally in Ballia, Modi thanked the people of the country for coming out in large numbers to hear him. Modi also told the huge crowd that in this election campaign, he interacted directly with voters from 5,800 places through meetings and TV interactions and that he travelled for more than 3 lakh kilometers across the countryand that it should be included in the Guinness World Records.[147]

Modi also told the crowd that this election had brought a spark of change for '*surajya*' (good governance) and it would be achieved. He asked the audience to remember Bal Gangadhar Tilak's iconic slogan '*Swaraj hamara janmsiddh adhikar hai aur hum isko lakar rahenge,* (Swaraj is my birthright, and I shall have it) and said that *surajya* was the birth-right of the people.)[148]

Modi came back in the evening to Ahmedabad having stopped at Varanasi, his constituency. Next day was Sunday, the first in eight months when he did not have to hit the road to address another rally. But, as habitual, he got up as usual at six and began his routine. After finishing his eight o'clock appointment he talked to Rajdeep Surdesai, at around 10:30, who had been trying to talk to him for the last two weeks. Rajdeep opened the conversation giving him advance congratulations. Modi had a laugh and asked Rajdeep: '*Kya number de rahe ho*, Rajdeep?' (How many seats are you giving, Rajdeep?) Rajdeep told him that BJP should expect 'between 270 and 280.' Unconvinced Modi told him that 'we shall reach 300, 'wave *hain,* wave.' (It is a wave) Rajdeep told him that it may be possible because 'you are sweeping north and west India, sir.' Then Modi gave an advice to Rajdeep: *'Yeh jo Dilli main baithe political pundits hain, kaho studio ke bahar jaaye!'* (Tell the political pundits sitting in Delhi to go out of their studio) And then, with an authoritative tone in his voice, he suddenly broke into English: 'First time since 1984, you will have a majority government in Delhi.' Before ending his conversation, Rajdeep ask for an interview to that Modi replied: '*Ab Dilli mein milenga.*' (Now we meet in Delhi)[149]

On the evening of May 11, Sunil Mittal of Airtel had invited few political leaders, media barons and corporate tycoons for dinner at his Amrita Shergill Marg. To make the evening interesting, Mittal announced a competition. Each guest was asked to guess the number of seats BJP would win on 16th. The guest who came closest was to get a Franck Muller watch and the farthest away was to hold the next dinner. Arun Jaitley was happy with 245 seats and a media leader gave a figure of 200. Only a lady from a prominent business family, Meenakshi Dass, came nearest with 266 seats.[150]

One-hundred-sixteenth day of 2014, May 16, was awfully hot summer day in Delhi. But it was a historic day in the Indian almanac as on that day a new era began in the annals of India. It was the day when the BJP, for the first time got clear majority in the Lok Sabha, an ability to form the Government on its own. It became a Party that could win a clear majority in three decades. It was the party that had many ups and downs since 1952 elections and had never ever dreamt of forming a Government on its own.

When the results began to be announced, the Indian voters began to give BJP and its lead candidate, Narendra Modi, a mammoth mandate for running the next government. In the beginning even Rahul Gandhi, Sharad Pawar's daughter, Supriya Sule and Shashi Tharoor were trailing behind their BJP opponents. The three, however, won finally though Rahul Gandhi's lead fell from 3.70 lakh in 2009 to just over one lakh votes. The margins of Sule and Tharoor had also fallen drastically. Within an hour of the beginning of the counting Rajdeep asked his producers to flash a breaking news on the video wall that BJP was 'set to win the 2014 elections; Narendra Modi poised to be India's next Prime Minister.' Within an hour all TV news channels were showing this breaking news.[151]

BJP got a commanding lead of 282 of the 543 seats in Parliament, Congress failing to get more than 44 seats. BJP got all the seats in Rajasthan and Gujarat and 73 out of 80 seats in UP. 'On our map in the studio, north, west and central India had only one colour—saffron. This was a rout of non-BJP parties. If it was a T20 match, they might have called it off after the first power play.'[152] For the first time in three decades a single party in India had won a clear majority. Ravi Shankar Prasad, the BJP leader, called it a 'tectonic shift' as the Indian voter had rejected the politics of dynasty, entitlement and inheritance in favour of the politics of initiative and accomplishment based on hard work.'[153]

Modi, on that day, got up very early and after his usual meditation, had a very light breakfast and began to watch TV. 'He, too, knew in the first two hours that it was all over.' He asked his aide to tweet from his account: 'India has won.' A little after noon, he came out of his home and drove to his village to pay his respects to his mother, Hiraben. 'The first television image post-victory was well thought out—Modi sitting on a chair being blessed by his mother and surrounded by a few smiling relatives.'[154] In his first public appearance, he addressed the voters in Vadodara, from where he had contested, along with Varanasi, and had won by 5.7 lakh votes, he said: 'I want to tell all my fellow Indians that in the letter and spirit, I will take all Indians with me.'[155] And speaking like a Prime Minister he said: 'I want to make the twenty-first century India's century; it will take ten years, not very long.' He had his last public function as CM a little after 8:30 in the evening and addressed a crowd of his admirers. He wrapped up his address saying: '*Desh chal pada hai, hamein kadam milana hai.*' (The country has begun to march ahead, we have to match its steps)[156]

Modi, undoubtedly, was the strategic mind behind the success of this Congress-shattering victory, but the miracle-man who gave Modi UP, entry door for power, on a platter was Amit Shah, who micromanaged that most difficult State. Surprisingly, he was the most relaxed person in the BJP. Unlike Modi, he got up late around 8:30 and switched on the news only around nine and soon switched it off when he was certain which way the wind was blowing. Rather the election results, he was more interested in knowing what was happening in UP. He switched on the channel that was showing the UP results. At the end, when Rajdeep asked him if he had expected such a big win, his reply was: *'Sahi kahen toh hamein bi anumann-ahitha ki itnibadi jeet hogi. Yeh tohvakaimeinek tsunami hi hai.'* (Even we did not anticipate the scale of this win, this is truly a tsunami)[157]

Election 2014 was the most expensive election campaign for the BJP costing Rs. 714.28 crore ($115 million). It was about Rs. 200 crore ($32 million) more than the Congress Party's expenditure and almost as much as the Rs. 791 crore ($127 million) that both the parties spent in the 2009 general elections. The biggest gainer were two firms—its media planner, Madison World founded by Sam Balsara and chartered aviation provider, Saarthi Airways, promoted by Delhi-based Gulab Singh Tanwar, known to be a close friend of Rajnath Singh.[158] Modi had flown more than 185,000 miles and addressed 457 rallies, which were seen at 5,800 places, in a slick, presidential-style campaign which began in September 2013 when he was declared Prime Ministerial candidate. Modi's exposure to voters was great as he received more than seven times the media coverage of his chief rival, one study showed.[159]

Modi, at last, fulfilled his long-cherished desire of becoming the Prime Minister of India. 'The boy from Vadnagar with the blazing eyes and burning ambition was going to be the prime minister of India. An RSS Swayamsevak was to take over as the country's chief executive. Long years in politics, the determined building of a massive personality cult in the face of the hard-work of controversy, had resulted in this extraordinary achievement. Narendra Modi deserved a good night's rest.'[160]

Eighteenth of May 2014, 'may well go down in history as the day when Britain finally left India. Narendra Modi's victory in the elections marks the end of a long era in which the structures of power did not differ greatly from those through which Britain ruled the subcontinent. India under the Congress party was in many ways a continuation of the British Raj by other means. The last of midnight's children are now a dwindling handful of almost 70-year-olds, but it is not the passing of the independence generation that makes the difference,' wrote *The Guardian* in its editorial of May 18, edition.[161]

****

Chapter Six

Indira Becoming PM

The Chinese attack in October 1962 had greatly shaken Jawaharlal Nehru. Though he had resumed his full responsibilities as Prime Minister, he was not in his normal self—dynamic, confident and active. The effect was that he became politically weak and mentally exhausted. It drained him of all power and strength, physical and emotional, causing a stroke early January 1964. He was partially paralysed on the left side while rising to speak at the Congress session in Bhubaneswar, Orissa (now Odisha). It made him weak and he had to make effort to rise in the Parliament to answer questions. Also, while walking he had to drag his left foot. Therefore, to reduce the burden of his work, he delegated most of his routine duties to Lal Bahadur Shastri, who was taken into the Cabinet as Minister without Portfolio after he got the stroke.

By the end of 1963, Nehru's health was declining. It made people to think seriously that who would takeover if Nehru dies. Therefore, for the first time in sixteen years since independence, New Delhi was rife with speculation about the question – "After Nehru, who?" This gave rise to a unique institution that became to be known as 'Syndicate.' It consisted five persons, who met at the Tirupathi Temple in the beginning of October, 1963 to consider 'who should be the PM after Nehru? The original four were: Kumaraswami Kamaraj, the former Chief Minister of Madras with wide mass appeal, Sanjiva Reddy, a powerful Andhra leader, Nijalingappa, the Chief Minister of Mysore and Atulya Ghosh, the President of Bengal Congress Committee. Later, S K Patil, an influential leader from Maharashtra joined them. Together, these men controlled the power in the Congress party in non-Hindi states.

Their meeting at Tirupati was secret. To give it a cover-up, they went to Tirupathi to offer worship at the shrine. But, in fact, they were together to discuss the future of the country and how to shape it after the death of

Nehru. The two questions they discussed were: Who shall be the next Prime Minister; and, who will become the next President of the Congress Party, a position that would be of tremendous importance after Nehru's death. When discussing who should be PM after Nehru and they all agreed that Morarji Desai should not be the next PM.

While the members of the Syndicate shared many ideological stands, the greatest factor that united them was that all the five disliked Desai. Though they did not disagree with Desai ideologically, as they were also conservative, pro-business and anti-socialism, their only fear was that Desai was too strong a political leader and too independent entity to be controlled by them. Many of them also had old grudges with Desai and that made them distrust Desai. Therefore, after Nehru's death in 1964, all the five rallied their support against Desai and supported Shastri as the Prime Minister.

Desai was the greatest Congress leader and was most likely to succeed Nehru. However, his very prominence was a threat to the Syndicate. If he were to become the Prime Minister, he would dominate the scene completely, reducing the Syndicate members to big zero. The Syndicate wanted someone malleable whom they could control absolutely. This in mind, they decided that a collective leadership, headed by Lal Bahadur Shastri, and not Morarji Desai, should succeed Nehru. This stymied the question of Desai becoming Nehru's successor, that Nehru also desired.

The moment for which the Syndicate was formed arrived on May 27, 1964 when Nehru died at the age of 74. He had, as usual, gone to sleep the previous night at 11:30, after coming back from a short vacation in Dehra Dun. He woke up at six in the morning and was fresh and fit. He went to the washroom. Coming back, he sat on his bed and complained to his valet of a pain in his shoulders, and soon lost consciousness. Indira came running and immediately called the three doctors who were attending him since his last stroke about six months ago. But before his physicians could arrive, he had a heart attack and fell unconscious. At noon, he was placed in an oxygen tent and an hour later his condition was described as 'grave and desperate.' He was declared dead at two in the afternoon. Soon after, Steel Minister, Coimbatore Subramaniam walked into the Parliament to announce Nehru's death saying: 'The light is out,' using the same words that Nehru has used announcing the death of Mahatma Gandhi on 30 January 1948.

Nehru died in a coma because of coronary thrombosis, the formation of a clot in a coronary artery of the heart. Nehru's face was neither tired out nor sad. It did not show any sign of pain and it did not look like an old man's face but was frozen into a mould of confounded will power. Even in death, his was not a face of dormancy but of eager, impatient discovery, as in life.

Draped in the Indian national Tri-colour flag his body was placed on an elevated platform in his study and Mahatma Gandhi's popular composition, '*Raghupati Raghava Rajaram,*' was being played in the background. After six hours, his body was taken to the front porch to lie-in-state. A red mark, made with a dab of sandalwood paste, on his forehead contrasted with the whiteness of his face. Indira sat on the floor by his side, her head covered with white sari. As the news of Nehru's death spread, hundreds of thousand people gathered at the gates of his residence. Men, women and children stood in mile-long queues in the hot sun, through the late evening. People wept as they filed past. Hundreds chanted holy verses. Thousands kept a vigil outside throughout the night.

On 28 May, Nehru was cremated in accordance with Hindu rites at the Shantivana on the banks of the Yamuna, witnessed by 1.5 million mourners who had flocked into the streets of Delhi and the cremation grounds.[1]

Despite the third consecutive victory of the Congress in 1962, Nehru began to face question mark on his leadership style because of a humiliating defeat in that year's war with China, whom he considered a great friend. It became greater when his Finance Minister Desai imposed heavy taxes on citizens, igniting widespread anger against the Nehru Government. Consequently, Congress lost heavily to three opposition leaders—Ram Manohar Lohia, J.B. Kripalani and Minoo Masani in the Lok Sabha by-elections in 1963. This made Nehru to think rejigging the Party.

Kamaraj was asked to take up the job and suggest ways to get rid of the unpopular leaders. What Kamaraj suggested, came to be known as 'Kamraj Plan.' According to it all senior ministers in the Nehru Government were to resign and go back to the Party and work to win the confidence of the people. He was the first, on October 2, 1963, to offer his resignation and then six cabinet ministers, including Lal Bahadur Shastri, Jagjivan Ram and Morarji Desai and five CMs, including Biju Patnaik, offered their resignations and work for the party. Kamraj became an instant hero and the most-known national figure and a week later he became Congress President. He proved to be one of the most active Presidents of the Party and closely monitored the performance of the Union Ministers and controlled the Party affairs when Nehru's health was falling. On his suggestion, Lal Bahadur Shastri was reinstated as a minister without portfolio, sharing most of

Nehru's responsibilities. He, in fact, became virtually the Deputy PM. It was also made clear by Kamaraj that Shastri would be the probable PM after Nehru and, therefore, he completely ignored Morarji Desai.[2]

The succession battle began soon after Nehru died, 'over Nehru's dead body,' as Krishna Menon later bitterly remarked. At that time, Desai, an ambitious politician, was the tallest leader in the Congress after Nehru. Therefore, he thought that he was the most natural claimant to be Nehru's successor. But he was disliked by both Nehru and the Syndicate for different reasons. Nehru did not approve of Desai's ambitions and his pro-business policies. Syndicate, on the other hand, feared that if Morarji became the Prime Minister he would leave no space for them. Therefore, they outmanoeuvred Desai after the death of Nehru and decided that Shastri, who was mild-mannered and whom Nehru had given many of his responsibilities, would be the next Prime Minister.

Three days after the cremation of Nehru, Shastri, just for formality, had asked Indira to become the Prime Minister. She was approached by other Congress leaders also with the same request. But she point-blank refused to all. By June 1, Shastri was the unanimous choice of the Congress Party to which Desai bowed and did not even accept any ministerial assignment. Soon after swearing in, Shastri realised that he had to have a Nehru in the Council of Ministers to maintain stability. He requested Indira and she accepted the invitation and was appointed Minister for Information and Broadcasting, though for the last two years she was writing to Dorothy Norman (Indira's best friend for 35 years. She first met her when she visited the United States with Jawaharlal Nehru in 1949. Norman was an activist in the India League.) that she was frustrated with politics and wanted to escape India. Then why she agreed to join active politics? It was believed that she needed a job and a house as Nehru had not made any provision for her maintenance after his death. She had already received a notice to leave the Teen Murti house. Reluctant to face an election of Lok Sabha, she was nominated to the Rajya Sabha.[3]

Indira developing into PM

Though India Gandhi was one of the most recognised faces in Indian politics, had international recognition and had a secular image capable of catching minority votes did not remain the most important person in the Congress after she joined the Cabinet. Strangely, though Shastri knew he needed Gandhi's support, he didn't give her much importance as he thought that she would become another power-centre and would endanger his own position. Therefore, he agreed to give her, as desired by her, the Information and Broadcasting Ministry that was quite unimportant at that time and to mollify her gave her fourth position in the Cabinet. But she was kept at a distance and was not consulted in policy-formulation and making important appointments.This made her more and more frustrated causing divisions between Shastri and her which kept on becoming wider and wider as time passed.[4]

She also thought that being Jawaharlal's daughter and having been his aide and confident, Shastri would consult her on all important issues before taking final decision. She, therefore, was upset when Shastri appointed Swaran Singh as the Foreign Minister when she was in London to represent Shastri at the 1964 Commonwealth Prime Ministers' Conference in October 1964.[5] She felt slighted and from this point developed unhappiness towards Shastri, thinking that Shastri was only using her being the daughter of Nehru and was not giving her any powerful political position. With a view to express her annoyance to Shastri that she was more acceptable to foreign nations she went from London to Yugoslavia to meet President Josip Broz Tito and from there to Russia and met the new Prime Minister, Alexei Kosygin. At both the places she was received warmly and her talks with both were reported widely to be very pleasant, constructive and guileless. Later she went to France, USA, Yugoslavia, Canada, Mongolia, Burma and USSR, not much to the liking of Shastri and Swaran Singh.[6]

After showing her annoyance successfully, she began to use every opportunity to put Shastri on the spot for coming into the limelight. The first such opportunity came in January 1965 when on January 26, fifteen years after the promulgation of the Constitution, Hindi became the official language of the nation. Nehru had given an assurance that English would remain official language as long as non-Hindi speaking States would want it. But since Shastri did not take any step and the Constitution provision became operative, widespread riots broke out in Madras (now Chennai) and some people publicly immolating themselves. President Radhakrishnan suggested to Shastri that in the broadcast that he was scheduled to give he should reassure the nation that the promise given by Nehru would be honoured. But he gave no such assurance and the two annoyed Tamilian Union Ministers, C. Subramanian, Minister of Food and Agriculture, and O. V. Alagesan, Minister of State, resigned. Even at that point, Shastri did not hear the advice of the President saying that the Cabinet was unwilling to make any commitment in law and went on to accept the resignations. The President accepted the resignation saying: 'You will lead the country to ruin and disintegration.'[7]

Shastri's silence caused violent demonstrations to continue in Madras. The President got really annoyed when his ancestral house that he had donated to the Tamil Nadu Government, along with a financial endowment, for setting up library and cultural centre, was burnt down. Though Radhakrishnan publicly condemned the violence and said that the rulers should ask themselves whether they had done all they could to avert such unhealthy developments. But the Home Minister Nanda ignored this also.[8]

While Shastri, on the advice from Kamraj, decided to wait and watch hoping that the situation would calm down, Indira Gandhi, took the first available flight to Madras and addressed the violent crowd. In Madras, she spoke to government officials, soothed the anger of community leaders and supervised reconstruction efforts for the affected areas. She told the Tamilians that Hindi would never be imposed on non-Hindi speaking people against their wishes. Shastri was unhappy as she did not consult him before going to Madras and giving the assurance to the people of Tamil Nadu. But her ability in diplomacy and calm in the face of a storm was established.[9] When Inder Malhotra, a journalist, told her about his feelings, she told him that she was not only the I&B Minister, but one of the national leaders. She also said: 'Do you think this Government can survive if I resign today? I am telling you it won't. Yes, I have jumped over the Prime Minister's head and I would do it again whenever the need arises.'[10]

Another opportunity to demean Shastri came in August 1965 when troops of Azad Kashmir Regular Force of Pakistan Army, disguised as locals, entered Jammu and Kashmir from Pakistan to provoke insurgency among Kashmiri Muslims. She was in Srinagar at that time on vacation and was asked to take the return flight as the situation was becoming serious. But she ignored the advice and stayed there. Not only she stayed there, but went to the front areas when the hostilities broke out. The media hailed the bold step by her and wrote that she was the 'only man in a cabinet of old women.' Though she returned to Delhi, she went back to Kashmir next month when the hostilities intensified and addressed a large gathering of Kashmiris in Srinagar telling them that India will not give an inch of her territory to the assailant. Not only that, she went to see the bombed areas on the Punjab border, visited military hospital in Ferozepur and went further to visit Abhor, Fazilka, Ambala, Amritsar and Gurdaspur. At all these places she was hailed by the waiting crowds.[11]

Indira, besides taking the liberty of taking bold political decisions to show that she was more respected than Shastri also formed a cabal who strongly backed her. It included: Dinesh Singh, who was a Minister when she became PM, Ashok Mehta, Deputy Chairman of Planning Commission,

Inder Gujral, who became her trusted fellow and Minister, Satish Gujral, a painter who had painted a portrait of her and Romesh Thapar, a prominent journalist of his times. Dinesh and Inder were always at her command.[12] Interestingly, Inder had become friendly with Indira when Satish was painting a portrait of Indira and he had to sit with her for hours to engage her in conversation as Satish was dumb and deaf. Since then Inder was her closest friend and had a significant influence on her. He was the person to give the last bath to Nehru and draft the resolution to accepting for contesting the election opposing Desai.[13]

When 1965 was ending, before leaving for Tashkent, Shastri skillfully eliminated his finance Minister, T.T. Krishnamachari, from his Cabinet. Indira considered him a friend and supporter and, therefore, was enraged and angrily told many people that she would be the next to be thrown out including Inder Malhotra. By that time, it was widely known that Indira Gandhi's sore relations with Shastri have reached to the point of breaking down.

Whatever Indira Gandhi was talking and doing was reaching to Shastri. He was a highly respectable politician for his unsullied deportments, unpretentious unassuming nature despite having held important and powerful positions in the Government and the Party. Nevertheless, he was indeed a strong and shrewd politician. He once told Inder Malhotra: I am not a *sadhu* (saint).' Both, Shastri and Indira,were politicians of the highest order and this became the main reason for complication in their relationship. He included her in his Cabinet thinking that her presence would give it strength. But he never wanted a strong political rival in his team. So, he began to show her all civilities and put her in all the important committees but never allowed her to be part of his policy-making team. Her reaction of annoyance towards Shastri was natural.[14]

Indira Gandhi was inducted into the Shastri's Cabinet being Nehru's daughter. But as she was accustomed of active political life and was highly respected in the Congress circles as she had considerable influence on Nehru, she was becoming highly frustrated by the political insignificance given to her by Shastri. But when Nehru was becoming politically weak and Shastri was being given importance by Nehru, she was becoming distressed. She began to feel lonely and isolated as she never had before feeling that her political fate in India was uncertain and therefore, she was seriously planning shifting to London for few years.

She is said to have written to her American friend, Dorothy Norman, whom she was very intimate and shared all her problems, that she plans to resign and settle down in London for some years at least. The reason may be that both her sons were in England at that time. Rajiv was studying at

Cambridge and Sanjay was learning about cars at the Rolls-Royce factory at Crewe.[15]

It was also believed that before Shastri left for Tashkent to negotiate peace deal with Pakistan, he too was distressed by the deliberate slights being inflicted by Indira and had almost decided to drop her from his Cabinet. He had offered her to become the High Commissioner in London for which she had agreed. But when she got the news of the sudden death of Shastri in Tashkent, she shelved her plan to move to London. With an eye on the Prime Ministership she made her moves to be in the good book of the Syndicate.[16]

****

It was Tuesday, a dull winter afternoon of January 11, 1966. A huge crowd of senior bureaucrats, selected politicians, high military officers, ambassadors of various countries in Delhi and many reputed citizens were awaiting a small Soviet aircraft at the Palam airport. They were waiting for the dead body of India's second Prime Minister, Lal Bahadur Shastri who had died suddenly in Tashkent, Uzbekistan only hours ago. More than the angst, most of those who mattered, were worried about the uncertainty over India's political future.

Shastri had died in Tashkent in the early hours of January 11 after a fatal heart attack. Indira was sleeping and was woken up by N. K. Seshan, her Secretary, to inform her the death of Shastri. He also told her that Nanda, the Home Minister, was also informed about the death of Shastri and he had gone to the Rashtrapati Bhawan to take the oath of the acting PM. She called for her car and dashed to the President's house. The Finance Minister, Sachindra Chaudhuri was already there. Nanda was sworn in as the acting Prime Minister in the early morning hours at 3:15 a.m.

When back at home, she rang up Romesh Thapar to come to her house straightaway. By now she was in touch with most of her advisors and all told her to compete for power this time. Thapar, instead of giving a definite advice asked her: 'What do you feel like doing.'

'Nothing,' was her reply.[17]

Thereafter, she wanted to know on whose side was the President. Therefore, a few hours later at 8:15, she went back to Rashtrapati Bhavan and told him that Nanda got in touch with her to enquire if she were interested in becoming the PM. Radhakrishnan replied: 'When your father was Prime Minister, I was against your being appointed a minister. Thereafter, I was for your joining the Cabinet. Now I am in favour for your being prime

Minister. We will all help you.' Feeling that she was not willing, he advised her: 'keep quiet, don't say yes or no.'[18] Radhakrishnan, in fact, besides advising Indira Gandhi on the timing of crucial moves, talked privately to many key Congress leaders and informed Indira of those who supported her.[19]

This indicates it was not true that she was not interested in the powerful position of the Prime Minister of India. She only wanted to be persuaded and not to ask for the PM's position.

Nineteen months later, the Syndicate and Desai were in 'as-you-were' situation; locked in the same struggle once again. In the post-Nehru situation there were only two contestants for PM's position, but this time the dynamics was entirely different as there were many contenders for prime ministership.[20] This made the situation grimmer because Shastri's death was sudden and bewildering whereas Nehru was suffering for a long time and his end was expected any time.

Four persons had joined the race of prime ministership. Besides Nanda, Morarji Desai, Indira Gandhi was also willing. So was Yashwantrao Chavan, who was Chief Minister of Maharashtra and Nehru had appointed him the Defence Minister after Menon's resignation. Radhakrishnan was not in favour of Nanda, Desai and Chavan. Nanda, he thought, was too limited, while Desai was too rigid and narrow, though he liked him personally. Chavan in his view had not proved to be good in Delhi and was a case of over-promotion. Though he thought little of her intellectual abilities, like Zakir Hussain, the Vice-President of India at that time, he felt that she had grown in stature and political imagination. Her going to the south at the time of a severe crisis had impressed him. So, he decided to support her and worked for her silently behind the scenes without compromising the dignity of his office.[21]

Soon a negative consensus began to develop against Nanda and Desai, both were determined to contest. Rajagopalachari, was in favour of Nanda and wanted him to remain the PM for at least one year. When Indira Gandhi was approached, she said that it was for the Party to decide. Radhakrishnan sent her a message that she should informally give her consent. Kamraj, who was in favour of Indira, passed a word around that the President's advice was that they should choose 'the best broad-minded person' without taking her name. But it was obvious to everyone whom he was referring to.[22]

Shastri was selected by the Syndicate hoping that he would be obliged to them and would consult them before taking any decision. But Shastri grew into a strong, independent leader, weakening the Syndicate's presumption that they were the lone puppet-masters in Delhi. Therefore, being not very happy with Shastri, the Syndicate wanted to be doubly sure that this time they would not be taken for a ride. After considering various names, Kamaraj was sure that the Syndicate would be successful in controlling Indira Gandhi and they would be able to be the power behind the throne. He was also sure that she would be 'pliable, weak … a lump of clay they could mould and remould according to need.' He also realised that she could be the only possible challenger to Desai because she had widespread respect in the Congress because of legacy of Nehru and name recognition that no one else did. Also, the next general elections were right around the corner, and they needed a Prime Minister who could win the elections for the Congress. But most importantly, the Syndicate no longer had a viable candidate like Shastri to challenge Desai's stature. Indira Gandhi was not a strong leader and, therefore, would need his support to run the country. He thought that he would control her through Congress committees and institutions all of which were ruled by the Syndicate.[23]

A significant development, that fully tilted the balance in favour of Indira Gandhi, happened four days before the election of the leader of the Congress Legislative Party when on January 15, eight Chief Ministers came forward to support her. Keeping all these factors in mind, Kamraj mustered his considerable influence and got her endorsements from most of the state Chief Ministers and eventually all the members of the Syndicate. Mrs. Gandhi, with such strong support behind her, became the strongest candidate to challenge Desai.

Desai, believing his long-standing work in the Congress Party, became adamant not to surrender easily and decided to fight through. He, therefore, asked for an open election within the Congress of all the MPs of the party. Syndicate members mobilised their home states and provided support to Mrs. Gandhi from their southern states, Maharashtra and West Bengal. Desai could only get support from his home state of Gujarat and the small factions from Bihar and Uttar Pradesh. The Congress Presidents from the eight supporting States managed their State's MPs votes from the lawns in the Parliament House.

Wednesday, January 19, the day the Congress Parliamentary Party was to elect its leader, was a cold misty day. Indira Gandhi got up early to get ready for the D-day (Designated Day when operations are due to commence) and carefully dressed up. She wore a white *Khadi* sari, that she had worn when she became the Congress President and, a string of dark brown beads, favourite talisman that she often wore in critical situations. The beads were given to her by Anandamayi, a Bengali saint and her mother Kamla Nehru's spiritual guru. She also wrapped a plain Kashmiri shawl. Then, before the traffic became dense, she left her bungalow at 1, Safdarjung Road to Rajghat and Shantivana, Gandhiji's and Nehru's cremation sites and prayed silently. After doing all this, she went to Teen Murti, where Nehru lived as PM and died and she walked silently in the corridors and stood silently before the portrait of her father. From there she went to Parliament House with Nanda and Subhadra Joshi, her bosom friend. Before entering the Parliament, she was presented flower bouquet from which Joshi plucked a red rose and pinned it to Indira's shawl. Then she entered the Parliament and later came out of it as India's new Prime Minister.[24]

The members of the Congress Parliamentary Party had gathered in full force by 11 in the morning when the election was to commence. The election by secret ballot began on dot and continued for four-and-a half-hours. When Indira's turn came for voting, she moved up to Desai and asked if he would vote. When he replied in negative, she also did not vote. When the 526 votes were counted, Indira Gandhi defeated Morarji Desai by 355-169 votes. After the counting was over and the result was declared, the Chief Whip of the Congress appeared on the balcony to announce the results to the waiting crowd, someone shouted: 'Is it a boy or a girl?' Á girl,' was said in reply and the crown roared with loud applause.[25]

After the result was announced, Indira Gandhi walked up to the podium and addressed the Congress MPs in Hindi: 'My heart is full and I do not know how to thank you…As I stand before you my thoughts go back to the great leaders: Mahatma Gandhi, at whose feet I grew up, Panditji, my father, and Lal Bahadur Shastri. These leaders have shown the way, and I want to go the same path.' Before leaving the Central Hall, she performed another act of deference when she went to Desai and with folded hands she said: 'Will you bless my success.'

Desai gave the curt reply: 'I give you my blessings.'

As she moved out of the Parliament House, the waiting crowd applauded her with slogans, 'Indira Gandhi Zindabad' (long live Indira Gandhi) and 'Lal Gulab Zindabad (Long live the red rose). It showed that people adored her perceiving her to be the progeny of Nehru.[26]

Five days later, on January 24, she was sworn in as the Prime Minister of India.

Desai was broken-heart because he was denied the prime ministership second time and this time by a lady who was thought to be a weak person.

In early 1960s, Desai was the most influential Congress leader, a centre of power within the Congress Party. He had emerged a strong right-leaning and pro-business conservative leader and had become an opposing pole within the party to left-leaning, liberal Nehru. When he was the Finance Minister in Nehru's cabinet, he had become so influential that many Congressmen thought that he was Nehru's expected successor. So strong was this view that during some of his foreign visits he was treated like a visiting head of state. Fearing that he would become his successor, Nehru had diplomatically eased him out of the Cabinet in 1963, through 'Kamraj Plan.' If that was not done, he definitely would have become the next Prime Minister automatically.

****

Epilogue

Narendra Modi and Indira Gandhi, no doubt, would remain two strong personalities as prime ministers, till a third one arrives on the Indian scene. A study and analysis of these two strong personalities was indeed interesting and revealing because the two came from two different directions, had different personalities and followings, had different upbringings, were differently trained for the political management and became the prime minister differently.

Modi was born in a large middle-class family and lived in an ordinary environment of a small town in western India. His was an on-the-street-family about whom no one was aware of in the town. It was a large family living in a small dingy house. It was so short of resources that his mother worked as house help in the neighborhood families and Modi had to work with his father and also pursue his studies. The family was nowhere near the power-Centre, not even the junior-most bureaucrat in the town. He went to an ordinary school in the town and could not attend the college after finishing the school. But, at the instigation of his mentor, Vakil Saab, he completed graduation and post-graduation through correspondence courses.

Indira was born in a small politically powerful, affluent and aristocratic family in a large metropolitan in northern India. She was brought up like a patrician should be brought up— raised by an English governess, ate food prepared by an English cook and moved in an imported perambulator. She attended the uppermost exclusive schools in India and Europe but never graduated, and made no efforts to graduate later, though Oxford honored her with an Honorary Doctorate in 1971. She became interested in dance and music while at Santiniketan.

The patriarch of the family, Motilal Nehru and her father Jawaharlal Nehru, were a name that every Indian was aware of. The family, right from its beginning in Delhi in 1716, was close to power—first the Mughals, then the British and finally the Congress, where her grandfather and father held top position. She also followed her father. It was a family of which every Indian, since the beginning of the freedom movement, was proud of whereas Modi's family lived in obscurity and oblivion.

Indira was greatly attached with her father, particularly after the death of her mother. She became his aid-de-com and looked after his household which became a cause of conflict between Feroze and her. She not only helped him in his political work but also accompanied him around the world assisting him with his political endeavours. Modi, it seems, had not much attachment with his father; he was rather too close to his mother whom he adored and loved. Still he often goes to meet her whenever he can.

Indira got her political training under her grandfather and father by actively participating in the freedom movement. Even as a child she organised a *vanar sena* (monkey brigade) to assist Congress volunteers in their political activities. She also travelled with her father to attend various Congress sessions. She was also close to Mahatma Gandhi whom she respected enormously. After the death of Nehru, she joined the Cabinet of Lal Bahadur Shastri and actively participated in political crises in Kashmir and Madras (now Tamil Nadu), much to the annoyance of Shastri.

Modi got his political training under the guidance of a staunch and much respected RSS pracharak, Vakil Saab, under whose guidance he joined RSS at the age of eight. He worked intensively and intimately for this disciplined organisation and inculcated its value-system. When assigned to the BJP, he became closer to the top BJP leadership at the State and Central levels. Organising Advani's Somnath to Ayodhya *Rath Yatra* established his credentials as an ace organiser and brought him closer to journalists. Later he organised Murli Manohar Joshi's Rath Yatra to Kashmir and his own Gaurav *Rath Yatras* in Gujarat. The 2001 Kutch earthquake brought him to the lime light when he effectively and efficiently organised the relief work operations while the State Government failed to look after the titanic devastation.

Indira, it may be said, was an accidental prime minister. When Nehru died, she was not considered eligible to become the Prime Minister by the powerful syndicate that had emerged when Nehru was becoming weak. Shastri had decided to get rid of her by sending her to UK as High Commissioner. If he had lived for another few years, Indira would never have become the PM. After the death of Shastri, she was chosen by the syndicate because it did not want Morarji Desai to get the PM's position. Also, she was considered pliable, though she proved it wrong. Moreover, powerful persons like President Radhakrishnan helped her to become the Prime Minister. In a way, she became the Prime Minister, being the daughter of Nehru and made not much efforts to get the position. In fact, it was being born in the Nehru family that made her the PM.

Modi reached to the ultimate political position by dint of his hard work and going through the various processes of knowing the people, their problems and aspirations. He left home at the age of 18 and for two years criss-crossed the country living like an ordinary man and meeting a large number of people. Later he joined the RSS at the lowest level and slowly moved upwards. He involved himself in organising various political activities and managing a number of crises, the last one was the relief work to Kutch quack sufferers. Then working for 12 years as the Chief Minister of Gujarat provided him excellent opportunity to prove his metal. No doubt he was selected by the RSS-BJP combine to contest the 2014 election as the prime ministerial candidate.

Modi and Indira, both strong willed and powerful personalities can be called history-makers of India. *India Today* magazine published a cover story in 2003, on '56 events that changed India.' One of the 56 events was *'Indira Gandhi defeats Morarji Desai to become P.M. in 1966,'* and declared that: 'She was the last of the strong leaders.'[1] The story went wrong at this point because 48 years later another strong leader, Narendra Modi became equally strong, if not stronger, than her. In fact, another survey by the same magazine in 2018, placed Indira Gandhi the second-best Prime Minister, with 20 per cent votes and Narendra Modi the best ever PM with 26 per cent votes.[2]

Knowing the personalities of Narendra Modi and Indira Gandhi is interesting as well as illuminating. Learning about their upbringing, education, family life and political life will make one to understand their prime ministership better.

References

Chapter one: Early Life of Narendra Modi

1. *Narendra Modi: Facts from His Childhood, Avinandan Choudhury, National Views; May 12, 2015; http://nationalviews.com/narendra-modi-biography-childhood-facts; Success Story Of Narendra Modi; The Journey From Being A Tea Vendor To The Prime Minister Of India; http://smilepls.com/stories/inspirational-stories/success-story-of-narendra-modi.html*
2. *Narendra Modi: Facts from His Childhood, Avinandan Choudhury, National Views; May 12, 2015; http://nationalviews.com/narendra-modi-biography-childhood-facts;*
3. Parsis - the Zoroastrians of India, SooniTaraporevala, the-south-asian.com; http://www.the-south-asian.com/april2001/Parsis-Arrival%20in%20India.htm
4. *Ibid.*
5. *Ibid.*
6. Gujarati showed Vasco 'da' way, The Times of India, October 3, 2010; https://timesofindia.indiatimes.com/city/ahmedabad/Gujarati-showed-Vasco-da-way/articleshow/6674395.cms; The Emperor Uncrowned: The rise of Narendra Modi, Vinod K Jose, Caravan Magazine, March 1, 2012.
7. *Caravan Magazine, opt. cit.*
8. Story of Vadnagar that PM Narendra Modi talked about at his birthplace in Gujarat, Prabhash K. Datta, India Today, October 8, 2017; https://www.indiatoday.in/india/story/vadnagar-narendra-modi-gujarat-hiuen-tsang-xi-jinping-xian-1060300-2017-10-08.
9. Caravan Magazine, opt. cit;The Childhood Years That Shaped Prime Minister Narendra Modi, Sudesh Verma, Huffington Post, September 16, 2016;http://www.huffingtonpost.in/sudesh-verma-/the-childhood-years-that-shaped-prime-minister-narendra-modi_a_21473370/
10. PM Narendra Modi: My brother and I kept the chulha going when my mother went out to work, India Today, January 9, 2019; https://www.indiatoday.in/trending-news/story/pm-narendra-modi-my-brother-and-i-kept-the-chulha-going-when-my-mother-went-out-to-work-1427157-2019-01-09.
11. National Views, opt. cit.
12. India Today, January 9, 2019.
13. Andy Marino, Narendra Modi: A Political Biography, pp. 17-19.

14. Caravan Magazineopt. cit.)
15. *Ibid.*
16. *Avinandan Choudhury, opt. cit.*
17. *Andy Marino, opt. cit.* pp. 16-17; *Nilanjan Mukhopadhyay, Narendra Modi: The Man, The Times, p. 30;* Avinandan Choudhury, opt. cit.
18. Caravan Magazine, opt.cit.
19. Andy Marino, opt. cit. p. 17; smilepls.com, opt. cit.
20. *Sudesh Verma, opt. cit.*
21. *Financial Express, February* 2, 2014.
22. In an interview to ETV; https://www.youtube.com/playlist?list=PLsPgF1U5iQ1AkT52MqycWCFI8RRmBvhlB
23. Andy Marino, opt. cit. p. 29.
24. Kamath and Randeri, Narendra Modi: The Architect of Modern India, p. 19.
25. Modi met him in 2013 in Belur Math in Kolkata and thanked him for his guidance. Swami died on 18 June 2017.
26. *Andy Marino, opt. cit. p. 27*
27. *Ibid, 25-28.*
28. *Ibid, p. 24.*
29. *Ibid, p. 29.*
30. Caravan Magazine, opt. cit.
31. Andy Marino, opt. cit. pp. 34-35
32. Caravan Magazine, opt. cit.

Chapter Two: Indira Gandhi Early Life

1. *Jawaharlal Nehru, An Autobiography, p.1; Katherine Frank, Indira: The Life of Indira Nehru Gandhi, pp.5-6; Lineage of the Nehru family; http://www.ikashmir.net/bnsharga/doc/Pt%20Bansi%20Dhar%20Nehru.pdf*
2. *Lineage of the Nehru family*
3. *KatherineFrank, opt. cit. pp. 6-7;* http://www.indiaonline.in/about/Personalities/Freedom-Fighters/Motilal-Nehru.html
4. *Ibid.* pp. 8-9.
5. *Ibid,* p. 14.
6. *Ibid.* p. 28.
7. *Ibid,* p. 15.
8. *Ibid,* p. 26.
9. *Ibid,* pp. 36-37.
10. *Ibid,* p. 38.
11. *Ibid,* p. 48.
12. *Indira Gandhi, Anand Bhawan Memories,* p. 13.
13. *Katherine Frank, opt. cit.* pp. 51-52
14. Katherine Frank, opt. cit. pp. 74-75

15. *Shanta Gandhi, 'When Indira was a student,' G. Parthasarthi and H. Y. Prasad, (eds), Indira Gandhi: Statesman, Scholars, Scientists and Friends Remember,* p. 185.
16. Katherine Frank, opt. cit. p. 89.
17. India after Gandhi: The History of the World's Largest Democracy, Ramachandra Guha, 2011, p. 809.
18. *Katherine Frank, opt. cit.* p. 91.
19. *Katherine Frank, opt. cit.* p. 118.
20. *Ibid.* p. 120.
21. *Ibid,* p. 121.
22. *Ibid,* p. 122.
23. *Ibid,* p. 130.
24. *Ibid,* p. 130.
25. Hindustan Times, 15 July 2017.
26. Katherine Frank, opt. cit. p. 139.
27. Indira Gandhi, What I Am, p. 25.
28. Sonia Gandhi (ed.) Two Alone, Two Together: Letters Between Indira Gandhi and Jawaharlal Nehru, p. 94.
29. Katherine Frank, opt. cit. p. 164.
30. Katherine Frank, opt. cit. p. 169.
31. https://blogs.timesofindia.indiatimes.com/bloody-mary/19th-november-2017-100-years-of-indira-gandhi-she-was-the-mother-of-every-indian-supremo/

Chapter Three: Modi: Political life in Making

1. *Narendra Modi, Jyotipunj, Ahmedabad, Pravin Prakashan,* 2008.
2. *Andy Marino, Narendra Modi:* p. 17.
3. *Ibid,* p. 30.
4. *The man behind Modi: Lakshmanrao Inamdar, Snadeep Unnithan, India Today, May 19, 2014; https://www.indiatoday.in/magazine/the-big-story/story/20140519-narendra-modi-lakshmanrao-inamdar-rss-802639-1999-11-30.*
5. *Caravan Magazine, opt. cit.*
6. *Nilanjan Mukhopadhyay, Narendra Modi: The Man, The Times,* p. 111.
7. *Andy Marino, opt. cit.* p. 36.
8. *Ibid,* p. 36.
9. *Nilanjan Mukhopadhyay, opt. cit.* p. 112.
10. *Snadeep Unnithan, India Today, May 19, 2014.*
11. *Immersed in Nation building from a very Young Age: Dedicated Life; https://www.narendramodi.in/the-activist-3129, May 23, 2014.*
12. *Caravan Magazine, opt. cit.*
13. *Unnithan, opt. cit. India Today.*
14. *Ibid, opt. cit.*
15. *Andy Mario, pt. cit.* p. 41.

16. *Chanakya Mehta, 'Emergency, Gujaratand Narendra Modi, www.narendramodi.in:citizen journalism, January 26, 2012; and, https://www.narendramodi.in/innovative-field-organizer-an-example-from-1980s-gujarat-522799.*
17. *Kamath and Randeri, opt. cit.* p. 30.
18. *Mukhopadhyay, opt. cit.*, p. 123.
19. *https://www.narendramodi.in/innovative-field-organizer-an-example-from-1980s-gujarat-522799*
20. *Andy Marino, opt. sit.*, p. 67.
21. *Andy Marino, opt. cit.*, pp. 67-68.
22. *Prashant Dayal, 'Latif was state BJP's first whipping boy,' The Times of India, June 12, 2008; https://timesofindia.indiatimes.com/city/ahmedabad/Latif-was-state-BJPs-first-whipping-boy/articleshow/3121443.cms?referral=PM*
23. *Ibid.*
24. *Rajdeep Sardesai, 2014: The Election That Changed India,* pp. 5-6.
25. *Caravan, opt. cit.*
26. *Andy Marino, opt. cit.* pp. 80-83.
27. *M. V. Kameth and Kalindi Randeri, Narendra Modi: The Architect of a Modern State,* p. 12.
28. *Andy Marino, opt. cit.* p. 86.
29. *Ibid,* p. 86.
30. *Kingshuk Nag, The NaMo Story: A Political Life,* p. 61.
31. *Rajdeep Sardesai, opt. cit.* p. 7.
32. *Andy Marino, opt. cit.* p. 87.
33. *Ibid,* pp. 87-88.
34. *Ibid,* p.10.
35. Ibid, p. 11.
36. *Ibid,* p. 90
37. *Ibid,* p. 90.
38. *Rajdeep Sardesai, opt. cit.*, pp. 8-11.
39. *Ibid.* pp. 9-10.
40. *Andy Marino, opt. cit.* pp. 91-91.
41. *Swapan Dasgupta,Gujarat earthquake: Gujarat CM Keshubhai Patel hard-pressed to explain sluggish response," India Today, February 12, 2001, https://www.indiatoday.in/magazine/cover-story/story/20010212-gujarat-earthquake-gujarat-cm-keshubhai-patel-hardpressed-to-explain-sluggish-response-775759-2001-02-12*
42. *Summer of '93: Check out young Narendra Modi hanging out in US*

    Firstpost, September 28, 2014;

    http://www.firstpost.com/world/summer-of-93-check-out-young-narendra-modi-hanging-out-in-us-1730697.html

    43. *Modi's Tryst with America: From Sangh Parivar Pracharak in 1990s to Indian PM By : Mugdha Variyar September 26, 2014, International Business*

Times http://www.ibtimes.co.in/modis-tryst-america-sangh-parivar-pracharak-1990s-indian-pm-610015

44. Ibid.
45. *Meet the future Prime Minister of India, they said at MIT, 25-09-2014, Uday Mahurkar, Daily O, https://www.dailyo.in/politics/scenes-from-modis-us-its/story/1/218.html*
46. *International Business Times, opt. cit.*
47. *Chidanand Rajghatta, Opt. cit., The Times of India, September 26, 2014.*
48. *Summer of '93: Check out young Narendra Modi hanging out in US, Firstpost, September 28, 2014, http://www.firstpost.com/world/summer-of-93-check-out-young-narendra-modi-hanging-out-in-us-1730697.html*
49. *http://post.jagran.com/peoples-blessings-wont-go-waste-narendra-modi-on-his-birthday-1379392038*
50. *http://news.bbc.co.uk/onthisday/hi/dates/stories/january/26/newsid_4666000/4666568.stm*
52. Ibid.
53. *How the 2001 earthquake changed Gujarat forever, Scroll.in, December, 01, 17;https://scroll.in/article/676529/how-the-2001-earthquake-changed-gujarat-forever*
54. *Gujarat Government's confused response to earthquake relief operations adds to loss and pain, Uday Mahurkar and Supriya Bezbaruah, India Today, February 19, 2001; https://www.indiatoday.in/magazine/states/story/20010219-gujarat-government-confused-response-to-earthquake-relief-operations-adds-to-loss-and-pain-775718-2001-02-19.*
55. *Gujarat Government's confused response to earthquake relief operations adds to loss and pain, Uday Mahurkar and Supriya Bezbaruah, India Today, February 19, 2001; https://www.indiatoday.in/magazine/states/story/20010219-gujarat-government-confused-response-to-earthquake-relief-operations-adds-to-loss-and-pain-775718-2001-02-19.*

    https://www.indiatoday.in/magazine/cover-story/story/20010212-gujarat-earthquake-gujarat-cm-keshubhai-patel-hardpressed-to-explain-sluggish-response-775759-2001-02-12.
56. *A Life Less Relieved, Davinder Kumar, Outlook, February 19, 2001: https://www.outlookindia.com/magazine/story/a-life-less-relieved/210882*
57. *Ibid.*

Chapter Four: Political Training of Indira

1. *Katherine Frank, Indira: The Life of Indira Nehru Gandhi, p. 17;* Indiadotonline.in, *http://www.indiaonline.in/about/Personalities/Freedom-Fighters/Motilal-Nehru.html*
2. *Katherine Frank, opt. cit.* pp. 21-22.
3. *Indira Gandhi, My Truth,* p. 22.
4. *Katherine Frank, opt. cit.* p. 60.
5. *Sonia Gandhi (ed), Freedom's Daughter,* p. 116, pp. 119-120.

6. *Katherine Frank, opt. cit.* p. 89.
7. *Ibid,* p. 90
8. *Jawaharlal Nehru, Autobiography,* p. 561.
9. *Sonia Gandhi, opt. cit.* p. 124-125.
10. *Katherine Frank, opt. cit.* p. 92.
11. *Ibid,* p. 95
12. S. Gopal (ed.), Selected Works of Jawaharlal Nehru I, p. 306-307 & 310.
13. *Katherine Frank, opt. cit.* p. 103.
14. *Ibid,* p. 106.
15. *Ibid,* p. 107.
16. Ibid, p. 110-111.
17. Ibid, p. 111.
18. *Ibid,* p. 114.
19. *Jawaharlal Nehru, The Discovery of India,* p. 43.
20. *Kathrine Frank, opt. cit.* p. 122-123.
21. TheSpanish Civil War from 1936 to 1939 between Republicans loyal to the left-leaning Second Spanish Republic, in alliance with the Anarchists and Communists and the Nationalists, a Falangist, Carlist, Catholic, and largely aristocratic group led by General Francisco Franco. It was a struggle between democracy and fascism, particularly due to the political climate and timing surrounding it. In early 1939, the Nationalists achieved victory, and ruled Spain until Franco's death in November 1975.
22. THE WIRE, May 22, 2016,https://thewire.in/37202/80-years-later-a-homage-to-catalonia-indians-and-the-spanish-civil-war
23. *Sonia Gandhi, Freedom's Daughter,* pp. 389-390.
24. *Katherine Frank, Indira: The Life of Indira Nehru Gandhi,* p. 138.
25. *Indira Gandhi, Remembered Moments,* p. 27.
26. Katherine Frank, opt. cit. p. 129.
27. *S. Gopal, Selected Works of Jawaharlal Nehru I,* p. 589-590.
28. *Arnold Michaelis, 'An interview with Indira Gandhi,'* p. 189; *Nayantara Sahgal, Prison and Chocolate Cake,* pp. 99-100.
29. *S. Gopal, opt. cit.* p. 457.
30. *Sonia Gandhi, opt. cit.,* p. 188.
31. Katherine Frank, pt. cit. p. 202-3.
32. *Ibid.* p. 204.
33. *Ibid.* p. 214.
34. Indira Gandhi, My Truth, p. 59.
35. *Ibid.* p. 70-71.
36. *Katherine Frank, opt. cit.* p. 229.
37. *B. K. Nehru, Nice Guys Finish Second,* p. 26.
38. Dorothy Norman (ed), Indira Gandhi: Letters to an American Friend, 1950-1984.

39. *Anand Mohan, Indira Gandhi,* pp. 203-205.
40. Katherine Frank, opt. cit., pp. 245-246.
41. *Ibid,* p. 239.
42. Sonia Gandhi (ed.), To Alone, Two Together, p. 614.
43. *Katherine Frank, opt. cit.* p. 241.
44. Sonia Gandhi (ed.), opt. cit. p. 616.
45. *Katherine Frank, opt. cit.* p. 241.
46. *Sonia Gandhi, opt. cit.* p. 619.
47. *Ibid,* p. 623.
48. Indira Gandhi, My Truth, p. 115.
49. *Katherine Frank, opt. cit.* p. 251.
50. *Ibid,* pp. 249-250.
51. Bertil Falk, Feroze Gandhi: The Forgotten Gandhi, pp. 251-252.
52. Uma Vasudev, Indira Gandhi, p. 276.
53. *S. Gopal, Jawaharlal Nehru III,* p. 59.
54. Katherine Frank, opt. cit. p.253)
55. *Ibid,* p. 253.
56. Ibid, opt. cit. pp. 255-256.
57. *Dorothy Norman (ed.), opt. cit.* p. 63.
58. *Sonia Gandhi. Opt. cit.* pp. 627-628.
59. *Ibid,* p. 59.
60. *Ibid.* p. 258.
61. *Ibid.* pp. 258-259.
62. PupulJayakar, Indira Gandhi, p. 187.
63. Katherine Frank, opt. cit. p. 267.
64. Ibid, opt. cit. pp. 279-280.
65. *Ibid.* p. 267.
66. *Ibid.* p. 281; *Inder Malhotra, Indira Gandhi,* p. 84.
67. Katherine Frank, opt. cit. p. 282.
68. Ibid, pp. 284-285.

Chapter Five: Modi Becoming PM

1. From Chaiwallah to Chief Minister: Modi's eventful journey, Ritika Katyal, Foreign Policy, June 24,2014; https://foreignpolicy.com/2014/06/25/from-chaiwallah-to-chief-minister-modis-eventful-journey
2. *Frontline, October 21, 2001, A new oarsman, Dionne Bunsha; https://frontline.thehindu.com/static/html/fl1821/18210300.htm*
3. India Today, Gujarat earthquake: Gujarat CM Keshubhai Patel hard-pressed to explain sluggish response, Swapan Dasgupta, February 12, 2001; https://www.indiatoday.in/magazine/cover-story/story/20010212-gujarat-earthquake-gujarat-cm-keshubhai-patel-hardpressed-to-explain-sluggish-response-775759-2001-02-12

4. BJP jettisons Keshubhai Patel in bid to keep party from sinking in next Gujarat elections, Uday Mahurkar, India Today, October 15, 2001; https://www.indiatoday.in/magazine/states/story/20011015-bjp-jettisons-keshubhai-patel-in-bid-to-keep-party-from-sinking-in-next-gujarat-elections-774405-2001-10-15)
5. New Chief Minister likely, The Hindu, Neena Vyas, September 27, 2001;https://www.thehindu.com/thehindu/2001/09/27/stories/1427206a.htm
6. Frontline, A New Oarsman, Dionne Bunsha, October 13-26, 2001; https://frontline.thehindu.com/static/html/fl1821/18210300.htm
7. *Andy Marino, Narendra* Modi.
8. Dillichhod do: When Vajpayee asked Narendra Modi to leave Delhi, India Today, Prabhash K Dutta, August 17, 2018; https://www.indiatoday.in/india/story/dilli-chhod-do-when-vajpayee-asked-narendra-modi-to-leave-delhi-1316702-2018-08-17.
9. *Narendra Modi – Leading the race to 7 RCR, Zee News.* 8 April 2014.
10. *Modi sworn in Gujarat CM amidst fanfare. The Hindu, October 7, 2001Dasgupta, Manas; The Emperor Uncrowned: The rise of Narendra Modi, Vinod K Jose, Caravan Magazine,* March 1, 2012.
11. Modi sworn in Gujarat CM amidst fanfare, Manas Dasgupta, The Hindu, October 8, 2001; http://www.thehindujobs.com/thehindu/2001/10/08/stories/02080001.htm
12. Ibid.
13. Caravan, Opt. Cit.
14. A victory and many pointers, Venkatesan, V. Frontline, March 1, 2002; https://www.frontline.in/static/html/fl1905/19050240.htm
15. *Caravan, opt. cit.*
16. Ibid, opt. cit.
17. *Andy Marino. Opt. Cit.* p. 104.
18. *Commission of Inquiry Report of Justice G.T. Nanavati& Justice Akshay H. Mehta ("Justice Nanavati Report" for short further below): p. 71-84: 97-125; p.86: 128; p.89-90: 130; p.170: 223; p.172: 226-27; p.174-175: 229; the integral text is available on the website of the Gujarat Government: http://home.gujarat.gov.in/homedepartment/downloads/godharaincident.pdf*
19. *Andy Marino, opt. cit.* pp. 105-106.
20. Ibid. pp. 107-108.
21. Ibid. p. 110.
22. Godhra: The True Story, Nicole Elfi, http://www.jaia-bharati.org/nicole-elfi/ni-godhra-ang.htm
23. *India Today, March 18, 2002; https://www.indiatoday.in/magazine/cover-story/story/20020318-gujarat-riots-is-narendra-modi-the-villain-who-allowed-mobs-to-seek-revenge-for-godhra-795729-1999-11-30*
24. *Ibid.*
25. *Ibid.*

26. *Caravan, opt. cit.*
27. Ibid.
28. Ibid.
29. *Andy Marino, opt. cit.* p. 142; *Huffpost*, August 16, 2016; https://www.huffingtonpost.in/2018/08/16/watch-how-modi-reacted-when-atal-bihari-vajpayee-reportedly-rapped-him-over-the-gujarat-riots-in-2002_a_23503197/; The Untold Vajpayee: Politician and Paradox, N P Ullekh, pp. 231-232.
30. *Scroll.in, How AB Vajpayee was foiled in his bid to have Narendra Modi removed as Gujarat chief ministerhttps://scroll.in/article/826433/how-ab-vajpayee-was-foiled-in-his-bid-to-have-narendra-modi-removed-as-gujarat-chief-minister; The Untold Vajpayee: Politician and Paradox, by Ullekh NP pp. 231-233U.*
31. N P Ullekh, opt. cit. p. 235.
32. *This was told to me by one of the BJP leaders who attended the Goa meeting in April 2002 in Delhi.*
33. *Caravan, opt. cit.*
34. *Andy Mario, opt. cit.* p. 149.
35. *Ibid,* p. 153.
36. *Ibid,* p. 155.
37. *Ibid,* p. 155.
38. India Today, 4 November 2002, https://www.indiatoday.in/magazine/states/story/20021104-narendra-modi-gaurav-yatra-acquires-sharper-political-edge-as-gujarat-polls-draw-near-794431-2002-11-04
39. *Ibid.*
40. *Ibid.*
41. Andy Marino, opt. cit. p. 159.
42. *Ibid,* p. 160.
43. *Ibid,* p. 162.
44. *https://in.reuters.com/article/india-modi-gujarat-bjp/special-report-the-remaking-of-narendra-modi-idINDEE96B00Y20130712*
45. *Andy Mario, opt. cit.* p. 166.
46. *Ibid,* p. 165.
47. *Narendra Modi Development model of Gujarat, LBDON, 28/4/2014, http://www.jbdon.com/narendra-modi-development-model-of-gujarat*
48. *Andy Mario, opt. cit.* p. 173.
49. *Ibid,* p. 174.
50. *Jabdon.com, opt. cit.)*
51. *Andy Mario, opt. cit.* p. 174.
52. *Ibid,* p. 176.
53 *Ibid,* p. 177.
54. *Ibid,* p. 240.
55. *Muslim businessmen in Gujarat no longer shunning Modi, Anilesh S Mahajan, India Today, December 12, 2013; https://www.indiatoday.in/india/west/story/*

narendra-modi-gujarat-riots-muslims-2014-lok-sabha-polls-220541-2013-12-12.

56. *Ibid.*
57. *Reuters, Special Report: The remaking of Narendra Modi,South Asia Review, July 12, 2013, https://in.reuters.com/article/india-modi-gujarat-bjp/special-report-the-remaking-of-narendra-modi-idINDEE96B00Y20130712*
58. *Andy Mario, opt. cit.* p. 195-196.
59. *Ibid.*
60. *Andy Mario, opt. cit.* p. 195-196.
61. *Understanding Panchamrut - Modi's Governance Philosophy,* Krishnarjun; https://swarajyamag.com/commentary/understanding-panchamrut-modis-governance-philosophy
62. WSJ, August 29, 2012; https://blogs.wsj.com/indiarealtime/2012/08/29/qa-gujarat-chief-minister-narendra-modi/
63. Ibid.
64. jabdon.com
65. *https://www.business-standard.com/article/economy-policy/jyoti-gram-yojna-to-help-rural-development-103122301073_1.html*
66. jabdon.com
67. *The Economic Times, November 13, 2006; //economictimes.indiatimes.com/articleshow/420963.cms?utm_source=contentofinterest&utm_medium=text&utm_campaign=cppst*
68. *Business Today, February 5, 2012; https://www.businesstoday.in/magazine/case-study/gujarats-power-sector-turnaround-story/story/21750.html*
69. *Hindu Businessline, February 5, 2012;* *https://www.businesstoday.in/magazine/case-study/gujarats-power-sector-turnaround-story/story/21750.html*
70. jabdon.com
71. *Why Gujarat's power story is hard to replicate, Sudheer Pal Singh, Business Standard, June 18, 2014; https://www.business-standard.com/article/economy-policy/why-gujarat-s-power-story-is-hard-to-replicate-114061801337_1.html*
72. *Understanding Panchamrut - Modi's Governance Philosophy,* Krishnarjun; https://swarajyamag.com/commentary/understanding-panchamrut-modis-governance-philosophy
73. *Ibid.*
74. *Ibid.*
75. *Ibid.*
76. *Ibid.*
77. *The Economic Times, Agriculture: Secret of Modi's Success, Swaminathan S. Anklesaria Aiyar, July 22, 2009, http://swaminomics.org/agriculture-secret-of-modis-success/*
78. *The Times of India, July 27, 2018; The Economic Times, Agriculture: Swaminathan S. Anklesaria Aiyar, July 22, 2009, http://swaminomics.org/agriculture-secret-of-modis-success/Secret of Modi's Success,*

79. *Jyotirgram Yojana scheme brings 24-hour power supply to Gujarat's villages, Uday Mahurkar. India Today, June 27, 2005;* https://www.indiatoday.in/magazine/states/story/20050627-jyotirgram-yojana-gujarat-govt-launches-24-hour-power-supply-scheme-in-villages-787454-2005-06-27#ssologin=1#source=magazine; *The Times of India, July 24, 2008*

80. *http://indiagovernance.gov.in/news.php?id=204)*

81. *http://cdn.narendramodi.in/newsletter/nl_250513.html*

82. *Plate to plough: PM Modi's Gujarat model on agriculture that other Indian states can replicate, Ashok Gulati, October 9, 2017; https://www.financialexpress.com/opinion/from-cm-narendra-modi-to-pm-modi-did-scaled-up-gujarat-model-work-on-pan-india-basis-find-out/886954)*

83. *https://en.wikipedia.org/wiki/Vibrant_Gujarat*

84. *Andy Marino, opt. cit. p.178.*

85. *https://www.jagranjosh.com/general-knowledge/vibrant-gujarat-global-investors-summit-2013-1359702462-1)*

86. *Special Report: The remaking of Narendra Modi, Ross Colvin, Satarupa Bhattacharjya, South Asia News, July 12, 2013,https://in.reuters.com/article/india-modi-gujarat-bjp/special-report-the-remaking-of-narendra-modi-idINDEE96B00Y20130712*

87. *Caravan, opt. cit.*

88. *Ibid.*

89. *Ibid.*

90. *Ibid.*

91. *Ibid.*

92. *Ibid.*

93. *Gujarat's Guru,Critics be damned, Modi has placed himself as the global Hindu leader, protector of Gujarat, Saba Naqvi, Outlook, 29 January 2007;https://www.outlookindia.com/magazine/story/gujarats-guru/233748*

94. *Ibid.*

95. *The Times of India, August 11, 2011 https://timesofindia.indiatimes.com/city/ahmedabad/Gujarat-roads-closer-to-international-standards-WB/articleshow/9559331.cms*

96. *Business Standard, January 20, 2013;https://www.business-standard.com/article/economy-policy/learning-from-gujarat-s-port-led-development-111071400023_1.html*

97. jabdon.com

98. *Business Standard, January 21, 2013·https://www.business-standard.com/article/economy-policy/gujarat-announces-new-land-acquisition-policy-110120900089_1.html*

99. jabdon.com

100. *The Economist,The Gujarat model: How Modi-nomics was forged in one of India's most business-friendly states, January 8, 2015; https://www.economist.com/finance-and-economics/2015/01/08/the-gujarat-model*

101. *Rediff.com; https://www.reddit.com/r/india/comments/2rum54/the_gujarat_model_how_modinomics_was_forged_in/*

102. *NDTV, October 8, 2018; Zhttps://www.ndtv.com/india-news/pm-narendra-modi-wanted-to-turn-gujarat-into-south-korea-when-i-was-chief-minister-1928265*

103. THEFAMOUSPEOPLE.com; https://www.thefamouspeople.com/profiles/l-k-advani-5506.php

104. Good bye, Mr Advani, Zafar Agha, National Herald, June 21, 2017; https://www.nationalheraldindia.com/politics/good-bye-lk-advani-presidential-elections-rss-modi

105. *Ibid.*

106. When LK Advani lost his job as BJP president for calling Jinnah a 'great man,'DNA, May 4, 2018; https://www.dnaindia.com/india/report-when-lk-advani-lost-his-job-and-standing-in-bjp-for-calling-jinnah-a-great-man-2611609

107. Devil's Advocate: The Untold Story, Karan Thapar, pp. 112-121.

108. *Ibid,* pp. 123-124.

109. *Advani salutes 'secular' Jinnah, Radhika Ramaseshan, The Telegraph, June 4, 2005; https://www.telegraphindia.com/india/advani-salutes-secular-jinnah/cid/873488*

110. *Jinnah created history: Advani, Beena Sarwar, The Hindu, June 5, 2005; https://www.thehindu.com/2005/06/05/stories/2005060507210100.htm*

111. *The Telegraph, opt. cit.*

112. *Ibid.*

113. *Who is Mohan Bhagwat?, Pavan Dahat, The Hindu, April 29, 2017: https://www.thehindu.com/news/national/who-is-mohan-bhagwat/article18311643.ece*

114. *BJP names Advani for PM, Reuters, December 10, 2007; https://in.reuters.com/article/idINIndia-30915420071210*

115. *End of the road for L.K. Advani? India Today, May 16, 209; https://www.indiatoday.in/election-news/story/end-of-the-road-for-l.k.-advani-47748-2009-05-16*

116. *Pavan Dahat, opt. cit.; Mint, 2014's RSS story, Sevanti Ninan, 25 Dec 2014.*

117. *Narendra Modi is BJP's PM candidate, Rediff.com, September 13, 2013;* https://www.rediff.com/news/slide-show/slide-show-1-its-final-bjp-to-declare-modi-as-pm-candidate-today/20130913.htm#1

118. *Narendra Modi is BJP's PM candidate for 2014, Advani disappointed* Ruchi Dua, September 13, 2013, India Today; https://www.indiatoday.in/india/north/story/narendra-modi-bjp-pm-candidate-2014-lok-sabha-polls-advani-disappointed-210945-2013-09-13

119. *Ibid.*

120. *Ibid.*

121. *Ibid* and *Rediff.com, opt. cit.*

122. *Ibid.*

123. *Just the Right Image, ShamniPande, June 8, 2014, Business Today; https://www.businesstoday.in/magazine/case-study/case-study-strategy-tactics-behind-creation-of-brand-narendra-modi/story/206321.html*

124. *2014 general elections: BJP plans to hold 250 Narendra Modi rallies, Amita Shah, The Economic Times, December 23, 2013; https://economictimes.indiatimes.com/news/politics-and-nation/2014-general-elections-bjp-plans-to-hold-250-narendra-modi-rallies/articleshow/27761478.cms*
125. *How India's BJP used data analytics to swing voters. PR Week, September 17, 2014; https://www.prweek.com/article/1312443/indias-bjp-used-data-analytics-swing-voters*
126. *Rediff.com, Battle for 2014: Tech-savvy BJP vs tardy Congress, August 7, 2013; Rediff.com Battle for 2014: Tech-savvy BJP vs tardy Congress August 07*
127. *Ibid.*
128. *How big data has changed India elections, Neerja PawhaJetley, CNBC.com* April 10, 2014; https://www.cnbc.com/2014/04/10/how-big-data-have-changed-india-elections.html
129. Ibid; 'Modi can never become PM, can sell tea,' Indian Express, January 17, 2014.
130. *How to do content marketing: Lessons from BJP's pre-election campaign,Nitan Jain, 16 August 2016; https://www.xorlabs.in/blog/how-to-content-marketing-lessons-bjps-pre-election-campaign/*
131. *Ibid.*
132. *2014 showed the power of Twitter, now every Indian politician wants a handle, T.V. Jayan, Smitha Verma, Sonia Sarkar and V. Kumara Swamy, The Telegraph, Kolkata, April 10, 2016 ;https://www.abplive.in/india-news/2014-showed-the-power-of-twitter-now-every-indian-politician-wants-a-handle-319116*
133. *Modi to use 3D version of his 'Bharat Vijay' rallies on April 11; https://www.narendramodi.in/narendra-modi-to-address-his-first-3d-rally-on-11th-april-6113*
134. *Ibid.*
135. *Gujarat Elections: Is BJP putting a new electoral strategy to test?M Manisha, Governance Now, December 9, 2017* http://www.governancenow.com/news/blogs/gujarat-elections-is-bjp-putting-a-new-electoral-strategy-to-test
136. *How India's BJP used data analytics to swing voters, PR Week; https://www.prweek.com/article/1312443/indias-bjp-used-data-analytics-swing-voters*
137. *Ibid.*
138. *Election Results 2014: 5 Factors that Helped BJP and Narendra Modi Win the Election, NDTV, May 16, 2014, https://www.ndtv.com/cheat-sheet/election-results-2014-5-factors-that-helped-bjp-and-narendra-modi-win-the-election-562309*
139. *Ibid.*
140. *Ibid.*
141. *Ibid.*
142. *Ibid.*
143. *https://www.greatlakes.edu.in/blog/six-marketing-strategies-behind-narendra-modis-election-victory/*

144. *Relearning Indian politics, the Prashant Kishor way, Mint, November 16, 2015, Srishti Gupta, Nikita Doval: https://www.livemint.com/Politics/z8ecilJSX0cpgom8dzZzeM/Relearning-Indian-politics-the-Prashant-Kishor-way.html*
145. *Narendra Modi's Citizens for Accountable Governance (CAG): Will it be disbanded or play bigger role? Vasudha Venugopal, The Economic Times, May 15, 2014; https://economictimes.indiatimes.com/news/economy/policy/narendra-modis-citizens-for-accountable-governance-cag-will-it-be-disbanded-or-play-bigger-role/articleshow/35131371.cms*
146. Men behind Narendra Modi's election campaign strategy, Indian Express, Archna, May 1, 2014 https://indianexpress.com/article/india/politics/men-behind-narendra-modis-election-campaign-strategy/
147. *Narendra Modi concludes his 2014 Lok Sabha election campaign with a rally in Ballia (UP), India TV, May 10, 2014; https://www.indiatvnews.com/politics/national/live-narendra-modi-to-address-five-rallies-in-up-today—17444.html/*
148. https://www.google.com/search?rlz=1C1CHBD_enIN807IN807&ei=HdkXL3eIML_rQHmyJbwDA&q=most+last+rally+in+Ballia+UP+in+May+00140&oq=most+last+rally+in+Ballia+UP+in+May+200140&gs_l=psyab.3...9180.29913..30665...1.0..0.287.7544.0j32j10......0....1..gwswiz.....6..0j0i71j35i39j0i131j0i67j0i22i30j33i21j0i13j33i22i29i30j33i160.YiXpDCYAEc
149. *Rajdeep Sardesai, 2014: The Election that Changed India, pp. 317-18.*
150. *Ibid,* p. 318.
151. *Ibid 328.*
152. *Ibid* 329.
153. *Narendra Modi's landslide victory shatters Congress's grip on India, The Guardian, May 16, 2014; https://www.theguardian.com/world/2014/may/16/narendra-modi-victory-congress-india-election*
154. *Rajdeep Sardesai, opt. cit.* p. 330.
155. Election 2014 results live: Modi's first victoryhttps://www.indiatoday.in/elections/highlights/story/live-lok-sabha-elections-result-2014-193048-2014-05-15 speech in Vadodara: good times are here, India Today, May 15, 2014;
156. Rajdeep Sardesai, Opt. cit. pp. 330-331.
157. *Ibid* 332.
158. *Quartz India January 16, 2015;https://qz.com/india/327771/it-cost-narendra-modi-100-million-to-win-the-indian-election-heres-how-he-spent-it/*
159. *The Guardian, May 16, 2014; https://www.theguardian.com/world/2014/may/16/narendra-modi-victory-congress-india-election*
160. Rajdeep Sardesai, opt. cit. p, 333.
161. India: another tryst with destiny, The Guardian, 18 May 2014; https://www.theguardian.com/global/2014/may/18/india-narendra-modi-election-destiny

Chapter Six: Indira becoming PM

1. *28 May 1964: The death of Nehru, India's first prime minister is dead following a stroke, leaving many anxious about the "after Nehru" era, Victor Anant, https://www.theguardian.com/theguardian/2013/may/28/death-of-nehru-archive-1964 and New York Times, 28 May 1964; https://archive.nytimes.com/www.nytimes.com/learning/general/onthisday/big/0527.html*
2. *Indira: The Life of Indira Gandhi, Kathrine Frank,* pp. 268-70)
3. *Kathrine Frank, opt. cit.* pp. 278-80.
4. *How Indira Gandhi became the Prime Minister: Prelude to the Congress Split,Sandeep Bhardwaj, Revisitingindia.com, June 24, 2013: Sandeep Bhardwaj; https://revisitingindia.com/2013/06/24/how-indira-gandhi-became-the-prime-minister-prelude-to-the-congress-split/*
5. *Kathrine Frank, opt. cit.* p. 280.
6. *Ibid,* pp. 278-280.
7. Radhakrishnan: A Biography, Sarvepalli Gopal, p. 336.
8. *Ibid,* p. 336.
9. *Kathrine Frank, opt. cit.* p. 281.
10. Inder Malhotra, Indira Gandhi, p. 84.
11. *Kathrine Frank, opt. cit.* p. 281.
12. *Ibid,* p. 282.
13. From memory by reading the newspaper reports in newspapers and articles in magazine when Indira Gandhi became the PM.
14. *Kathrine Frank, opt. cit.* p. 281.
15. *Kathrine Frank, opt. cit. pp* 275-276; *What If Shastri Hadn't Died Suddenly in Tashkent? Inder Malhotra, Outlook, August 23, 2004; https://www.outlookindia.com/magazine/story/what-if-shastri-hadnt-died-suddenly-in-tashkent/224865*
16. India Today, Indira Gandhi, a goongigudiya who went on to become Iron Lady, India Today, Prabhash K Dutta, November 19, 2017;https://www.indiatoday.in/india/story/indira-gandhi-a-goongi-gudiya-who-went-on-to-become-iron-lady-1089668-2017-11-19What; If Shastri Hadn't Died Suddenly in Tashkent? Inder Malhotra, Outlook, August 23, 2004; https://www.outlookindia.com/magazine/story/what-if-shastri-hadnt-died-suddenly-in-tashkent/224865
17. Katherine Keith, Opt. Cit. p. 284.
18. *Gopal, Opt. Cit.* p. 345.
19. Gopal's interview to Katherina Frank, Opt. Cit. 291.
20. *Sandeep Bhardwaj, opt. cit.*
21. Gopal, Opt. Cit. p. 345.
22. Gopal, Opt. Cit. 346.
23. Katherine Keith, Opt. Cit. p. 289-290.
24. Kathrine Frank, opt. cit. p. 292.
25. *Ibid,* p. 292.
26. *Ibid,* pp. 292-93.s

Epilogue

1. India Today, August 18, 2003; https://www.indiatoday.in/magazine/cover-story/story/20030818-56-events-that-changed-india-indira-gandhi-defeats-morarji-desai-to-become-pm-in-1966-791874-2003-08-18.
2. Financial Express, August 21, 2018.

Index

A

A K Sharma and Principal Secretary, 133
A.C.N. Nambiar, 66
Aam Aadmi Party, 130
Abdul Latif, 46
Abhor, 144
Achyut Yagnik, 46
Acting PM, 80
Adani Group, 110
Adani Port, 101
Additional Chief Secretary, 97
Additional Principal Secretary, 133
Advaita Ashram, 22
Advani, 92
Advani arrived in Pakistan, 119
Advani ji, 44
Advani-Qazi meeting, 118
African, 17
African coast, 16
Agra Summit, 52, 118
Agricultural community, 17
Agricultural growth, 107
Agricultural land, 101
Agricultural products, 112
Agricultural sector, 106
Agricultural wages, 114
Agriculture in Gujarat, 106
Agro-Processing, 108,104
Ahmedabad, 17, 23, 40, 41, 42, 49, 59, 62, 82, 86, 87, 88, 89, 91, 97, 102, 108, 134
Ahmedabad floods, 54
Ahmedabad Municipal Corporation, 46
Ahmedabad municipal elections, 45
Ahmedabad Police Commissioner, 89
Ahmedabad, Vadnagar, 17
Ajay Singh, 124
Akhil Bharatiya Vidyarthi Parishad, 24
Akshardham Temple, 95
Albright Stonebridge Group, 98
Alexei Kosygin, 143
All India Students Council, 24
All-India Organisation Secretary, 84
All-rounders, 53
Allahabad, 28, 32, 63, 64, 69, 80
Almora, 22, 37
Almora jail, 64
Alternate methods of farming, 107
Alwar, 117
Amarsinh Chowdhry, 45
Ambala, 144
Ambassador, 71
Ambassadors of various countries, 146
Amit Shah, 53, 136
Amol Sharma, 102
Amrita Shergill Marg, 134
Amritsar, 144
Anand Bhawan, 28, 29, 30, 35, 61, 69
Anand Bhawan lawns, 62
Anant Kumar, 48
Ancient Manipuri school, 32
Ancient Vedic ritual, 16
Andhra Pradesh, 45, 78, 91
Andy Marino, 39
Anglo-Indian, 31

Anil Bakeri, 110
Anna Hazara, 130
Annual Congress meeting, 62
Annual Congress session, 62
Annual farmers' events, 107
Anthony Eden, 71
Anti-Hindi violent agitation, 79
Apparels and Gems-Jewellery, 108
Arab, 17
Arabia, 17
Arabian Sea, 37
Arabs conquered Persia, 16
Archaeological excavations, 17
Arid and semi-arid, 106
Armed Hindus, 89
Arnab Goswami, 51
Arun Jaitley, 52, 53, 85, 93, 134
Arun Shourie, 91
Arvind Gupta, 126, 128
Ashok Mehta, 80, 144
Ashok Narayan, 97
Ashraf Qazi, 118
Ashram, 22
Ashwin Mehta, 86
Asian, 17
Asian ports, 17
Assassination of Indira, 45, 46
Assembled servants, 29
Assembly election, 49
Assembly polls in Gujarat, 132
Atal Bihari Vajpayee, 12, 39, 56, 60, 82, 115, 123
Atal ji, 44
Atlanta, 55
Attock, 123
Atulya Ghosh, 78, 139
Auctioned gifts, 104
Awakening or rebirth, 22
Ayodhya, 81, 87, 117
Azad Kashmir, 144
Azim Premji of Wipro, 109
Azizuddin Shah, 27

B

Babri Masjid, 46, 47, 49, 81, 117
Babri Masjid demolition, 48
Babubhai Nayek, 20
Badenweiler, 34, 65
Badminton School, 35
Bakeri Engineers, 110
Bal Bhawan, 72
Bal Gangadhar Tilak's iconic slogan, 134
Balbir Punj, 93
Ballia, 134
Balwant Rai Mehta, 42
Bandung, 71
Bandung Conference, 71
Bangaru Laxman, 85
Bangladesh, 57
Bangladesh front, 40
Banks of the Yamuna, 141
Barak Obama, 126
Beatrice Webb, 68
Becoming an Oxford graduate, 36
Bellary, 53
Belur Math, 22
Bengal Congress Committee, 139
Bengali saint, 149
Berlin, 34
Bermuda, 60
Bhachau Taluka, 57
Bhairon Singh Shekhawat, 85, 116
Bharat Darshan, 40
Bharat Lal, 133
Bharatiya Jan Sangh, 20
Bharatiya Janata Party, 20, 81
Bhartiya Jana Sangh, 46, 117
Bhartiya Janata Party, 46
Bhathiji Maharaj, 95
Bhathiji Maharaj temple, 95
Bhowali, 64, 65

Bhuj earthquake, 81
Bhullabhai Char Rasta, 42
Bibek Debroy, 97
Bibi Amma, 30
Bihar, 22, 90, 110, 132, 148
Biju Patnaik, 78, 141
Bill Clinton's technique, 131
Biotech- Pharma, 108
BJP High Command, 82
BJP National General Secretary, 50
BJP President M. Venkaiah Naidu, 95
Black Forest region, 65
Bofors scam, 46
Bombay, 37, 69, 78
Bombay State, 76
Boston, 55
Boy from Vadnagar, 136
Brahmanwada, 21
Brain-storming sessions, 97
Breakfast, 23
Brew foreign coffee, 60
Britain, 11
British Commander-in-Chief, 71
British Government, 29, 120
British intelligence, 71
British PM, 71
British pram, 29
British Premier, 63
British Raj, 137
British rule, 61
British school, 30
British style, 71
British tutors, 28
British-style education, 29
Brother-in-law of Sarojini Naidu, 66
Buddhist centre, 17
Buddhist monks, 17
Budget day, 88
Bundi, 117
Bureaucratic circles, 80
Burma, 67, 143
Burn them all, 87
Burned alive, 88
Burning compartment, 87
Business tycoons, 72

C

C. Subramanian, 143
Cabinet minister, 90
Cadila Pharmaceuticals, 110
Calcutta, 22, 51
California, 55
Cambodia, 91, 92
Cambridge, 78
Cambridge University, 28
Campaign Committee, 125
Campaign in Varanasi, 124
Campaign Strategy, 124
Campaigners, 23
Canada, 143
Canned Florida orange juice, 60
Cans of tinned sardines, 60
Capital of United Provinces, 28
Captain-Major Vasco di Gama, 16
Captivating slogan, 131
Caravan magazine, 20
Cardinal de Richelieu, 11
Central Election Committee, 73
Central Hall, 72
Central Parliamentary Board, 74
Chair Professor of Marketing, 130
Chamanpura area, 89
Chandan Banerjee, 55
Chandigarh, 51
Chandra Shekhar, 12
Chandupatla Janga Reddy, 45
Charan Singh, 12
Chariot procession, 81
Charles M Vest, 55
Cheaper power, 103
Check dams, 102, 106

Chestnut trees, 31
Chhattisgarh, 123
Chicago, 55
Chief Election Commissioner, 94
Chief Minister G B Pant's, 71
Chief Minister Keshubhai Patel, 60
Chief Minister of Haryana, 41
Chief Minister of Mysore, 78
Chief Minister Suresh Mehta, 83
Chief Scientist, 55
Child volunteer, 19, 20
Children's University, 105
Chimanbhai Patel, 48
China, 17
Chinese attack, 139
Chinese humiliation, 78
Chinese traveller Huan Tsang, 17
Chinese War, 78
Chou En-lai, 71
Citizens for Accountable Governance, 133
Citizens of Accountable Governance, 128
Civil Lines, 28
Classical dance, 63
Classical Indian dance, 32
Clean Gujarat, 105
Cleaning utensils, 40
Clement Atlee, 68
Clinics and sanatoria, 65
Coalition governments, 11
Cold mountain nights, 23
Cold-blooded decisions, 78
Collector of Kutch, 59
Commonwealth Prime Ministers' Conference, 143
Communal disturbances, 91
Communal riots, 95
Communal violence, 117
Communist block, 72
Communist government, 76
Communist Party, 67, 111
Complete offering worship, 87
Comptroller and Auditor-General, 59
Confederation of India Industry, 108
Congress candidates, 73
Congress circles, 145
Congress flag, 62
Congress headquarters, 75
Congress leader Mani Shankar Aiyar, 133
Congress leaders, 73, 126
Congress Legislative Party, 148
Congress MP Ehsaan Jafri, 89
Congress Parliamentary Party, 148
Congress Party, 41, 130, 148, 150
Congress President, 66, 72, 74, 78, 141, 148
Congress session, 62, 78
Congress session in Bhubaneswar, 139
Congress volunteer, 33
Congress Working Committee, 72
Conservative MP, 68
Conservative MP Nancy Astor, 68
Constituent Assembly of Pakistan, 120
Controlling corruption, 130
Controlling riots, 97
Cooking oil, 15
Corn flakes, 60
Corporate Affairs, 93
Corporate tycoons, 134
Corruption-free environment, 100
Council of Ministers, 142
Cripps Mission, 69
Crocodile-filled lake, 20
Cuttack, 123
Czechoslovakia, 68

D

D G Vanzara, 124
Dahej port, 113
Daily Telegraph, 76
Damodardas Mulchand Modi, 15

Database Marketing, 132
Daughter of Sarojini Naidu, 67
Davinder Kumara, 60
Defence Minister, 118, 147
Dehra Dun jail, 64, 69
Delhi, 22, 23
Delhi Darbar, 53, 73
Dense forest, 22
Deputy Chairman, 80
Deputy Chairman of Planning Commission, 144
Deputy Prime Minister, 78, 117
Desalination plants, 102
Designated Day, 148
Development of Gujarat, 96
Development road plan, 113
Dhirendra Brahmachari, 73
Dina Nath Mishra, 93
Dinesh Singh, 80, 144
Director-General, 110
Distribution systems, 104
Doon School, 77
Doordarshan, 60
Dorothy Norman, 71, 145
Dr A. P. J. Abdul Kalam, 106
Dr AK Patel, 45
Dr Bharat Barai, 54
Dr Madan Atal, 34
Dr Panna Barai, 54
Dr Steffan, 65, 66
Dravida Munnetra Kazhagam, 90
Drinking water, 102
Drip irrigation, 102, 107
Durban, 37

E

E. M. S. Namboodiripad, 75
East India Company, 27
Economic development, 108
Election Commission, 94
Ellis Bridge, 100
Emergency medical, 105
Emergency medical help, 105
Emergency services, 105
Emperor Aurangzeb, 27
Emperor Bahadur Shah Zafar, 27
Empower rural women, 105
Enemies of Hindus, 90
Energy resources, 102
Engaged the best brains in advertising, 131
Engineering colleges, 105
England, 29
English chauffer driven car, 29
Ernst Toller, 30
Establish eight restaurants, 100
Europe, 64
European music, 32
Evening snacks, 23
Ewing Christian College, 33
External Affairs Minister, 92

F

Farrukhsiyar, 27
Fascists and Hitler, 68
Fast-unto-death, 63
Fatal heart attack, 146
Fazilka, 144
Federation of Indian Chambers of Commerce & Industry, 108
Ferdinand T. Brooks, 28
Feroze, 35, 36, 37, 66, 77
Feroze Gandhi, 64, 68
Feroze lived alone, 70
Ferozepur, 144
Fifty-eight passengers, 88
Finance Department, 99
Finance Minister, 72, 80, 129
Finance Minister Desai, 141
Financial assistance, 114
Fine arts and culture, 32
Fire brigade, 89

Fiscal subsidies, 101
Five lakh hectares, 102
Five pillars of his development, 101
Flag-raising ceremony, 70
Focus on agriculture, 106
Food Bazaar, 107
Food for Spain, 68
Food packets, 60
Ford and Maruti Suzuki, 113
Foreign affairs, 79
Foreign Minister, 79, 143
Forensic Science University, 105
Former Chief Minister, 90
Former Prime Minister, 123
France, 143
Franck Muller, 134
Frank Oberdorf, 32, 64
Free market economy, 45
Freedom movement, 33, 61
French and Swiss borders, 65
French teacher, 64
Full cream milk, 60
Future Prime Minister, 121

G

G C Murmu, 133
Gallant fire brigade workers, 58
Gandhi, 33
Gandhian culture, 31
Gandhidham, 60
Gandhinagar, 81, 88, 95
Gandhi's assassination, 20, 71
Ganga Dhar, 27, 28
Gas grid, 104
Gas-based economy, 104
Gauhati, 22
Gautam Adani, 110
General Motors,, 113
General Musharraf, 52
General Pravin Togadia, 56
General Secretary, 43
Geneva, 30
George Fernandes, 85, 88, 118
Georgia State University, 55
German-Jewish poets, 30
Germany, 34, 36, 65, 66
Ghanchi community, 15, 86
Glimpses of World History, 63
Global perspective, 51
Gloomy environment, 31
Goddess Kali, 102
Godhra, 86, 88
Godhra burning, 88
Godhra burning of Hindus, 93
Godhra episode, 95
Godhra station, 92
Godhra train burning, 91
Godrej and Bajaj, 110
Gokul Apartment, 59
Good governance, 134
Gordhan Zadaphia, 97
Govind Ballabh Pant, 74
Govindacharya, 55
Graduation course, 68
Great Britain, 67
Great Lakes Institute, 130
Greatest Congress leader, 140
Greece, 17
Grocery-cum-tea-shop, 15
Ground level data, 104
Ground water level, 102
Guard of honour, 120
Guinness World Records, 134
Gujarat, 16, 22, 41, 47, 76, 83, 89, 95, 102, 103, 132
Gujarat Assembly election, 109, 128
Gujarat burnt, 90
Gujarat Gaurav, 95
Gujarat General Secretary, 49
Gujarat Industrial Development Corporation, 101
Gujarat issue came up, 91

Gujarat Lok Sangharsh Samiti, 43
Gujarat model, 114
Gujarat Riots, 90, 92
Gujarat Special Economic Zones Act, 101
Gujarat Special Investment Region Act, 101
Gujarat State Electricity Board, 103
Gujarat State Road Transport Corporation, 23
Gujarat State Wide Area Network, 98
Gujarat under Emergency, 44
Gujarat unit, 20
Gujarat University, 24
Gujarati, 17
Gujarati businessman, 100
Gujarati families, 43
Gujarati Kanji Malam, 16
Gujarati merchants, 17
Gujarati people, 90
Gujarat's Industrial Policy, 101
Gujral, 12
Gujrati dresses, 16
Gulab Singh Tanwar, 136
Gulf of Kachchh, 56
Gurdaspur, 144

H

H. D. Deva Gowda, 12
Handle-less terracotta cup, 17
Handsome Bihari, 73
Happiest moment, 50
Harappan sites, 17
Haridas Mundra's company, 72
Harold Laski, 68
Haryana, 50, 51, 81, 85
Hawala scam, 117
Hazira port, 113
Healing touch, 18
Health expert, 132
Hedgewar Bhawan, 23, 40
Her foreign origin, 115
Her official status, 72
Hermit, 22
High Commissioner in London, 146
High Court in Agra, 28
High military officers, 146
High value cash crops, 107
High-quality power supply, 107
High-value crops, 107
Higher yields, 107
Himachal Pradesh, 22, 50, 51, 53, 81, 85, 90, 118
Himalayas, 22
Hindi as the official language, 79
Hindu seats, 63
Hindu-Muslim riots, 81
Hindu-Muslim unity, 120
Hindutva, 48
Hira Lal, 64
Hiraben, 15, 21, 136
Hiren Joshi, 133
Holographic technology, 127
Home Affairs, 97
Home Department, 97
Home Minister, 80, 100, 117
Home Minister Nanda, 144
Home Minister Nanda ignored, 144
Hometown of Jinping, 17
Hong Kong, 71
Hooghly River, 22
Huge ballroom, 71
Huge tribal population, 105
Human development, 104
Human resource, 104
Hundreds of rallies, 131
Hungry, 68
Hyderabad, 116
Hydro carbon exploration, 104

I

IDFC Institute, 115
Image of Modi in Kutch, 59
Important decisions, 79

Inamdar, 21, 39
Independence Day, 62
Inder Gujral, 12, 80, 145
Inder Malhotra, 80, 144
India League, 37, 142
India League in London, 67
Indian ancient philosophy, 102
Indian businessmen, 101
Indian Congress, 120
Indian culture, 31
Indian girls, 31
Indian High Commissioner, 80
Indian Institute of Teacher Training, 105
Indian Majlis, 36, 67
Indian Muslims, 120
Indian Ocean, 37
Indian ports, 113
Indian territory, 80
Indian tutors, 28, 30
Indian University, 32
Indian vegetarian food, 61
Indira, 74
Indira Gandhi, 12, 43, 79, 80, 144, 145, 147, 148
Indira Gandhi Zindabad, 149
Indira Gandhi's cabinet ministers, 67
Indira Priyadarshini, 28
Indira sat on the dais, 72
Indira was married to Feroze, 38
Indira's political maturity, 68
Indo-Pak War, 23
Indonesia, 17, 93
Indravadan Modi, 110
Indu-boy, 29
Indulal Yagnik, 41
Industrial development, 102
Industrial Extension Bureau of Gujarat, 108
Industrial Investment, 108
Industrial minister, 57
Industrial Policy, 101
Industrial use, 101
Inflammatory speech, 42
Information and Broadcasting, 79
Information and communication technology, 127
Infrastructure, 108
Infrastructure development, 112
Inns of Court School of Law, 28
Inns of Court School of Law in London, 28
Inspector-General of Karachi police, 120
Interlinking small rivers, 102
Interlinking small rivers and streams, 102
International Court of Justice, 100
International recognition, 142
Irish tutor, 28
Islamic terror, 52
Islamic terrorism, 52
Island of Diu, 16
Israel, 107

J

J P Mathur, 52
J.B. Kripalani, 141
Jadi Rana, 16
Jafri fired, 89
Jahandar Shah, 27
Jakarta, 71
Jalalabad, 85
James Michael Lyngdoh, 94
Jammu and Kashmir, 144
Jana Krishnamurthi, 82, 83, 85, 93
Janata Dal (United, 90
Janata Dal alliance, 48
Japan attacked China, 68
Japanese company, 102
Jashodaben, 21
Jaswant Singh, 92
Jawaharlal, 12, 30, 61
Jawaharlal and Indira, 35
Jawaharlal Nehru, 139, 142

Jayaprakash Narayan, 73
Jayawanti Mehta, 85
Jehangir, 32
Jehangir and Coonverbai Vakil, 32
Jehangir Faredoon Ghandy, 33
Jehangir Vakil, 63
Jhalawar, 117
Jinnah Mausoleum at Karachi, 117
Jivraj Mehta, 42
John of Are, 63
Joshi and Sushma Swaraj, 123
Journey for justice, 46
Jungfrau, 66
Jyoti Gram Yojana, 107

K

K Jana Krishnamurthy, 82
K Kailashnathan, 133
K. B. Hedgewar and M. S. Golwalkar, 121
K. Kamaraj, 78
K. N. Govindacharya, 53
K. R. Malkani, 117
Kabul, 85
Kalraj Mishra, 85
Kamala, 62, 64, 65
Kamaraj, 73
Kamdhenu University, 105
Kamla, 34
Kamla and Nehru, 32
Kamla to Calcutta, 32
Kamlesh Lulla, 55
Kandahar, 85
Kanyakumari, 47
Karachi, 116, 120
Karachi branch, 116
Karan Thapar, 118
Kargil war, 115
Karnataka, 53, 113
Karsan Patel, 110
Kashiram Rana, 49, 85
Kashmir, 27, 80, 110
Kashmir to Kanyakumari, 123
Kashmiri Muslims, 144
Kashmiri shawl, 149
Kaul-Nehru, 27
Kerala, 75, 124
Kerala episode, 77
Kerala government, 75, 113
Keshavbhai Solanki, 60
Keshavrao Deshmukh, 43
Keshubhai, 53, 54, 96
Keshubhai Patel, 48, 49, 50, 56, 81, 82
Key areas for development, 109
Khajuraho, 50
Khali near Almora, 70
Khanpur, 49
Khorasan, 16
Khurshid Kasuri, 119
King Edward VII Sanatorium, 64
Knowledge Computing Center in Ohio, 125
Kolahoi glacier, 79
Kota, 117
Kotwal of Delhi, 27
Krishna, 62
Krishna Menon, 142
Kumaon region, 22
Kumaraswami Kamaraj, 139
Kutch area, 56
Kutch District, 56, 57
Kutch quake, 82

L

L.K. Advani, 85, 100, 121
L.N.S. Mukundan, 58, 59
Lahore, 75
Lahore session, 62
Lakshmanrao Inamdar, 20
Lakshmi Narayan, 61
Lal Bahadur Shastri, 12, 72, 73, 78, 140, 141, 146, 149

Lal Chowk, 47
Lal Krishan Advani, 46, 116
Lalan grounds, 60
Lalu Prasad Yadav, 117
Land to industrial units, 101
Landslide victory, 128
Large drawing and dining rooms, 71
Large water bodies, 17
Large-scale rural electrification, 104
Large-scale rural electrification programme, 108
Larsen and Toubro, 86
Late Shri Dattopant Thengadi, 44
Late Shri Nanaji Deshmukh, 44
Latur, 60
Lausanne, 66
Law University, 105
Lawyer, 27
Laxmanrao Inamdar, 19, 39
Laxmi Narain Nehru, 27
Leader of Opposition, 117, 121, 122
Leadership of Gandhi, 63
League of Nations, 30
Leave Kashmir, 73
Left-wing friends, 36
Left-wing Jewish, 71
Leftist organisations, 67
Lekha Pandit, 70
Life Insurance Corporation, 72
Linguistic basis, 76
Lodhi Road, 133
Lok Kalyan Marg, 84
Lok Sabha, 48, 50, 122, 142
Lok Sabha by-election, 45
Lok Sabha Elections, 41, 53
Lok Sabha seats, 45
London, 28, 36, 37, 66, 67, 68, 76
London School of Economics, 34, 65
Long corridors, 71
Long live Indira Gandhi, 149
Long live the red rose, 149
Long-life Plan, 105
Lord Krishna's birthday, 95
Lord Lothian, 68
Lord Ram, 39
Lord Ram's birthday, 24
Low importance ministry, 79
Lucknow, 61, 70, 71

M

M J Akbar, 100
M O Mathai, 73
Macroeconomic policy, 11
Madagascar, 37
Madan Bhai, 64
Madanlal Khurana, 85
Madeline Albright, 98
Madhav Sadashiv Golwalkar, 43
Madhav Singh Solanki, 44
Madhukarrao, 122
Madhya Pradesh, 50, 87, 88, 123
Madison Square Garden, 54
Madison World, 124
Madras State, 79
Mafatlal Patel, 21
Maharajas, 28
Maharashtra, 20, 73, 76, 88, 139, 147, 148
Mahatma Gandhi, 38, 61, 63, 140, 149
Mahmuna Sultana, 72
Major defence decisions, 11
Makeshift warehouse, 60
Making India a strong economy, 129
Making tea and serving, 40
Mal-nutrition among children, 105
Malaya (now Malaysia, 66
Malaysia, 17, 35, 93
Mamta Banerjee, 111
Mani Shankar Aiyar, 126
Manjula Subramaniam, 103
Manmohan Singh, 12, 115, 116, 121, 129
Manmohan Singh Government, 129

Manmohan Singh regime, 11
Manmohan Singh's Government, 132
Manohar Lal Khattar, 41
Manoj Ladwa, 133
Mansion, 27
Marathwada, 17
Marching songs, 19
Margaret Thatcher, 115
Marginal farmer, 114
Married Feroze, 69
Massachusetts Institute of Technology, 55
Massive heart attack, 77
Mathura, 17
Mausoleum of Mohammed Ali Jinnah, 120
Media barons, 134
Media Conference Room, 123
Medical aid in China, 68
Meenakshi Dass, 135
Mega projects, 101
Mehsana district, 21
Mehsana station, 19
Memoranda of Understandings, 108
Men behind Modi's election campaign, 132
Mendicant, 22
Menon and Agatha Harrison, 68
Menon's resignation, 78
Mental shock, 77
Metropolitan Council, 117
Mexico, 78
Micro-irrigation, 106
Micro-irrigation projects, 106
Mid-day meal scheme, 105
Militant Hindutva, 90
Minimum agricultural wages, 114
Mining, 108
Minister for Information and Broadcasting, 142
Minister of Food and Agriculture, 143
Minister of State, 97
Minoo Masani, 141
Miss Baker, 35
Miss Zahir, 70
Mobile tanks, 102
Mod exam, 68
Moderations exam, 36
Modi Administration, 114
Modi created a history, 85
Modi helped Muslims, 100
Modi must go, 92
Modi reached Kutch, 56
Modi travelled across, 22
Modi-regime, 109
Modi's determination, 103
Modi's marketing strategy, 130
Modi's resignation, 94
Mohammad Ali Jinnah a, 118
Mohan Bhagwat, 121
Mohan Kumaramangalam, 37, 67
Mongolia, 143
Morarji Desai, 12, 41, 73, 78, 140, 141, 147
Most valuable treasure, 41
Motilal, 61
Motilal and Jawaharlal, 31
Moulvi Liaqat, 120
Mrs Advani, 119
Mrs Indira Gandhi, 41
Mud-bricks house, 15
Mughal Court, 27
Mughal Emperor, 27
Mughal Emperor Babur, 81
Mughal ruler, 27
Mughals, 61
Mughlai food restaurant, 100
Mumbai, 115
Mundhra Scandal, 72
Mundra, 101
Mundra port, 113

Munich Conference, 68
Murli Manohar Joshi, 47, 81, 85, 122
Musharraf, 118
Muslim fundamentalists, 95
Muslim League, 75, 120
Muslim property, 89
Muslim shops, 90
Muslim women, 46
Mussorie, 31
Mutiny against the British, 27

N

N K Seshan, 80
N. K. Seshan, 146
N. R. Narayana Murthy, 109
Nadiad town, 95
Nagpur, 24, 42
Naini jail, 63
Naini jail in Allahabad, 63
Nainital, 22, 37
Na Mo tea cups, 126
Nanaji Deshmukh, 43
Nancy Astor, 68
Nandlal, 28
Nano plant, 101
Narendra Modi, 12, 56, 83, 131, 135, 136
Narendra Modi's victory, 137
Nathalal Jaghda, 20
Nathalal Zagda, 43
National average, 102
National Cadet Corps, 19
National Coordinator, 47
National Democratic Alliance, 85
National economic growth, 97
National Election Committee, 47
National Executive, 92, 93
National figure, 69
National headquarters, 24
National Herald, 70
National Rural Employment Guarantee Scheme, 116
National Secretary, 81
National Security Adviser, 92
National Technology Head, 128
National Volunteer Society, 19
Natural Gas and Oil, 108
Nehru, 12
Nehru became the Prime Minister, 79
Nehru dismissing, 71
Nehru family, 32, 38
Nehru sent a telegram, 65
Nehru was cremated, 141
Nehru's daughter, 37
Nehru's expected successor, 150
Nehru's successor, 78
Nehru's trusted advisor, 76
Neo-imperialism, 72
Nepal, 57
New Chief Minister of Gujarat, 109
New Jersey, 54
New York, 54, 85
New York City, 55
Next Prime Minister, 80
Nijalingappa, 139
Nikhil Chakravarthy, 37, 67
Nilanjan Mukhopadhyay, 41
Nirma Group, 110
Non-cooperation movement, 29, 61
Non-food crops, 107
Non-Hindi speaking States, 143
Non-Hindi states, 139
Non-overlapping mandate, 103
Non-violent protest, 23
North-western Gujarat, 56
Number of bedroom, 71

O

Oberdorf, 34
Oberdorf appeared in Europe, 65
Odisha, 124
Officer Training Camp, 24, 42
Om Prakash Chautala, 85

One-roomed apartment, 37
ONGC helicopter, 88
Opposed Nehru's meeting, 68
Orange juice, 63
Organisational skills, 41
Organise funeral rites, 57
Organised travels, 94
Organising secretary, 68
Organising Secretary of Gujarat, 46
Orrisa, 78
Other Backward Community, 15
Oxford, 34, 35, 36, 65, 68
Oxford admission test, 35
Oxford MP Sir Arthur Salter, 68

P

P N Haksar, 37, 67
P. V. Narsimha Rao, 12
P.C. Pande, 89
Padmaja, 36
Padmaja Naidu, 67
Pak-terrorists, 118
Pakistan, 116, 146
Pakistan border, 88
Pakistan Government, 118
Pakistani soldiers, 80
Palme Dutt, 68
Panchmahal district, 87
Pandara Road house, 118
Pandit Deendayal Petroleum University, 105
Pandit Raj Kaul, 27
Paris, 36, 68
Parliament House, 149
Parliamentary Affairs Minister, 93
Parliamentary Board meeting, 122, 123
Parliamentary Board of BJP, 121
Parsees, 16
Parsi couple, 32
Parsoli Motors, 100
Party President, 75
Persia, 17
Persian, 27
Persian Gulf, 17
Pervez Musharraf, 46, 119
Petroleum refinery, 101
Pipavav port, 113
Piyush Goel, 124, 125
Piyush Pandey, 131, 133
Planning Commission, 80, 103
Planning Commission study, 112
Political activities, 29, 32, 36, 63, 69
Political advisor, 67
Political analysts, 12
Political decisions, 80
Political journey, 40
Political science, 24
Political speeches, 29
Politically stronger and powerful, 72
Pollution Control Board, 101
Polytechnics, 105
Pondicherry, 57
Port of Hormuz, 16
Portuguese, 17
Post-death formalities, 78
Post-earthquake relief, 59
Post-Nehru situation, 147
Power deficit, 104
Power distribution companies, 104
Power supply, 103
Power-surplus state, 103
Prakash Javadekar, 52
Prakash Swamy, 55
Pramod Mahajan, 53, 93
Prashant Kishor, 132
Prasoon Joshi, 131, 133
Pre-election meetings, 84
Pre-electronic voting machine era, 49
Prem Kumar Dhumal, 85
Premal Nathwani, 56
Preparing tea, 23

President Josip Broz Tito, 143
President Radhakrishnan, 143
Press conference with Modi, 91
Prime Minister, 56
Prime Minister Atal Bihari Vajpayee, 52
Prime Minister L.K. Advani, 95
Prime Minister of J&K, 71
Prime Minister Shaukat Aziz, 119
Prime Ministerial candidate, 121
Prime ministership, 79
Prime Minster of Ceylon, 71
Prince of Wales, 63
Principal Secretary, 67
Principal Secretary R. K. Lahiri, 58
Privy Council in London, 28
Pro-Modi forces, 93
Pro-Pakistani movement, 80
Professor S. Bharadwaj, 130
Pt. Prithvi Nath Chak, 28
Public Distribution System, 105
Public lectures, 36
Public-Private-Partnership, 113
Punjab, 51, 70, 76, 88
Punjab border, 144
Pupils' Own School, 63
Pupils' Own School in Poona, 32
Pure vegetarian, 55

Q

Quaid-e-Azam Mohammed Ali Jinnah, 120
Quality enhancement initiative, 105
Quality technical education, 105
Quit India, 70
Quit India Movement, 38

R

R. K. Narayan, 56
Rabindranath Tagore, 32, 65
Race Course Road, 83, 84
Radhakrishnan, 147
Radhakrishnan publicly, 144
Radhakrishnan replied, 146
Radical organisation, 37
Rahul Bajaj, 110
Rahul Gandhi, 130, 135
Railway station, 15
Raj Bahadur Kakkar, 33
Raj Kaul, 61
Rajagopalachari, 147
Rajas, 28
Rajasthan, 23, 88, 117, 123
Rajdeep Surdesai, 134
Rajendra Prasad, 73
Rajghat, 149
Rajiv, 77
Rajiv Gandhi, 12, 45, 46
Rajiv Gandhi Foundation, 97
Rajkot, 22, 86
Rajnath Singh, 85, 116, 122, 123, 136
Rajya Sabha, 142
Rajya Sabha Member, 125
Ram idols, 46
Ram Janambhomi Campaign, 46, 117
Ram Janmabhoomi temple, 117
Ram Mandir, 46
Ram Manohar Lohia, 141
Ram Rath Yatra, 117
Ram Temple movement, 117
Ram Vilas Paswan, 85
Ramakrishna Math, 22
Ramakrishna Mission, 22
Ramdas Agarwal, 85
Ramsay Macdonald, 63
Rangoon, 67
Ranjan Bhattacharya, 91
Rashtrapati Bhavan, 80, 146
Rashtrapati Bhawan banquet, 118
Rashtriya Janata Party, 53
Rashtriya Swayamsewak Sangh, 19
Ratan Tata, 111
Ravi Shankar Prasad, 135

Reaching Badenweiler, 66
Reception rooms, 71
Red flag, 82
Red tape, 97
Regular Force of Pakistan Army, 144
Reliance Fresh, 107
Relief agencies, 60
Remove poverty, 42
Renewable energy generation, 104
Republic Day parade, 57
Republicans, 68
Resident Commissioner in Delhi, 133
Resident Editor, 79
Resident Senior Fellow, 115
Resurgent Group of Gujarat, 110
Right to Information, 116
Rigorous daily routine, 23
Robert Walpole, 11
Rohtak, 74
Rolls-Royce factory, 146
Roman Catholic Church, 36
Roman Rolland, 30
Romesh Thapar, 80, 145, 146
Ronald Reagan, 115
Royal court, 27
RSS chief Mohan Bhagwat, 122
RSS national headquarters, 42
Rural electrification, 104, 107
Rural electrification resulted, 104
Rural Feeder Segregation Programme, 103
Rural migration, 104
Russia, 29, 143
Russian Revolution, 28, 63

S

S K Patil, 78, 139
S Nijalingappa,, 78
S Radhakrishnan, 80
S. S. Bhandari, 117
Sabarkantha Lok Sabha, 60, 81
Sabarmathi, 102
Sabarmati Ashram, 32, 62
Sabarmati Assembly, 81
Sabarmati assembly seats, 60
Sabarmati Express, 86, 92
Sachindra Chaudhuri, 80, 146
Sacred force, 101
Safdarjung Road, 149
Saffron-robed sanyasi, 44
Sainik School, 19
Sales tax incentives, 101
Salt produced in the hinterland, 57
Sam Balsara, 124, 131
Sangh leaders, 90
Sanjan, 16
Sanjay, 77
Sanjay Joshi, 49, 93
Sanjiva Reddy, 78, 139
Sanjoy Joshi, 53
Sanskrit, 27
Santiniketan, 32, 34, 63, 64, 65
Sardar Patel Stadium, 96
Sardar Patel Statue of Unity, 54
Sardar Sarovar project, 102
Sarojini Naidu, 120
Satish Gujral, 80, 145
Saurashtra region, 22
School-teacher, 20
Science and technology, 55
Scientific testing, 107
Second World War, 70
Secret engagement with Feroze, 36
Secretaries of all Departments, 99
Secretary of State for India, 65
Selected politicians, 146
Senior bureaucrats, 146
Separate bank account, 114
Separation of feeder lines, 104
Sexual advances towards female, 73
Seychelles, 37

Shah Bano case, 46
Shakha, 19
Shankar singh Vaghela, 42
Shankersinh Vaghela, 48, 49, 95
Shanta Gandhi, 35
Shanta Kumar, 90
Shantivana, 141, 149
Shashi Tharoor, 135
Shastri as the Party leader, 79
She needed surgery, 64
She reached Berlin, 65
She wanted to marry Feroze, 69
Sheikh Abdullah, 70, 71
Short of food and blankets, 58
Shri George Fernandes, 44
Sidney, 68
Sikh gentleman, 44
Silk Road, 17
Silver Jubilee celebrations, 118
Singapore, 35, 66, 91
Single-phase line, 103
Singur, 111
Sip chicken soup, 60
Sit-in strike, 40
Sleepless nights, 77
Social media, 129
Social media campaign, 133
Soft loan, 101
Soho Square, 124
Sohrabuddin, 46
Soil-health cards, 107
Sola Civil Hospital, 89
Sole mate, 71
Sombhai Modi, 20
Somerville College, 35, 36
Somnath in Gujarat, 117
Somnath Temple, 47
Somnath to Mumbai, 47
Sonia Gandhi, 53, 97, 115, 121, 129
South America, 78
South Korea, 115
Southeast-Asian countries, 66
Southern States, 104
Southwestern Germany, 65
Soviet policies in Hungry, 76
Spain-India Committee, 68
Spanish Civil War, 67, 68
Spanish democrats, 68
Special Economic Zones, 101, 112
Special medical treatment, 32
Spice Route, 17
Sri Lanka, 39, 72
Srinagar, 47, 70, 77, 80, 144
St Mary's School, 31
Stanley Baldwin, 68
Starched and ironed cloths, 42
Statue of Liberty, 54
Steel Minister, 140
Stones in the kidney, 77
Straight fight, 49
Strong Prime Ministers, 12
Strongest rival, 49
Sub-transmission, 104
Subba Rao, 58
Subhadra Datta, 70
Subhadra Joshi, 72, 149
Subhash Chandra Bose, 66
Subramaniam Swami, 44
Subsidised farm sector, 103
Sudden death, 146
Sunil Mittal of Airtel, 134
Sunil Shastri, 85
Supreme Court, 94
Supriya Sule, 135
Surat, 21, 86
Suresh Jani, 54
Suresh Mehta, 57
Suresh Prabhu, 85
Sushma Swaraj, 52, 53, 121, 122, 123
Swami Vivekananda, 18, 22
Swamiji today, 55
Swapan Dasgupta, 53, 96

Swaraj and Ananth Kumar, 122
Swaraj Bhawan hospital, 62
Swaran Singh, 79, 143
Swarup Rani, 62
Swiss dresses, 30
Swiss university, 65
Switzerland, 29, 30, 34, 35, 65, 66
Syama Prasad Mookerjee, 117

T

T.T. Krishnamachari, 72, 145
Talk over tea, 126
Taluqdars, 28
Tamil Nadu, 79, 91
Tamil Nadu Government, 144
Tapti river, 21
Tarakeshwari Sinha, 72
Tarun Das, 110
Tashkent, 145, 146
Tata Motors, 101, 113
Tea seller, 126
Tea-kettle, 17
Teen Murti, 149
Teen Murti house, 71,142
Telugu Desam Party, 91
Temple town, 78
Ten children, 88
Ten-roomed building, 23
Texas, 55
Textiles and Gems, 108
TheTimes of India, 79
Third-class compartments, 62
Tihar jail, 40
Tirupathi Temple, 139
Tirupati, 78
Togadia, 97
Top priority to irrigation, 106
Tourism, 108
Traditional Gujarati sweets, 49
Train tickets, 24
Transmission losses, 104
Travel for change, 84
Tribal areas, 105
Trinamool Congress, 91
Trinity College, 28
Trivandrum, 76
Twelve-year-old girl, 86
Twenty-seven, 88
Two low budget hotels, 100
Two-month tour of Africa, 78
Typical British home, 61

U

U. N. Dhebar, 72, 73, 74
U.K. Premier, 69
Uday Mahuhrkar, 95
Uday Shankar, 68
UK Government, 100
Underground guide, 42
Underground network, 43
Understanding voter perceptions, 131
Uninterrupted electric supply, 104
Union Defence Minister, 88
Union Disinvestment Minister, 91
Union Home Minter, 81
Union Law Minister, 110
Union Ministers, 143
United Nations Aid Mission in Chad, 132
United Nations Industrial Development Organisation, 108
United Progressive Alliance, 115, 116
United States, 24, 54, 71, 78, 85, 142
Unity Journey, 47
University Labour Club, 36, 67
University of California study, 127
University of Delhi, 24
Unpalatable food, 62
Upper castes, 44
Urgent treatment, 65
US Administration, 100
Using technology in the campaign, 130
Uttar Pradesh, 22, 74, 81, 85, 110, 132, 134, 148

Uttar Pradesh and Bihar, 110
Uttarakhand, 22
Uttarakhand Investors Summit, 115
Uzbekistan, 146

V

V K Krishna Menon, 31,67
V. K. Krishna Menon's India League, 37
V. P. Singh, 12
Vadnagar, 15, 17, 19, 20, 21, 23, 54
Vadnagar Railway Station, 15, 17
Vadodara, 54
Vaghela, 49, 96
Vaghela joined Congress, 95
Vajpayee, 92
Vajpayee and Advani, 93, 123
Vajpayee Cabinet, 117
Vajpayee Government, 90
Vakil Saheb, 20, 23, 24, 39, 40, 41, 43
Vallabh Kathiriya, 85
Varanasi, 134, 136
Vasant Gajendra Gadkar, 20
Ved Prakash Goel, 85
Veteran journalist, 67
VHP volunteers, 89
VHP's International Secretary, 56
Vibrant Gujarat, 109
Vibrant Gujarat Global Investors Summit, 108
Vice-President of India, 147
Viceroy, 65
Vijay Chowk, 52
Vijay Kumar Malhotra, 51
Vijay Laxmi, 29, 32, 64
Vijaya Lakshmi Pandit, 31
Village of Chobari, 57
Villages of Rajkot, 44
Vinod K Jose, 20
Vishwa Hindu Parishad, 46, 117
Visited military hospital, 144
Visiting temples and monasteries, 66
Vivek Dehejia, 115

W

Wall Street Journal, 102
War broke-out, 80
Water is life, 102
Water resources, 102
Weekly protection money, 100
Welcome to Gujarat, 111
Welfare of the children and women, 72
Wengen, 34
West Africa, 132
West Bengal, 78, 91, 111, 124, 148
Western outskirts of Ahmedabad, 89
White House, 55
White sarees, 77
Winston Churchill, 69
Women force for development, 102
Worked under Inamdar, 23
World Bank, 112
World Economic Forum, 111
World Peace Conference, 68
World Trade Center, 85
World War, 68

X

Xi Jinping, 17

Y

Yashwantrao Chavan, 147
Yervada jail, 63
Yervada Prison, 63
Yoga, 73
Young Muslim girl, 70
Young tea-seller, 133
Youth-oriented development, 130
Yugoslavia, 76, 143

Z

Zadaphia, 97
Zafar Sareshwala, 100
Zakir Hussain, 100, 147
Zamindars, 28
Zoroastrian religion, 16
Zurich, 111